THIS BOOK BELONGS TO

Matt Neumann !

Searching for O'Sensei

Learning and Living the Wisdom of the Warrior

By Thomas Barclay Collings

Library of Congress Control Number: 2014905870

CreateSpace Independent Publishing Platform, North Charleston, SC

Published by Long Island Asian Studies Center, LLC

Long Island, New York

Design & Typography: Mammen Thomas

Typeface: Baskerville 11/17

Second Printing, January 2016

Front cover photo—mountain path to Chogen-ji Zen Temple,
Kannami Village, Japan

DEDICATION

The inspiration for this book is my amazing daughter Lien Bi Wang Gui Collings, may she discover the depth of ancient wisdom in her Asian roots. It is also an expression of appreciation to my teachers and training partners. I also wish to single out my first two sempai, Howard Pashenz and Edgar Kann, men of great honor and compassion.

ACKNOWLEDGEMENTS

My sincere appreciation to the following friends for their feedback and support: Oscar Mercado, Ed Whele, Richie Basso, Jason Mallia, and Bill Morris. Many thanks to Mammen Thomas for his design skills. Thanks also to Andrew Pannullo, Adam Brodsky and Eugene Duvidzon for editing assistance.

TABLE OF CONTENTS

Kisshomaru Ueshiba　　　　　　*Morihiro Saito*

INTRODUCTION

WHEN we look at the broad spectrum of human activities, martial arts is surely one of the most peculiar. To transform fighting and violence, the ugliest form of human behavior into an art form would seem to be completely irrational. Is it not more sensible to concentrate on the lighter and happier side of life? Most people, and especially my fellow law enforcement officers, prefer to forget the "dark side" of life during leisure hours. They enjoy ball games, TV, movies, and other relaxing activities.

But what movies do they enjoy? The most popular are action films about embattled heroes overcoming villains of all kinds, and good guys prevailing over predators, terrorists, and other evil. The theme of violence, conflict, and danger not only fills popular culture, it permeates great literature of all types including epic novels. Danger and conflict are even prevalent in our dreams.

Human conflict and the struggle for safety in a dangerous world is an archetypal theme, expressed in all art through the ages. Primal fears of danger have always been a part of the human experience. From cave dwellers' drawings on ancient rocks to biblical tales of David and Goliath, right up to movies such as *Star Wars* and *Rambo*. Monday Night Football on TV is symbolic warfare. My favorite team, the Oakland Raiders "battle" opposing teams with well practiced "attacks" and a "strong defense." In the theatre, whether it be Macbeth or Japanese Kabuki, there is no shortage of desperation and mayhem.

One of the foundations of modern psychology, Maslow's hierarchy of human needs begins with safety and security. All other needs and aspirations defer to safety. This is just who we are. Safety has always been the primary human concern. But in our modern world we have perfected and stockpiled hi-tech weaponry of mass destruction to such a degree that our survival as a species is in doubt. My most poignant moment in Asia was standing at the burned-out remains of Hiroshima City Hall, ground zero of the first nuclear holocaust. In their infinite wisdom, the survivors left it for all to see — the only structure that remained standing for a mile in any direction. It is a terrifying sight.

In today's world art and recreation that merely reflect our violent nature is no longer acceptable; it is a luxury this world can no longer afford. For the human race to survive the violence of our nature must be harnessed, disciplined, and transformed. It is our obligation to future generations, and it must happen soon.

One source of such transformation is the Asian discipline known as *budo, or traditional martial arts*. The authentic lineage incorporates martial training, strict self discipline, and purification. This ancient hybrid of mind-body training engages the full spectrum of human needs from physical survival to the spiritual. It is a multi-dimensional approach to human evolution, encompassing all components of our nature, both mental and physical. It has little in common with the current fad of MMA, or any form of sport fighting, and little relation to the violence portrayed in martial arts films.

Budo is historically an intensely private tradition, born of monks and holy men (and women) with roots in temples and monasteries. Like the original Shaolin Temple of China, it was intended only for seekers of enlightenment. But, with humanity in dire need of such transformation, a training system which disciplines the violence within us, and harnesses our passions must expand its presence in our culture. It has the potential to make a far greater contribution.

This book could have been two or three books. There is a memoir of a young man's bumpy road to the martial arts in the 1960's, and how it altered the course of his life. A journey through Asia, encountering martial arts masters, spiritual teachers, and training partners of the highest caliber. Then a return to the mean streets of Brooklyn, New York, during the crack cocaine wars of the 1980's and 90's, attempting to apply this Asian wisdom to the harsh realities of the street, and seeking the meaning of "peace officer" in the gritty world of law enforcement.

It is also about war and peace, in personal relations and on a global scale — What does it mean to act with a warrior spirit in daily life? What decision does a warrior make when ordered to join the death and destruction of war?

As both a lover and critic of martial arts training, I search for something beyond the "workout," beyond the acrobatics, theatrics, and mythologies which often overshadow the heart of these precious Asian disciplines. You may follow the common thread linking all these stories and places, or pick and choose whatever may be of interest. For me there is only one story here — a search for the true meaning of "warrior."

Tom Collings
Long Island, New York

DISCLAIMER

The opinions expressed in this book are my own, and do not necessarily reflect the opinions of my teachers or law enforcement agencies where I worked. I have tried to recount events faithfully, without fabrication or embellishment. Perception of events is always subjective, but an effort was made to be reasonably objective. In some cases, I used only a first name or changed a name to protect the privacy of an individual, but the stories are true.

"If you have life in you, you have access to the secrets of the ages, for the truth of the universe resides in each and every human being."

MORIHEI UESHIBA was a twentieth-century Japanese sword master, martial arts genius, and spiritual teacher, born December 14, 1883. He spent his life studying budo, the discipline of applying battlefield skills to modern life, for both physical and spiritual survival. He created a training system called "aikido," a response to conflict which expands our choices beyond the limitations of "fight or flight." He passed away on April 26, 1969. Those who knew him, and those inspired by his vision, refer to him as "O'Sensei."

I.

FINDING THE PATH

1. Dedicated to the Six-Pack

SOMETIME in the mid-1960s, there was a high school kid in New York who tried but could not seem to make the grade — academically, socially, or athletically. He was nervous, hyperactive, and self-conscious. To make matters worse, he had a bunch of learning disabilities (the word back then was "slow."). He was generally on the losing team, warming the bench, and in classrooms could be found sitting as far in the back as possible. No high fives, trophies, cheering crowds, or varsity patches for this kid. In his teenage world, most messages clearly announced "loser." That kid was me.

My only fun seemed to be getting wasted at parties, a vacation from the awkward self-consciousness that ruled my life. By age fifteen, the high school yearbook clearly defined me: "Tom Collings — dedicated to the six-pack, buddy of Andy and Phil." That was it, the entire entry. The sum total of who I was. I remember thinking, at least I was known for something. Better to be a drunk than a complete nobody.

Through the years, I have worked with a lot of kids like this who never made it, kids convinced they were losers. Kids with no parents to support them or no parents there for them at all. But I was blessed with parents who were there for me all the way, convinced I was a slow starter with great potential. Though I never believed it, their belief never wavered. Having one or two people who believe in you seems to be all it takes for some kids. Most of the parolees, drug addicts, and juvenile delinquents I have worked with never had that one person with absolute faith in them. It can make all the difference.

Catherine Collings was a kind, unshakably polite Christian lady with a tough inner core that was acquired growing up on the Canadian frontier of British Columbia. One day, she visited my polished, impeccably dressed, Harvard graduate guidance counselor who barely knew my name, since his main focus was the school's best and brightest. Politely ignoring his arrogance and condescending objections, she gently insisted he move me from the low level classes to the highest, even though my grades were poor. What was her rationale for this outrageous request? "It will be good for him, he can do it."

I am sure most mothers would have accepted the school's "profession-al" judgment against such a change. Most parents would not have the nerve to even bring up such an outrageous request. But there are warriors in this world, and they come in all shapes, sizes, and sexes. With her sugarcoated but laser-like intent, she politely ignored all professional objections and insisted the changes be made. They finally gave in and waited to tell her, "We told you so."

So, did Thomas become a straight *A* honors student, or quickly flunk out of the higher level classes? Neither happened; he simply went from being a *C* student in the lower classes to a *C* student in the higher classes. Mom expected that. She joked, "Thomas, you will have no trouble being a *C* student anywhere, even Harvard, so why accept any lesser placement?" How can you argue with logic like that?

2. The Path of Karate

WHEN Mom saw a stack of martial arts magazines in my room, a kid who never read anything, she loaded me in the car, and off we went to a martial arts school. The dojo atmosphere was very different from that of high school sports, and something about it fired my soul. I always gave 100 percent. For the next three years, she drove me there three times a week without complaint. She had found a place I was not content to be a *C* student.

Tom Collings, Sr. had been a pretty good amateur boxer, always grabbing me to put on the gloves and go a few rounds with him. Even in his eighties he rarely missed a day pounding his heavy bag hanging in the shed. I guess you have to learn how to fight when you are the only Jew on your block in Wheeling, West Virginia, and they are burning crosses in your front yard. Being a Jew in Appalachia definitely was no picnic, and it shaped who he was. So, while he did not understand why we wore funny suits and called it a "dojo" he supported my training.

My dad always tapped his knuckles along whatever wall or building he was walking past. He was a workaholic who had a reserve of nervous energy that never seemed to be fully discharged. Back then, I just thought of him as a little "hyper," like me, but it's clear to me now he had Tourette Syndrome, a neurological condition causing muscle twitches and strange sounds. It was part of his DNA, as it is mine. My childhood ADHD is still with me, I just learned to cope better, and channel all that extra energy. I inherited some of the Tourette thing too. Mine is a nervous tension in my jaw and fingers that never quits except when confronting danger, or in deep meditation. I guess, it is no mystery why I was drawn to the Asian disciplines and police work.

But hyperactivity definitely has its strong points. That knuckle rapping thing gave Dad very strong hands. One day, mom showed me an old newspaper article about a guy who almost died on a New York subway. When his leg got caught in a closing door, the train began to drag him down the subway platform. The paper reported: "The hammer used to break the thick glass covering the emergency stop switch was missing, but an unidentified Good Samaritan put his fist through the glass and stopped the train." Mom said the

Good Samaritan was "unidentified" because dad refused to give his name. He had a fiercely private side to him, and that subway event became another private event never to be discussed.

He was impulsive as well as hyper. I remember him engaging in near violent arguments with people over dumb things like parking spaces, and yet, just as impulsively reaching out to help people in distress many times, when others passed them by. Although not the easiest person to be around, if you got in trouble and needed help when my dad was near, it was your lucky day.

One day, dad came to my karate *dojo* and watched our drills — front kicks, side kicks, back kicks, flying side kicks, combinations of punches and kicks together. I was sure it would impress the hell out of him. After class, he told Sensei, "When I was a kid, they called that dirty fighting; now it's an art!" I thought Sensei would be offended, but he laughed so hard he almost fell off his chair.

The dojo was so different from high school, where I was lost toward the bottom of a large pecking order. The dojo students were mostly adult blue collar guys from the streets of New York City: cops, firefighters, auto mechanics, train conductors, etc. I was "the kid." There were also Vietnam vets with recent scars and war stories that were real. None of these guys cared that I was a lousy athlete, and socially awkward. All they saw was a teenaged kid who kept showing up and training hard. That was enough. That was enough to be accepted and respected.

Sensei was very different from high school athletic coaches. Mel Sutphin was an ex-marine whose full-time job was tending a bar down the street. Just like me, he was skinny as a rail. He was also lightning fast. He had some serious personal baggage that hampered his status and career in the martial arts, yet he was a natural leader who commanded respect with just a look or a quiet word. He had that "presence" that many great teachers have. To me, he was a mystical master, my ticket out of loser's hell. Mom had given me the gift of a lifetime, and I took it and ran with it. I remember her pride my third year of training, when I became the first brown belt registered in the newly formed American Isshin-Ryu Karate Association.

3. Sempai John

THE only other teenager in my dojo was a wild Brooklyn kid named John Snidersich, who seemed to have everything I lacked. He was only a year older than me but had it all — he was strong, athletic, and already had earned his black belt. John could have really beaten on me or worse — ignored me. But, instead, he just pushed me hard in training to get better. He gave me some bumps and lumps but no serious injuries, and most importantly, he never embarrassed me. At my high school, he probably would have been just another arrogant jock, but there was something about the dojo that brought out the best qualities in people.

Although John had very good karate skills, he was from the streets and even as a teenager had no use for martial arts fantasies. He came in one day with a huge bandage over the eight-inch gash on his forearm. A mugger had demanded John's wallet, and when John responded with a "fuck you," the guy attacked with a meat hook. John caught him dead on with a front snap kick to the groin, lifting the guy a foot off the ground. But, to his amazement, the guy just kept on coming at him with that meat hook. John shot up a strong block that stopped the weapon, but it tore a long gash in his arm. Then he ran like hell and got away, but needed a lot of stitches to close his arm.

He seemed to love trashing my martial arts fantasies. "Tom, let me tell you another story of real Brooklyn-style martial arts. I was hassled by this big guy in Bay Ridge who started pushing me around. We exchanged a few shots, and the guy went down but started getting right back up, so I grabbed a nearby garbage can and crashed it over his head a few times. He did not get up for a long time after that. That's called 'Brooklyn karate' — use whatever you got."

Shortly after that, John entered the Marine Corps and was shipped to Vietnam. I worried a lot about him. About nine months later, he came into the dojo walking really slowly with a cane. He was in a foxhole during some mortar attacks but just "had to" piss really badly, so he waited for things to get a little quiet then got up to pee. A mortar landed a few yards away and opened up his leg from his ankle to his hip. I can't remember how many hundreds of stitches he said it took to close his leg, but the injury got him out of Vietnam. I guess it's better to piss in your fox hole. I heard the Viet Cong soldiers had no problem doing that. It's one reason they won the war.

I lost track of John after that. But, twenty years later, I saw him on the TV show *Top Cops*. He had rebuilt his leg and joined the NYPD. Working in the street crimes unit, he was chasing down a bank robber, when he received a shotgun blast to the chest (with no vest) and a .45-caliber bullet to his belly. The bullet to the belly would have been the fatal shot, but his big Marine Corps belt buckle stopped the slug. He described how, in the ER, they needed to saw open his chest but had to keep him conscious since his blood pressure had dropped dangerously low. That meant no anesthesia. I cannot even imagine what that must have been like, wide awake, watching and feeling a guy saw your chest open. John was one tough bastard.

After that, he led support groups for NYPD officers severely injured like him in the line of duty. He is probably damned good at that. As a tribute to John, and his lucky belt buckle I always wore my heavy silver Crazy Horse belt buckle when I worked the streets. It served me well. Thank you John.

4. Sparring Days

THROUGHOUT high school and college, my martial arts training became increasingly incompatible with the drinking and drugging that seemed to be all around me. So, the drugs and alcohol lost. It did not suddenly end, it just gradually faded away. It is a trick I share with recovering addicts. Find a passion that is incompatible with getting high. It creates a conflict, and sometimes the addiction loses the contest.

At a college in Pennsylvania, I trained with this Okinawan Shorin-ryu karate guy who had little more than a front snap kick in his repertoire. He knew very little of the cool stuff I knew — the flying kicks, spinning kicks, and all those neat hand combinations. Trouble was, he practiced that stupid little front snap thousands of times until it was like greased lightning. These were the days when no one wore protective gear — stupid, yes — but that was then. So, every time I launched one of my awesome combinations, that nasty little snap kick caught me right in the gut. Lesson learned — stay focused on the basics, practice the simplest, boring stuff thousands of times, then practice them some more. I can still feel that fellow's foot in my gut today.

I had a big Isshin-Ryu sempai who skillfully side stepped my attack and nailed me with a high roundhouse kick right in the mouth. It came out of nowhere. So clean, and so beautiful that I hardly noticed the teeth it knocked out. It is hard to believe we were too stupid in those days to wear mouthpieces; those were for "wimpy boxers." My dentist got rich off that.

There was another fellow I used to meet and spar with at the Lafayette College gym. He had very fast hands, often getting through my blocks and nailing me good. Most of the time, he managed to avoid my back kicks, which were not that fast but very powerful. One day, my timing was just right, and he walked right into a back kick I fired at his center just before he got within range to use those hands. My heel caught him dead center of the solar plexus. He dropped to the floor, motionless. His eyes were still open, but he couldn't speak or move or breathe. I panicked, trying everything I knew to get him breathing. After two or three minutes, he was turning blue, so I ran to call 911, but as soon as I reached the door, he started coughing and gasping, then started breathing normally.

I helped him up, then helped him to his car. I tried to apologize, but he would have none of it. "It was a real good shot, I never saw it coming," he said. "No apology necessary." He had a great attitude, but my heart was still racing. It really scared the hell out of me — I thought I killed him. We never trained together again, but several months later, I read that he won the Pennsylvania State Karate Championship.

I was beginning to lose interest in sparring, but those trophies still attracted me   they were so tall and shiny. My last day of karate sparring came a year later at a big East Coast tournament around 1969 or 1970. It was at the Manhattan Center, a big, old New York City auditorium with a huge, open main floor. I fought a guy who was very good and beat me by one point, one lousy point. I was really jealous when he got to face the top-ranked guy. I kept thinking, "That should be me, it should be me."

Sitting at ringside, I was only a few feet from the action. Immediately after they bowed, there was a ferocious exchange of kicks and punches. During the exchange, the guy who beat me took a blow to the head and went down. It did not seem like much of a punch. "I could have taken that shot no problem," I told myself. But he must have gotten hit in the temple because he never got up. After ten minutes, an ambulance drove right into the auditorium and up to the ring. They took him away on a stretcher, still unconscious. I never learned what happened to him, but he was definitely in a coma. The words still echoed in my head "that should be me." After that incident, trophies lost their glitter. After that I never sparred again.

5. Buffalo, New York — One Rough Town

*A*FTER my first year at a private college in Pennsylvania, I had to find a cheaper school if I wanted to stay in college. Dad had built a company around this little night light he had designed in the early 1950s. It paid the family bills and allowed us to live well. It was a useful little thing with a mushroom-shaped shade and a little clip for the base, convenient for attaching

to a book, bed side table or a baby's crib. He called it the "D-light." It used only a tiny ten watt bulb, but was more than sufficient to read by. As an energy saver, it was fifty years ahead of its time.

There was also a little brass one called the "Book 'n Bed" light. It was a handy thing you could clip on a book or just about anywhere that needed a little bit of light. With a few part-time employees, and my dad working his usual sixty hour weeks, we sold two million of the little suckers, all made by hand. I say "we" because I must have made a few hundred thousand of them myself from around age ten or eleven. I was a high roller for a ten-year-old; I always had ten dollars for candy on payday, so I had lots of friends.

They say child labor is cruel, but I disagree. I loved it. Just dump a pile of parts in front of any ADHD kid like me, offer him a little money to build something, then leave him alone — and presto! You get perfect attention and laser-like focus. A lot of young kids who hate school and are lousy students would be great workers if given the chance.

Working with dad was also a chance to hang out with him, since he was rarely at home. Unfortunately, all good things must end. A Japanese company made a cheap knockoff of our light, which caused some house fires.

Consumer alerts went out with pictures of the light, but they used a photo of our light. That was the end of Dad's business. We slid down the ladder from our upper-middle-class lifestyle to barely middle. So, I transferred to a cheaper college — the State University of New York at Buffalo. But I did not mind since the catalog showed a beautiful day with beautiful girls walking on a beautiful campus. The caption read: "The Berkeley of the East." Only a dummy like me would believe that about Buffalo; it turned out to be more like East LA.

After getting settled in Buffalo, I started to look for a dojo. My search gained impetus as I realized what this town was like. The first week the Robbery Squad busted down the door of the college dormitory room next to me, dragging away two guys in handcuffs who committed several armed robberies. A few weeks later, a girl in the dorm laundry room was robbed at gunpoint, with a sawed-off shotgun put to her head. I quickly realized, these boys in Buffalo play rough!

Even the dogs in Buffalo have an attitude. It must be all that nasty cold weather. One day, while stopped at a traffic light on my motorcycle, I spotted a big German shepherd about twenty feet off to my right. Standing guard in the front yard of a house, he kept giving me the evil eye and staring at my leg. I could feel what was coming so I cocked my leg just as he charged. I nailed him pretty good in the snout with a hard side kick, as he went for my ankle. No one on this planet loves dogs more than me, but this Buffalo beast deserved it. Unfortunately, the laws of physics say something about each action having an equal and opposite reaction, so the power of my kick sent the motorcycle flying sideways into oncoming traffic. To this day, I will never understand how that guy was able to swerve with zero warning, missing me by inches.

The next week, I met my old high school buddy, Andy, and persuaded him to join me at one of Buffalo's many rowdy bars. It was a jock bar, where the UB football team hung out — drinking, tending bar, and beating people up. Why would anyone go there? Young and stupid are about the only reasons I can think of. It was not a good place to get into a fight with a football player, but thats just what we did. Perhaps I had a death wish back then.

During a short-lived, pleasant night of drinking, a guy kept pushing into Andy. Andy pushed back, not recognizing the behavior for what it usually is — a setup for an attack. The moment Andy pushed back, all hell broke loose. In Buffalo, one push is all it takes to start a war. That night two young karate hot shots discovered the hard way that after four or five beers, the coordination needed for our wonderful karate techniques was long gone. We also learned that those great karate kicks did not work so well in a barroom of wall-to-wall bodies, with Neanderthal sized jocks, who were feeling no pain and coming from all directions.

After getting slugged several times from the front, side and rear, Andy went down, and the biggest Neanderthal of them all started pounding on him mercilessly. That moment, although many years ago, is still crystal clear in my memory because of a critical decision I made. I still had a beer bottle in my hand and felt the impulse to smash the big monster with it, but I hesitated. That let him slam a few more shots into Andy's face before I grabbed his arm and screamed in his ear, "Enough!" After that, about half the football team threw us both out on the cold frozen sidewalk.

I describe my decision not to use that beer bottle as critical because years later I supervised a guy on parole for deciding the use his beer bottle in the exact same situation. He cracked a guy who was beating his friend during a high school brawl. Unfortunately, the bottle broke and cut the guy's neck. He quickly bled to death. That decision cost him ten years upstate in Sing Sing from age eighteen to twenty-eight. That's how fast simple fights can turn deadly. So, was my decision right? I don't know, because those last few blows to Andy's face did some serious damage.

Buffalo is so damn cold in winter that my car's engine block froze solid, even with antifreeze in it. So, we had to walk the two miles back to Andy's college. It was so cold, and we were so drunk, that Andy did not feel any of the broken bones in his face until the next morning. My injuries were mostly damaged pride. In the morning, in addition to a hangover, Andy lost his vision. He was rushed to the hospital for the first of many surgeries to save his eyesight and rebuild the many shattered bones in his face.

Andy's dad, John Colletta, was a very decent and hard working blue collar, Italian guy from Brooklyn. A skilled artist who lettered the trucks of many companies in the city, he knew lots of good guys and lots of very bad guys. Within a few days, he had the necessary information on the big jock who pummeled Andy and was getting the money together to have him taken care of. Andy was not sure if that meant his knee caps would be shattered, both legs broken, or if he would just disappear. He was not interested in the details.

When my dad got wind of this, he kept pushing Mr. Colletta to forget

the hit. "Let's just go up there together and beat the hell out of the bastard." The fact that their target was a 21 year old, 290 lb. football player, and dad was 59 years old and 160 pounds did not seem to matter. Apparently, the call from my dad meant word of the hit had gotten out, so it had to be called off,

Andy and me in our Frogman phase

pissing off Mr. Colletta, but saving him a lot of money. They never did go to Buffalo to find the guy, placing their faith in the justice system. However, back then UB football players were untouchable, since UB football meant dollars to the city and the top cop was a big UB football fan. So, nothing ever happened to the bastard. Somewhere in Buffalo today, there walks a big, stupid, aging jock who owes his life, or at least both knee caps, to my dad messing up a well-planned hit.

While I felt bad for Andy, and visited him a lot in the hospital, I noticed he actually was having a good time there. He surely did have the resilience of a warrior. He got to know a lot of doctors and nurses, including one nurse, who he ended up marrying. In fact, he liked being around doctors and nurses so much, he decided to go to medical school. Two little problems; the cost of medical schools in the US, and his grades. Imagine — a "B" student having the audacity to be a doctor! But, he said "none of that bullshit" would not stop him, and I believed him. In high school Andy was the Italian kid who hung out with Collings and Blackburn, so to his "guidance" counselor he obviously was not college material. They set him up for a trade school, but he ignored "that trade school bullshit" and got himself into a good college. Andy is my poster boy for "where there is a will there is a way."

After having several medical schools and financial aid applications rejected, he simply caught a plane to Mexico. He spent the first few months learning Spanish, then got into a medical school in Guadalajara. He learned to hit the floor fast in the library, when bullets of the Mexican Federales flew by during shootouts in the streets with the cartels. He studied hard, and used those doctors contacts from all those operations he had, to get internships and residencies back home. Ten years later he was one of the top orthopedic surgeons in New York.

On January 25, 1990, Avianca Airlines Flight #52 arriving in New York from Columbia ran out of fuel, and crashed in a wooded area of northern Long Island. If you had to crash a plane back then, that was the place to do it, because it was right by Andy's house. It was also near Glen Cove Hospital, where Andy worked the emergency room. Within a few minutes, he was at the scene, and then at his ER doing forty-eight hours of nonstop surgeries.

Many of the eighty-four survivors of that crash were operated on by Andy. None of them know they owe their lives to a drunken brawl at a scummy Buffalo bar, way back in the winter of 1971.

❧ ❧ ❧ ❧

I resumed my Okinawan karate training in Buffalo, but I met a teacher newly arrived from Korea, and felt an immediate bond. He built a small dojo in a room behind his Korean grocery, so I started Tae Kwon Do with Mr. Lee. I used to watch the shop, while he and his wife went to the wholesale fish market. Somehow, I got the correct change without being able to read any of the prices or knowing a word of Korean. Those Korean customers were very honest and never took advantage of Mr. Lee being away; maybe it is an Asian ethic.

Mr. Lee would have us sit in meditation before training for "reflection." That was just about the only English word he knew. I still remember the wonderful feeling of sitting quietly there with the aroma of those strange foods from the store filling each breath. In the back of that little food shop I learned to love meditation.

I wanted to learn more about meditation, but Mr. Lee spoke no English so I signed up for a three-day Transcendental Meditation course. I discovered that some serious release of tension can happen at intensive meditation retreats — and I mean serious. It was held at the teacher's apartment that was filled with expensive antiques. On the third day, my left leg was twitching a lot but I just ignored it. Suddenly — and involuntarily my leg shot to the side sending a beautiful antique wooden stool across the room, shattering it against the wall. It freaked me out, and the TM instructors. What had just happened was apparently not in the TM instructor's manual. They graduated me early, and politely sent me on my way.

I enjoyed both the meditation and Tae Kwon Do workouts with Mr. Lee, but I was the only student not entering tournaments, and this soon became an issue. He tried to understand my self-imposed ban on participation in tournaments, but never could. I felt I was letting him down, since other students brought him back trophies. He was a very kind man, and let me stay anyway. I really loved that training.

To pay for my training, I got a job on campus — a job no other student would take. Thinking back, it was a job no human in their right mind would take. I was the test tube washer at the New York State Department of Health

Virus Research Laboratory, located on the university campus. I called it the "Virus Factory." All the lab did was grow viruses, lots of pretty green, blue and black viruses. How stupid (or poor) do you have to be, to take a scrub brush to hundreds of scummy test tubes full of dead (they claimed they were dead when I got them) virus goo, for $2.50/hour ? I learned that there is a silver lining in having the worst job on earth — the only direction from there is up!

When I finally quit that job, the lady in charge of part-time workers followed me down the hall in shocked disbelief. "Thomas, this is an excellent campus job, why do you want to leave?" She insisted it was an "excellent" campus job. An excellent job? Was I missing something? Test tube cleaner in a virus factory? She was a middle aged lady, not a hippie, but I remember thinking that she must be on some kind of drugs. Another possibility was the viruses got to her brain, confirming my worst fears about working there. Scrubbing viruses is my last memory of Buffalo, New York.

6. Disorderly Warrior for Peace

*A*LONG with all the death and destruction, the Vietnam War demolished most of my boyhood dreams. The few books I ever read as a kid besides martial arts magazines were about ninjas, Green Berets, and Army Rangers. Every self conscious awkward boyhood moment got buried under feel good fantasies of "Commando Tom." Not an uncommon boy's fantasy, but I went all the way with it. Starting at age 11, summer camp for me was all about the rifle team. Getting that NRA marksmanship badge sealed the deal.

Next was my frogman training. The Navy had just created their new elite SEAL Teams, which I decided must have been created just for me. I immediately searched for a diving class and finally found an ex-navy UDT diver starting a class in something called "scuba." I had no idea what that was, nor did anyone I asked, but if it would make me a frogman I was in! There were no certification organizations back then so the UDT guy gave us little cards that read certified by "Carl Frank Funes, 1ST UDT Unit, United Sates Navy." Now I was both a marksman and a frogman!

I already had karate training to make my hands registered weapons. I was not sure where you go to get them registered, but I could take care of that later. To seal the deal (pun intended) I needed to become a paratrooper so I found what had to be the world's cheapest jump school on a farm somewhere in Maryland. Why Maryland? I could find no other $35.00 parachuting schools on the planet.

Shortly after arriving at the school I discovered why it was so cheap. The equipment was beat up old World War II army surplus stuff, and the "flight instructor" looked more like a drunken farmer. Now thinking back, you have got to be one of the cheapest little sons of a bitches around to bet your life on a beat up 25+ year old parachute with a ripped harness and rusted buckles. If my parents had seen it they would have dragged me out of there fast, but to a young fool with a dream it was "jump school!" How that ragged equipment ever held I will never know but I floated down from 3000 feet in ecstatic fantasy. Ignorance (and stupidity) is bliss.

My military hero dreams were taking shape nicely when the Vietnam War began to mess it all up. Like most Americans I knew nothing about Vietnam, and trusted the wisdom of our leaders. Harvard grads like Robert McNamara, who advised president Kennedy. I remember mom saying "He is from Harvard, a very brilliant man." We were just recovering from the Cuban missile crisis and saw everything in the world as Communist aggression. When I was assigned the anti-war side in a social studies class debate, I knew I was in trouble, especially since they picked Bruce Ferron, the brightest kid in the school to argue the pro war side. Bruce was confident, articulate, and had God and the American flag on his side. I recall thinking this might be a good time to quit school.

Everyone I knew was a patriotic American who believed in "my country right or wrong." Even my mother, who was the most loving and spiritual person I knew, assumed we were defending democracy against the evil North Vietnamese. They were the 1960's equivalent of today's "Islamic terrorists." Having learned her world history in Canada, and knowing that much of American history I was being taught was bogus, she still believed in America and trusted our leaders. In fact, as girl scout troop leader, PTA president, and chairperson a dozen charities, hardly anyone knew she was not an American citizen. I guess she had to support the war.

I tried to educate myself fast about this "Vietnam thing," so I would not sound like a complete fool when I lost the debate. But there were so few articles against the war, and nothing in the library on the history of Vietnam. I finally found one book, by a World War II general named James Gavin. To my amazement, he insisted that our involvement there was a big mistake, but he was the only one I found who expressed that opinion. The eloquent letters from Ho Chi Minh to US presidents Kennedy and Johnson, asking for help to liberate his country from French colonial rule "just like the American war for independence," were kept classified for years.

Finally, I found one person who argued forcefully against the war. To my shock, it was my father, a guy who had no interest in politics. The moment I mentioned the debate he opened up as never before. "Tell them how damn stupid this war is. Tell them we are creating a Goddam mess over there. We should get the hell out of there now! We have no Goddam business being there! Your debate will be easy. Tell them the truth, even if they don't want to hear it." I was shocked to hear my own father express these "radical" ideas. It did not sound very patriotic. But, the more I educated myself about this little country called Vietnam, the more I realized he was right.

It seemed strange that mom was a very loving religious person, but she supported a war that was wrong, while dad was a short tempered atheist, but his opposition to the war was not only correct, it was more humane. That contradiction still confounds me.

While the Vietnam War had put a damper on my military dreams, I figured it would be a short war, then joining the military would be honorable again. After all, we were the greatest military power on earth fighting a tiny country with no Air Force, no Navy, and rag tag soldiers recruited from rice paddies. I figured wrong; by the early 1970s those skinny guys from the rice paddies were kicking our ass, and holding their own against impossible odds. The draft board sent me a nice welcome letter with a shiny new draft card, number #37 (out of 365). That meant I would be stomping through hot jungles, and wrestling in the mud with some Viet Cong fellow the moment I left college. Stomping through a jungle in a war I did not believe in was not acceptable, but worse was the thought of killing people I had no argument with.

As I held that draft card I thought of Muhammad Ali, and the simple truth in his statement "I got no quarrel with those Viet Cong," when he was drafted and refused to go. It would have been so easy for him in the military. He would have been treated as a celebrity. But he said no, so they took away his title, and banned the champion of the world from boxing. He lost everything, except his honor and integrity. That is a true warrior. Ali was a powerful role model to me, and many other young men both black and white during the Vietnam war.

I decided this war had to end before I could realize my dreams, so in college I joined protests, marches, rallies, and led a few non-violent but very disruptive war resistance activities. One night in 1971, I found myself sharing the stage at a big Washington, DC, peace rally with a hero of mine, Pete Seeger. Pete was a veteran war resister, who played his banjo brilliantly while I urged the crowd to join me the next morning, blocking traffic on the Key Bridge. That is the bridge many senators, congressmen, and other government leaders must cross to get to work each morning from Virginia. Blocking that bridge would literally shut down the government. I knew that, and so did all the undercover FBI agents in the crowd.

After the rally, the agents alerted the Arlington police department to prepare for an invasion of "radicals." Since I was organizing the action I figured I should get there first, so at 5:00 am my buddy and I drove across the bridge from Washington to Arlington. We would wait until the start of rush hour, then halfway across the bridge, block several lanes of traffic with my old Chevy Nova, hopefully beginning a massive traffic jam.

At 5:00 a.m. the downtown streets of Arlington were completely empty. All of downtown had been evacuated. Only a few police in riot gear were visible; it appeared they had declared martial law. It was ominously quiet, and I had a bad feeling. As we drove around the deserted streets waiting for the start of rush hour, a lone motorcycle officer began driving next to us. I turned left, then he turned left. I turned right, he turned right. We played this little game for about five minutes, then I nervously turned down a one way side street as he instructed. When I did all hell broke loose.

Dozens of police in full riot gear surrounded us. From every direction I heard the unmistakable sound of pump shotguns being racked. Soon twelve gauge barrels were pointing in every window. The Southern accents were thick and angry. One guy kept repeating "Boy, give me a reason to pull this trigger, come on boy just give me some reason!" A cop in the rear kept repeating "do it Lem, come on Lem, do it"!

We had invaded their state. These were good old Southern boys from Virginia farm country who came in to Arlington for work, then headed back out to their farms in the sticks. This was their country, and we were invaders. They were defending God and Country from the tidal wave of social and political chaos going on in America, now spilling into their state. After watching all the trouble in America on the evening news for years, they were getting to see the enemy up close and personal. Wearing my uniform of the antiwar movement, long hair and old jeans, I was the face of the enemy. I felt there was a good chance I would die that morning.

My buddy was given ten minutes to get (run) out of town, and cross the bridge back into Washington, "or you gonna die boy." They followed him closely, guns drawn, as he ran in the direction of the bridge. Then there were

twenty very angry riot cops, and me. No one else around at 5:15 a.m. Moments of such intensity can be quite strange; although scared shitless, I could not stop thinking "Who names their kid Lem? What kind of name is that?" I remember being so curious what "Lem" looked like, but with several shotguns aimed at my back, it seemed like a bad idea to turn around and look. So, I followed their every command, moving very, very slowly. I was taken away in a big paddy wagon designed to hold at least a dozen prisoners, which I had all to myself. I remember thinking how amazing it was to still be alive.

By 6 a.m. I was behind bars in the Arlington County Jail. The charge on my paperwork first read: "Radical." When I questioned the legality of that charge, it was changed to "Disorderly Conduct." When no one could testify to any disorderly behavior, the charge was changed yet again to "Excessive Tread Wear on Tires." To this day, I believe I may be the only citizen of this good country ever to be arrested for tire wear.

After I got locked up, every person coming over that bridge who even vaguely looked "radical" was arrested. So much for blocking traffic. However, I was only the first of more than 1,800 people arrested that day. The jails couldn't hold us all; there would be no business as usual in Washington that day, and on many other days we came to town. We were bringing the war home. Americans, and especially government officials, were far removed from all the pain and suffering in Vietnam. Bringing a bit of chaos and aggravation here was the least we could do.

When I got out of jail, my car had been towed to an impound lot ten miles outside of town. I had to purchase and carry four new tires with me before they would release my car at the lot. A few hours later, after hitchhiking out to the middle of nowhere, carrying the 4 new tires, I walked up to the gate of the impound lot. From a big cop wearing jet black sun glasses, I heard "What you doin' here with all those tires?" I prepared to be hassled and jerked around by another good old boy with a badge, this one carrying a big pearl handled revolver. But, my stereotype of Southern cops was blown away by this sympathetic, intelligent man, who had been banished out to "the lot" as an attitude adjustment.

Apparently Officer Masterson's gentle manner and liberal ideas ran counter to the red neck expectations of his bosses. He had been passed over for promotion for years, and placed far from town where he could do no harm. We talked for hours, and I learned a lot from him about the South, about cops, and about life. He was a gentle warrior who refused to be a bigot, or to hate anyone. I have since met a lot of Southerners like that. As he helped me change all four tires, I remember him sadly saying, "this used to be a hell of a good country, I just don't know where all the hate is coming from." I never felt so close to anyone in such a short time. We parted as good friends.

Before long I found myself back in Washington, this time camped out near the Washington Monument at another big peace rally. By evening, all protesters were being ordered out of the area by a ring of a few hundred Federal Park Police on horseback. More than a thousand people left as ordered. That left me and a few hundred diehards, who prepared to get arrested. I hoped it would be a peaceful arrest, and manage to avoid injury a second time.

I got separated from my friends, ending up in another camp, with a lot of military-type tents and guys in army fatigues. At first, I thought I had stumbled into a national guard camp, since I knew they had been called up to deal with the massive protests. But a lot of these guys had beards and long hair. Their combat fatigues were dirty, and they looked like they had been camped there for weeks. Then I saw the banner: "Vietnam Veterans Against the War." I did not feel I belonged there, but they asked me to stay and support them. A guy with an army ranger insignia on his shoulder handed me a two-foot long piece of iron shaped like a pipe, with a .50- caliber machine gun shell casing welded on the end. "You are in the army now, man, so take a hit." I sucked in the strongest smoke I had ever had, then stumbled backwards a few feet, and fell on my butt. "Best blow in Vietnam, man. He's one of us now, boys." Then they all laughed and applauded, and called me "brother."

We sat all day in a huge circle, sharing bottles of juice and wine, and a weeks worth of sandwiches and snacks from my pack. I listened to their stories about being in Vietnam. Some were hilarious, some hard to hear, really heartbreaking. They spoke about friends who never came back, and about the horrible things war makes you do. A lot of huts with kids and old folks were blown up, and burned down because someone had shot at them from somewhere. They were good guys with important information that America needed hear, but no one was listening.

The stories were shattered by the roar of a cobra helicopter with "National Guard" written on the side. It kept flying very low over us, with the loud speaker blasting, "Leave the area immediately or you will be arrested." It was so loud that some of the mounted park police one hundred yards away had trouble controlling their horses. One vet in the group started screaming at the copter, "Fuck you, the Washington Monument is ours, we earned it, and we ain't movin!" Another guy, jumped up screaming, going completely crazy. His buddies grabbed him and held him tight until he calmed down. I did not know about PTSD back then, but that is clearly what the roar of the helicopter and aggressive police confrontation was triggering in some of these guys.

I was witnessing a great tragedy unfolding before me; even veterans who had fought in Vietnam, were being treated as criminals. If anyone had a right to camp at the Washington Monument it was those guys. More warnings were blasting from megaphones, as hundreds of mounted police began to close in. It looked like a battlefield just before the battle begins, and it was frightening. But none of these guys were frightened, just angry. They defiantly held their ground. They were used to battle.

Maybe it was flashbacks from the war, but one guy with a big scar on his neck jumped up and pulled a bayonet from his belt, yelling at the helicopter, and threatening to kill the first mounted policeman who invaded their camp. After trying unsuccessfully to calm the guy down, the Army Ranger with the big pipe took one last puff, then got up saying, "This is gonna get ugly around here guys, I think its time to retreat." He walked around and hugged every guy who was staying, telling them "God bless you, man". A guy who was crying ran up and gave him a long hug. "Love you, man, I hope you and the kid (me) get out safe." No one was pressured to stay. About a dozen of us left, a few dozen stayed. I left them my water bottles, my sleeping bag, and the phone number to the antiwar legal defense group that had helped me get out of jail.

The ring of mounted Park Police let us through. I never found out what happened to the guys who stayed. There was nothing about it on the evening news. I worried about them for a long time.

Back in New York, some Quakers helped me apply for conscientious objector status, but they warned me the draft board would reject it, and to be prepared to go to jail. I was not a real conscientious objector in the government's eyes, because my refusal to kill was not based on "religious" principles. I refused to kill Vietnamese people because there was no good reason for it. That was deemed "political," and not religion. So, I prepared myself for some serious jail time.

The Quakers knew I was half Canadian, so they urged me to take advantage of that, and move to Canada. No way! I would not let Tricky Dickie Richard Nixon and his boys run me out of town. They would not get rid of me that easily! I waited for draft number thirty-seven to be called, waited for my chance to refuse, and got ready to do my time.

I became aware that my father had refused induction in WWII. He had been assigned to a civilian munitions factory after refusing to fight. He was angry about the Soviet invasion of Finland, and said he would only fight if he could first go in to liberate Finland from the Soviets. But when you agree to be a soldier, you fight whoever they tell you to fight. It was such a strange and unusual request, I guess they thought he was crazy, so they just assigned him to an aircraft factory as a civilian worker.

This war resistance thing really must have been in my DNA because my great, great grand dad, Thomas Servos, was killed in a run-in with George

Washington's militia for being a vocal loyalist, and refusing to support the Revolutionary War. Before my mother passed away, she gave me a well worn old booklet entitled United Empire Loyalists. It describes old Grandpa Servos being shot while running George's militia off his farm in upstate New York. His influential objections to a war with England, had apparently made it back to Washington, so George sent some soldiers up to Schoharie County, upstate New York to set him straight. After he was shot they burned down his farmhouse.

When all his sons returned from the fields, and discovered what had happened, they packed up and moved to Canada, becoming Canadian citizens along with many of their neighbors. Most of Thomas's sons, became soldiers fighting against Americans in both the Revolutionary War, and the War of 1812. A lot of Servos family members are buried in a military cemetery in Toronto, reserved for United Empire Loyalists.

My mother saw to it that I learned the Canadian version of American history during my school days. Her history books told of America's many attempts to invade Canada, during the War of 1812, and how they were defeated every time. I was probably the only parole officer in New York State who knew the derivation of the word "parole," and who the first parolees were. After one of the big failed attempts to invade Canada, three thousand American prisoners of war were put on ships, then sent back to America across the Great Lakes. Before being released, they had to sign a promise, or "parole" in French, to stay out of Canada. So far, we Americans have honored the conditions of our parole.

🎋 🎋 🎋 🎋

As fate would have it, a few weeks before my draft number #37 was called, the government ended the draft. Not long after that the US military pulled out of Vietnam. It seems that too many people were refusing to go, so they had to call the whole war off. When we left Vietnam, Communists did not take over the world as feared, or invade Brooklyn. But, the government learned their lesson, and converted to an "all volunteer" military. That made it a lot easier to engage in military adventures that had little popular support, since the draft had impacted rich and poor alike, and even the sons of government officials.

I was happy when the war ended, but I wish it had ended sooner because my friend, Francis, died there. I respect the guys who served in Vietnam, but I also respect the war resisters and protesters who helped stop that fiasco. The fifty-thousand Americans who died, was a great tragedy. A greater tragedy was the death of nearly three million Vietnamese people. We should keep the scale of human suffering in proper perspective. We should also hold politicians accountable, who involve us in unnecessary wars. Would it not be a fair rule?

The events during this period of my life taught me that there are many kinds of warriors, and many kinds of courage. Sometimes it takes greater strength not to fight. In that sense, Dr. Martin Luther King Jr., was greatest warrior of my lifetime. Receiving death threats every day, and harassed rather than protected by the FBI, he never backed down. He never toned down his aggressive voice for justice, or his nonviolent civil disobedience. The man had nerves of steel. Although remembered fondly now, he was very unpopular during his lifetime, considered an agitator and trouble maker. He was disliked for pushing so hard for racial justice, and later for his outspoken opposition to the Vietnam War. More than any other individual, he was the conscience of America.

Without Dr. King lending his moral authority to the anti-war movement, the Vietnam war would have gone on much longer. I would have been drafted, refused induction, then gone to prison. I owe a personal debt to Dr. King.

7. Finding the Aiki Path

𝕱ROM the moment I read about O'Sensei and aikido, I got excited. This guy, Ueshiba, was offering a possibility beyond "fight or flight." The image kept coming to me of a black-belted Gandhi, romantic and naïve perhaps, but hopeful and optimistic. This "ai-ki-do," or "way of harmonizing energy" offers possibilities essential for this world. My mother, would load the family into the car every Sunday morning for a trip to the local Quaker meeting house. It was the only church my atheist father would attend. But the Quaker pacifist thing was just too hard for me when dealing with bullies. Aikido seemed to offer the perfect Quaker backup plan!

Sempai Edgar Kann, Sensei Eddie Hagihara, and Sempai Howard Pashenz

Eddie Hagihara was a Japanese American martial arts teacher who projected the same mystical Asian presence which captivated me in the television program *Kung Fu,* with it's misty ancient monastery setting and enlightened masters. Eddie had a small cult following that I threw myself into with abandon. My inspiration for martial arts training was reignited, which led to five years of dedicated training under his guidance. Eddie did not teach so much as he "performed," but it was really quite beautiful. I tried to be just like him — relaxed, graceful, effortless, and magical. After 5 years I at least had the relaxed part down. I also learned to become light when being throw (light things do not break as easily). For Eddie, holding tightly and not cooperating with the person trying to throw you was unacceptable "rough stuff".

I learned Eddie's ways well and within a few years rose to become a "big fish" in that little bowl. Unfortunately, once you became a big fish you had to leave the stream and plunge into the ocean. Since Eddie's senior, Yoshimitsu Yamada, supervised our dojo and administered all examinations we were required to train often at his big dojo in New York City. When I went to Yamada's Manhattan dojo, this big fish quickly became bait for much bigger fish. In the early 1970s, New York Aiki Kai was a wild and crazy, free-wheeling place. It was not the tame, gentle, "spiritual" dojo I was used to. This place was rough, and to put it mildly, cooperation was not a priority. This was the big time, the school of hard knocks.

There was a black belt named Henry Smith who practiced his martial art as if he was performing in the Bolshoi Ballet. I was sure this guy would be a piece of cake, I would handle him easily. Henry was, in fact, a professional dancer, and I was too dumb to realize that dancers are among the world's strongest athletes. He wore me out in the first five minutes, the rest of the hour I was dying.

There was this cocky eighteen-year-old kid, Bruce Bookman, who was five years my junior, but had already earned his black belt. I was almost his rank and five years older, so I was sure he would be no problem. But, he kicked my butt even worse than Henry did. This tough city kid had it in for us suburban softies with our airy-fairy "mystical" teacher, Eddie. So, every time I went in to the city to train, it seemed like Bookman always spotted me, and like a young predator on the prowl, would show the world he was no longer a kid by pounding me into the floor. He loved the fact that he could wipe the mat with guys in their twenties. I hated that kid for being so damn good.

It was frustrating feeling so weak after almost eight years of martial arts. It got me thinking about heading to Japan, where I could learn the secrets to kicking butt. I was questioning the value of a cooperative aikido style — in a less than cooperative world. My hope of becoming an unbeatable martial arts master was to go to the source, in Asia. If I failed at that, the backup plan was to become an enlightened spiritual master. Better yet, why not become an enlightened spiritual — martial arts master! Yes, I would shoot for the whole enchilada.

Yamada sensei and New York Aikido friends

8. Bull in A China Shop — Unforgettable Terry Dobson

A while before leaving for Japan, I recall a big, bearded man entering the changing room after class at the Manhattan Dojo. He was wearing a worn-out, ragged training uniform (gi) and a thing that may at one time have been an old black belt, but now looked like an old grayish rope he found in the street. He must have trained in class, but I was too busy getting bounced around the mat to notice him.

He was pleasant enough and shared something about his last trip to Japan with one of the senior black belts as they dressed. He was pretty much ignored, almost as if he was just some bum off the streets who had wandered into the school. Only later did I learn this guy had trained for ten years in Tokyo, the only non-Japanese live-in disciple, with an intimate 10 year relationship with O'Sensei. Why did he receive so little respect? I never understood that.

When I learned who he was, and that he had a little dojo downtown I had to go. No one I knew in New York City had visited Terry's dojo, apparently it was off limits. With my rebellious nature, something off limits is guaranteed to peek my curiosity, and draw me to it. Forbidden fruits always seem to taste best.

Even if he had not been an outcast, the location of his dojo in the Bowery would have kept most students away. I was a suburban kid, not thrilled with going to the city at all, let alone the sleaziest part of downtown Manhattan. The Bowery was synonymous with bums, drunks sleeping on sidewalks, and puddles of vomit. Only

Terry would choose such a place — what a character he was.

It was a true Bowery dojo, with a bum lying on the sidewalk near the front door, and the smell of piss and other unpleasant organic substances all around. You had to watch where you stepped very carefully. I kept asking myself why I was even going there, the training hours there were "unofficial," meaning they would not be counted toward the next rank. That was a big deal back then, it was how they controlled the troops.

The dojo was as small as Terry was big, with a weapons rack consisting of a wooden sword, a big branch from a tree, and some kind of club Terry had found in the dumpster. The class was small, with a mix of the traditional and the outrageous. It was strange being taught by a guy who looked and sounded like a cross between a big furry mountain man, and a beatnik poet from the 1950s. His language was sprinkled with a unique mix of old jazz lingo and no-nonsense blue collar working class talk from his days working on oil rigs out west, and work as a bouncer in biker bars. This guy was one of a kind. He did not seem to quite fit in anywhere. He definitely did not fit my Asian master image.

Both Terry's martial practice and demeanor were a strange combination of a no-nonsense bouncer and devout spiritual seeker. It was one-of-a-kind "kick butt — but resolve conflict peacefully" style. He was still mesmerized by his master's spiritual teachings. He was also absolutely eloquent in his clarity and simplicity, when translating O'Sensei's complex ideas. No one ever translated the profound and elusive principles of O'Sensei into useable-practical terms as well as Terry Dobson. His martial practice was definitely not polished or artistic; in fact, he often seemed awkward and clumsy. But he had a spontaneity and authenticity like no other teacher. He seemed always to be searching and experimenting. He was not afraid to risk looking foolish, in fact, how he looked held little interest for him. (I know where I got that from!) Many of his experiments and exercises bombed, but he was the teacher unafraid to try.

Some of the weird exercises he had students do to explore O'Sensei's concepts of non-resistance and conflict resolution really made the point, while others were awkward and clumsy, but his efforts all had heart and passion. He used all kinds of props, from a rag doll snatched from the dumpster, to a bull whip; anything to get his point across.

At his best, he ignored style and was all substance. Many teachers' demonstrations were more graceful and artistic, and some appeared more "dynamic" or powerful than Terry. But, Terry was real. He had traded sweat and blood on the football field with the Green Bay packers, and been a bouncer in rowdy bars. He did not need to "look" powerful, he was powerful. As for grace and elegant movement, it held little inter-

est for him. What was a Terry Dobson class? You never could be sure, like this memorable class:

We were in the midst of Terry's rough and tumble class when he announced that we needed to meditate. A teacher stopping a class in the middle to meditate was a first for me. After a few minutes sitting, I heard him quietly get up and walk to the back of the dojo. You could hear him pushing and moving things around, apparently looking for something. As the minutes passed, the sounds gradually became louder and more forceful. It started to get scary when things were being knocked over and throw around — like some kind of rumble back there, or a grizzly bear on the loose. Maybe some bums had broken in the back of the dojo and a battle was raging! Do we continue to sit or run in the back to help?....Then... everything fell silent; he had found what he was searching for. His soft, quiet footsteps meant the danger had passed. He had returned, and then...the gentle sound of the meditation bell which he had finally found, signified the end of our meditation.

Terry would teach Verbal Judo seminars at a Human Potential Center in Greenwich Village for non-martial artists. Since I was the only one who could take falls, he took full advantage of me being there to dramatize his points. He would describe O'Sensei's concepts like nonresistance, but would not be getting through to them, or he would sense their boredom — so I knew it was coming. He would motion me up to strike him then bounce me off the walls, or reverse some strangle hold he demanded I put on him. They would all applaud and start paying attention. I think it was fun for him to bounce somebody around in the same way that O'Sensei used him for a demo prop countless times. I felt so honored, what a thrill.

He claimed his best barroom bouncer technique was to imagine with great intent that the mean drunk trashing the place was his brother. He would go up to the guy, put his arm around his shoulder, call him brother, and quietly speak heart to heart. He claimed that it almost always worked, but had the muscle and skill to back up his gentle requests. They could sense that. He would not let someone lose face in front of his buddies or his woman, which is why he rarely had to get physical. I sat there in coffee shops listening, hypnotized by the tales he would tell. His language was tough New York street talk, punctuated with continuous literary and historical references that revealed a great depth of knowledge of both European and Asian history.

Some of his tales were beyond outrageous, and I believe they were all true because they were not as much "war stories" as they were painful confessions. Like almost starting World War III:

"After I got out of the Marines Corps, I found myself sitting around my mother's Manhattan apartment, restless and lonely. I saw Russian Premier Khrushchev on TV give his famous 'we will bury you' speech at the United Nations. Her uptown apartment was right across the street from the Russian embassy, so later in the day, the fool struts out onto the balcony waving to the crowd like he is a big star. That pissed me off. I decided I would do the world a favor by blowing the son of a bitch away. In my mind I would become a big hero, that's how messed up I was. I got out my rifle, and I had him perfectly centered in my sights. I was all excited as I prepared to squeeze off the shot, but then her damn face got in the way. It was my mother's face. That mean, angry face, scolding me for screwing up again! So, I finally put down the gun, and the bum got to live another day. I guess you could say my fear of that woman kind of prevented World War III."

Shortly after that, his mother shipped him off to a Peace Corps-like missionary job in a rural village in Japan, where he could do less harm. Isolated, even lonelier, and not able to speak the language, he sank into a deep depression. It got worse. He started criticizing some corrupt village bosses, and really pissed them off. Wanting to get rid of him and knowing how depressed he was, they left a loaded pistol in his room. "I considered it a welcome gift. I put it to my head and pulled the trigger, but the damn thing jammed on me. I was even a failure at killing myself!"

Feeling the new energy and elation that often comes to severely depressed individuals who have made the decision to end it all, he decided to spend a night in Tokyo getting drunk and getting laid in a brothel. Then he would come back, fix the gun, and end it all. "Maybe I could have one happy day that somehow would not get fucked up."

It was a windy day in Tokyo, and no sooner had he gotten off the train, when a big gust of wind blew a cloud of dust in his eyes. He wiped his eyes, and it just got worse. Now, unable to see at all, he stumbled down a Tokyo street, helpless and completely disgusted. A Good Samaritan, seeing this big, blind foreigner stumbling down the street, led him to a clinic. After getting his eyes washed at the clinic, he saw the poster advertising a martial arts demonstration and decided to add that to his last day's itinerary. He had practiced a lot of martial arts but never heard a thing called ai-ki-do. "Seeing this aikido thing changed everything, I do not know why, it just did. Suddenly there was something to live for."

He insisted that the young man who performed the demonstration take him to his teacher. O'Sensei must have heard the commotion as this huge, brash, obnoxious foreigner pestered everyone for a meeting with the master. Against all their objections, O'Sensei came out of his room and met with Terry. Maybe it was out of compassion, or maybe he thought it was the only way to get rid of this big clumsy gaijin. Whatever the reason, they hit it off right away. It had to be something beyond words, since neither could speak the other's language. So, Terry gave up his planned suicide, and became the only foreign live in disciple, or "uchi deshi" of Morihei Ueshiba.

I asked Terry who the young Japanese man was who gave the demonstration that changed his life, and who took him to meet his master. "It was Yamada (Yoshimitsu). We have always had a kind of hatred for each other that is......organic, just meant to be. I am sure he has never forgiven himself for taking me to O'Sensei, and letting me in the door of Hombu Dojo. He must have really caught hell from the other Japanese, students and teachers alike. But I gotta give the guy credit, he saved my life."

9. Moving To Japan

SITTING on a plane heading to Japan in the mid-1970's, I wondered if quitting my job and selling my car was such a great decision for a twenty seven year old. A letter from Jay, the only martial arts bum I knew over there, said he was leaving a temp job way out in the middle of nowhere, and heading for Tokyo. That job, in the foothills of Mount Fuji, was about three hours from the city, "if you can find the place." It seemed as good a place to begin my Asian journey as any.

I had heard stories about foreigners getting beaten up pretty badly in Japan, so I tried to prepare myself. I figured I could not become big and powerful in a few months, but I could develop great stamina. So, in addition to martial arts I began running every day, twelve miles a day, seven days a week. I think I had my father's obsession with work. We cope with stress by working longer and harder than is reasonable. My response to high anxiety over my black belt examination had been to rise at 4:00 a.m. the day of the exam, and stay home from work practicing all day. Twelve hours training with imaginary opponents, taking a ten-minute break every hour to rest and calm my nerves with meditation and wine.

So, in the months before heading to Japan, I ran a lot, which would have been fine if I had known anything about running. Stores back then probably sold good running shoes, but I was happy with my four-year-old US Keds, a good, twelve-dollar sneaker. The result of all that running in junk shoes, with no days off, was improved stamina and the near destruction of both my knees. When I eventually boarded the plane to Tokyo, I was limping down the aisle looking more like a ninety-year-old with severe arthritis than a twenty-seven-year-old aspiring athlete.

My last memory of leaving America was a gift from my mother. I had been told the straw tatami training floors chewed up foreigners' knees like a meat grinder during the suwari waza groundwork training. But I had a secret weapon. Mom had asked what going away present I would like, so in one of my rare inspired moments, I asked her to sew knee pads into my training uniform. She got to work and created hidden pockets with three or four layers of soft, thick towels sewn into the pants at the knees. I may have limped my way to Japan, but I was the only foreign student without bloody knees during the first several months of training.

II.

SEARCHING FOR O'SENSEI IN JAPAN

1. Mt. Fuji's Boeki Kenshu Center

I left America with enough money to last me a few weeks, even though I planned to be in Asia for a few years. So, the temp job Jay had written me about seemed like a good start, even if it was far from anything. It was an English teaching job, and I remember reminding him that I knew nothing about teaching English. His letter responded to my concerns with "You can speak English, that is all you need to help a few guys practice their English." That sounded reasonable. So, I ignored the fact that my grammar was lousy, my spelling was worse, and that I had always been a marginal student. But, how hard could it be to give a few folks a little conversation practice in some remote village far from civilization?

From the airport I found the right train which took me way out there, until there was nothing but rice fields and one giant mountain, Mt. Fuji. Getting off in the village of Fujinomiya, as Jay had instructed, I searched for some little English tutoring place but could not find anything like that. I asked around in my broken Japanese, but no one knew anything. Finally, someone answered "Boeki Kenshu?" and pointed halfway up Mount Fuji, about five miles away. I saw nothing up there but mountain forest. What had Jay gotten me into? I met a cab driver who seemed to know of the place, so after twenty minutes winding up a long, mountain road, he dropped me off at a huge iron gate with a large highly polished bronze sign reading:

BOEKI KENSHU CENTER
Institute for International Studies and Training
Japan Ministry of Trade and Industry

This was not the little tutoring place I envisioned from Jay's letter. This was an elite and prestigious government institute. It could not be the right place. I was disgusted with myself for letting the cabbie leave me there. It was a long way back down so I figured I would walk up to this place then get a cab back down from there. I limped my way up the mountain road past the front gate. Several times, shiny black limos with darkened windows passed. Was this a school or the giant estate of some Japanese mafia boss?

The road continued past the front gate for over a mile. When it finally ended, what I saw was a damn palace! Boeki Kenshu, as it turned out, was an elite college campus built and operated by the Japanese government's Ministry of Trade and Industry (MITI) with, what seemed to be, unlimited funding. I walked into the first building, and into an ultra modern big classy looking lobby. There were pamphlets in English explaining what this place was. The brightest young executives from the top corporations in the country were sent there for a few months of training in international finance and English before being sent abroad to represent the biggest Japanese corporations in New York, London, Hong Kong, and other financial centers around the world. There was a small army of British college professors from places like Cambridge. The place was a combination of Harvard, Yale, and MIT, built for the best and brightest, who were being groomed to be the next generation of corporate executives.

I checked some papers Jay had sent me that helped me get a working Visa, and freaked out! Buried in the Japanese documents I found the words "Boeki Kenshu." This was the place. I was totally out of my league here. Jay was an A student from a top university, but I was a C student who barely made it through college. It would not take long for them to find out who I really was and throw me out. Worse yet, this was a government institution, so they could revoke my visa and have me deported! How did Jay get me into this? I had to get out of there fast. But, my cab was long gone. I decided to limp my way out of there as fast as my screwed up legs would carry me, then maybe catch a cab at the bottom. But, as I started to make my escape, I was approached by an old man in a very expensive black business suit.

"Good afternoon sir, would you be Mr. Collings." I nodded, wanting to run. "It is extremely wonderful to meet with you, sir. I am Udo, Dean Toru Udo of Boeki Kenshu Center. Please, you will follow me." Now there was no easy escape; he knew my name and saw my face. When he discovered how Jay had conned them into hiring me I would probably be deported, or maybe arrested for fraud. After serving a long jail sentence…..my mind continued to spin out, projecting the dire consequences.

He escorted me into his office, his very large elegant office. I scanned the windows for a possible escape route. "Mr. Jay recommended for you highly." He then proceeded to explain in his less than perfect English that most Japanese receive English language classes from first grade through college, but actually can hardly speak English at all. They know all the rules of English grammar, but rarely get conversation practice, and never with a native speaker. The joint government/industry council realized that they needed something other than English classes if young executives were to go overseas with effective communication skills. They were smart enough to realize language skills were not enough. These guys needed to understand how Americans thought and behaved. They also needed them to feel less awkward in social situations with foreigners.

Accomplishing all that would not be easy. But they had a strategic plan — brilliant in it's simplicity. Their plan was — me! They recruited "teaching associates," a polite title for young gaijin bums like me who did not know much of anything, except how to speak English and party:

"You mean, I do not need to know Japanese?"

"No, sir. No Japanese, please," he replied.

"Mr. Udo, I know nothing about business."

"No, sir. No business, please."

"You mean, I do not have to know how to teach English, either?"

"No, no teaching English, please. Only speak English."

I was starting to really like this guy. "You live in dormitory and talk to my students after they have long day of international business class. Your job to have fun with them, and they have fun. Then they know Americans and use English. Can you drink? At night, my students can drink a lot and not so nervous can practice English with you. We have very best sake, whiskey, beer, is this OK for you, Mr. Collings?" You receive salary every Friday.

Now I am loving this guy. "Room for you is very nice, and we have finest food in Japan. All the best food brought up to here because government ministers visit here many times. Is this OK for you?" I shook his hand and told him, "Yes, sir. For your students, I will drink and eat. I will help your students have a good time and speak English."

My mind was now racing in a new direction. I hit the jackpot, a gold mine. Was this really possible, a job where they paid me to do nothing but party with their students? It didn't matter what I said. I could say any stupid, useless thing that came to mind — and get paid for it! Free room and board, the best food and booze, and two hundred dollars a week to drink with a bunch of guys every night until we all passed out. A professional partier — I was up to this task! So, for the good of international relations and world peace, I accepted the job.

This place was beyond cool. The banquets were immense and designed to impress visiting government ministers and corporate CEOs who were constantly visiting. The students were young, hardworking executives, getting the chance to briefly relive their college days before being sent off to a strange land, devoting their lives to the corporation. After a long day of classes, they were ready to let loose in the dormitory lounge and enjoy having a "real American" to drink with. Just as Dean Udo had said, after a few drinks, their nervousness and awkwardness disappeared, and so did mine. Then, their bad English flowed effortlessly like the beer and sake. Every night was a laugh a minute.

I taught them how to tell some good dirty jokes in English. They tried to teach me how to get laid in Japan, although they were not that sure themselves. I would lead them in singing the few American songs I knew, their favorite being, "Take Me Out to the Ball Game." Hearing twenty drunk Japanese guys singing that really cracked me up. More than once, I fell off my chair in hysterical laughter. I really enjoyed being with these guys, and they seemed to have a great time, too. It was not just the drinking, although that added to the fun. Most Americans have stereotypes of foreigners. Mine was that the Japanese were all mystical masters or deadly martial arts experts. I am sure they had their stereotypes, too. But there, we got to know each other as real people.

Two things happened that I never expected. I realized that most of the other teaching associates were graduates of business schools who made a strategic decision to come there to make business contacts in the corporate world. Most of them were brighter and much more ambitious than a martial arts bum like me, but my guys were definitely having the most fun. They became more than just students or drinking buddies, we became good friends. They helped me understand how Japanese people were different from me, and the ways they were the same. They shared their hopes, fears and dreams with me, and let me enter their lives.

At the banquets and formal affairs, I learned all the proper etiquette and protocols expected and appreciated in Japan. But in the dorm and around campus, these guys were my buddies, and cultural differences disappeared. We spoke the universal language of all young men, including girls, sports, and silly guy stuff.

Sato was a young executive from the Kirin beer company, a big fellow who resembled a sumo wrestler. He would make a call every Friday afternoon to the company, ordering another "hayaku" (urgent) delivery of ten cases of beer, as well as a few cases of sake and whiskey. One Friday I was kidding

around with him and called out, "No, not "hayaku" — "hyaku!" (one hundred) cases!" Before I could explain it was just a joke, without a pause, he had changed the order to one hundred cases. I thought to myself, it just does not get any better than this. It must be God's way of making up for my virus lab job, he owed me for that one. Maybe it all balances out.

One Saturday, the guys took me on the hiking trail to the top of Mount Fuji in early spring before it was officially open to the public. That's because in spring, the whole mountain is a giant mud pie as the volcanic ash thaws from the winter freeze. We hiked right up through patches of snow and the waves of mud. It was a very slow messy climb but loads of fun, and the views were breath taking. Like walking up to heaven — you go into — then above — the clouds several times. The only person we saw the whole morning was a lone skier zooming down past us.

Coming down was ridiculous, slipping and sliding down the steep, muddy trails. It was like climbing down a giant mountain of melting ice cream. One of the guys muttered "sho ga nai" (what the hell) then started sliding down the snowy side of the mountain on the seat of his pants. It worked much better than tramping through the muck for 3 hours. We all left the marked trail and slid down the mountain after him on our butts. Zooming down so fast that the bottom of our jeans wore right through. At the bottom all ten of us had bright red frost bitten butts. It took almost five hours slipping and sliding up, but less than an hour to slide down. It was outrageous fun. Let the world know I conquered Mount Fuji on my butt!

After my three-month tour of duty at Boeki Kenshu, it was hard for me to leave those guys, but they had to leave, too. I made friendships that lasted several decades. Why was I the most well liked teaching associate? A socially awkward, antisocial fellow by nature? It was because I had no ambitions and no agenda. I was not there to "make contacts," I was there just to learn about Japan, make friends and have a good time. I was innocent and genuine. I did not realize, at the time, how special that is. But, it was special, and they appreciated it. So, they shared their lives and their culture with me. I will never forget them.

2. Seigo Yamaguchi — My Introduction to Hombu Dojo

𝕴N the City of Tokyo, I somehow found the big martial arts school known as Aikido Hombu Dojo, without too much trouble. It is an ugly four-story building on a side street in the Shinjuku section of the city. I even registered at the first floor office without too much trouble; they were used to the broken, half-baked attempts by foreigners struggling to speak Japanese. What made my language struggles easier was seeing how the Japanese appreciated any foreigners' attempts to speak their language. This was, in fact, what separated students of Japanese culture from tourists in their eyes. The struggle to speak their language showed humility and respect for their culture.

I headed up the stairs, excited to take my first class and passed the big, empty dojo on the second floor. Then went up another flight, where I found myself on a big, open landing, looking out onto the main dojo. There was a big class of maybe sixty students in progress. I was not sure where the dressing room was, so I sat down on the stairwell and watched the class. This teacher was a real showman, thin but not frail, he moved with silky smoothness. He handled the young black belts who reached out for him like an elegant matador, treating the bulls like toys.

Before he had finished demonstrating, he was already giving me the evil eye. When he finished demonstrating and had the students practice he walked to the edge of the mat toward me, and obviously pissed, let loose with a ferocious barrage of angry Japanese, none of which I understood. Even with months of study tapes and books, I had no clue what he was saying. All I could do was stand there and look stupid. I tried bowing, but that did not work. I started backing down the stairs, but that got him even madder so I just stood there frozen. His tirade did not seem to distract the students training, so I guessed they were used to this. I just stood there and watched as the guy kept going off on me, a wonderful way to introduce myself at Hombu dojo, I thought.

Something of this situation felt familiar. My mind shifted to three thousand feet in the sky, standing outside the cockpit of a small, single-engine plane in parachute school. I was being screamed at by the jump master. He had said, "When you climb out onto the wing, wait for my commands to jump. If I give a different command, do not jump, got it?" No problem. Trouble was, with wind rushing past your ears at 130 miles per hour, and the roar of the plane engine blasting, you cannot hear anything. You see the guy's mouth is moving and all kinds gestures but you do not have clue what he is saying. So, regardless of what he was saying, I let go of the wing and flew into space. His fading sounds gave way to the gentle flapping of my parachute, floating down like a leaf off a tree. Very quiet, with no one yelling any more. Ah,… peace.….

Still on the stairwell of Hombu Dojo — and getting yelled at in Japanese by this nut job? I finally spotted a little curtain that looked like a storage closet, so I ducked in there. Eureka! It was not a closet, it was the locker room! For the moment I was safe.

I thought of hiding in there until class was over but reminded myself I traveled halfway around the world to train there, so I changed into my gi and found the entrance to the training hall. There was another guy who was late for class sitting there in the formal *seiza position*, still and erect on the wood floor, in the back of the training hall. I bowed onto the mat and sat next to him. Together we waited to be recognized and granted permission to join in the class. In a few minutes, the teacher spotted us and approached. I prepared myself for getting yelled at some more, but he simply nodded, motioning for us to join the class.

I later learned the instructor was eighth degree black belt Seigo Yamaguchi. Although I never got yelled at by him again, the chemistry never was very good between us, kind of oil and water. He was the most popular and influential teacher at Hombu, more so even than O'Sensei's son, Kisshomaru Ueshiba. Most students, especially the large contingent of French, were mesmerized by Yamaguchi Sensei's elegant style of movement. This was the dominant style in most of Japan, and clearly becoming the future of this aikido martial art. I spent several months attending his classes, joining the atmosphere of fluid — graceful — artistry. Yamaguchi had the demeanor and style of the great Spanish bull fighters. Trouble was, I don't like bull fighting.

Yamaguchi Sensei was more selective than other teachers about who he would let strike or grab him. The very thing that made him so popular — elegance and beauty, was a performance orientation that lacked the martial intensity I was seeking. It seemed more suited to a stage than a dojo, but that was clearly a minority view. I spent many hours immersed in the atmosphere of his classes, but it just was not me. It was a bad fit. I finally had to face the hard truth about myself, I was just not made to be "elegant."

3. Ichiro Shibata — Steal the Knowledge

ON the streets of Tokyo, I quickly discovered all those months of Japanese study in America proved quite useless. Little of my Japanese made sense to Japanese people, so I would struggle like a babbling idiot to pay for toothpaste, communicate with my landlord, or ask where a public bathroom was. The assurances I had received that most Japanese spoke some English was dead wrong. More accurately, they "wanted" to speak English, or "thought" they spoke English. But their English was even worse than my Japanese. However, the sight of a struggling young foreigner drew out an innate kindness from Japanese people. They were always patient and tried to be helpful. My ineptitude and awkwardness consistently revealed the warm and generous nature of these people.

On my second day in Tokyo, I wandered the streets, unsuccessfully searching for a post office. I repeated a phrase I had memorized well, "Excuse me sir, where is the post office." I got a blank stare. It was incomprehensible babble as far as the drug store clerk was concerned. Another customer in the store overheard and came to my assistance. He was a young Japanese man, not much older than me, clean cut and athletic looking. Without a word, he smiled and motioned for me to follow him. He led me four or five blocks to the post office, then disappeared down a side street before I had a chance to thank him.

Back at Hombu for my second week of training, Jay was eager to introduce me to another foreign student from New York. His name was Bruce, and he had been training in Tokyo for several months. "He is a wild and crazy kid but really good, you will love training with him." Could it be? No, it could not be Bookman. Not the same Bruce who had been kicking my ass at the New York City Dojo for three years. Yes, he had moved to Japan too. Months before me. He would now continue to kick my butt on this side of the world, but with more power and style. No matter how strong I became, he would become stronger too. Whatever secrets I learned, he would learn them too. Their was no escaping it; Bruce Bookman would remain my sempai for life. More than thirty years later I am still hot on his heels, training hard, but so is he. Sempai for life.

Both Bruce and Jay warned me that the next class was taught by a tough as nails monster man named Shibata. He was the baddest of the uchi deshi, who they heard had started his training at around age four. Recently promoted to instructor status, he had been a private student of the ferocious Kazuo Chiba Sensei. Rumor was, that he had become even stronger than Chiba, so he was made an instructor.

I sat as far back from the front row of students as possible, waiting for "the killer" to arrive. Trouble was, not many students showed up for his class, so there were very few others to hide behind. In a school of five hundred, just a handful of students came for this class. Bruce and Jay nervously sitting beside me. A few Japanese guys. This was going to be intense. As I waited for the "Thursday Afternoon Terror" to arrive, I wondered why I was sitting there.

Shibata Sensei walked onto the mat like a slow-moving Sherman tank. His demeanor was that of a Roman gladiator entering the coliseum, expecting to battle tigers and lions — but seeing only men. With deliberate intent, he perused the battlefield to see who had dared attend his class — like showing up was a provocative act, a personal challenge to him. But, his face and walk were slightly familiar. Was it possible? Was this the nice young man who had gone out of his way to help me find the post office? It was definitely the same guy.

But here he was a totally different person.

True to his reputation, he blasted black belt students into the tatami like a jack hammer, pushing both Japanese and foreigners to the limits of their ability, then a little further. In this special world called "Shibata's class," pain was a certainty, injury a possibility, and death …? Minor injuries were just part of training in this class. Which was fine since young men heal quickly, and only young men were crazy enough to attend. Shibata Sensei offered a clear window into Japanese character, in all of its complexity — generous, selfless, but on the battlefield ruthless and terrifying.

As the months passed, Shibata Sensei became a friend, as well as a teacher. Extremely intelligent and very cultured, he knew more about classical music than anyone I have met. That helpful young stranger in our first encounter was a big part of who he was; it was a part of his warrior ethic, service, part of his personal bushido. He embodied both soft and hard, both fire and water. He dedicated his life to the most philosophical and nonviolent of the martial arts, at the same time serving as dojo bouncer. Happy to lead trouble makers down the block and dutifully beat the hell out of them.

Like many great martial artists at "Humble Dojo," as we called it, long after Shibata became an instructor, he still trained in other teachers' classes. It was not long before I was the lucky fool bowing in to him for an hour of one-on-one training. Some of those were the longest hours of my life. If you knew Shibata back then, you would be surprised that I am still alive.

He never blocked or stopped my attempts to throw or pin him. That would have been more merciful, and much easier. He just responded very, very slowly, and became very, very heavy. His body moved one centimeter at a time. Which meant that with a sustained, all out effort I could complete one throw or pin in maybe 2 to 3 minutes. It felt longer. He timed his resistance perfectly so that I completed each technique just before passing out.

Shibata never tried to hide the fun he had watching me struggle, with sweat drenching my uniform within the first five minutes. He also never hid the respect he had, for those willing to train that hard with him. Struggle takes courage. In the budo tradition it builds "kokoro" and "kiryoku." This intense level of training, or "seishi tanren" is not pretty, or comfortable, but it has heart. It is of great value for those committed to going deep into their practice, and deep into themselves. It also builds strength.

The prevailing view of such training in the noncompetitive martial arts is that not cooperating is mean-spirited and competitive. This is not necessarily true. At his dojo in Iwama, O'Sensei emphasized *katai keiko and tanren*, which are intensely rigorous and demanding forms of practice. It is designed to take serious students to deeper levels of understanding and skill. This level of training is perhaps more suitable for potential teachers, than typical students. It quickly reveals all weaknesses in one's movement and understanding, and defies attempts to "muscle through" resistance. On one cold winter day, a senior Japanese black belt approached me after training with Shibata, and touching my sweat soaked gi he commented: "Good for you, hour with Shibata equal one month training anyone else." It certainly felt that way.

Years later, at a New York martial arts seminar, he spotted me from the far side of a college gymnasium. Running at top speed across the gym, he leaped onto my back as I was stretching on the floor. "Tom-San, how are you!" It was a little stretching assistance, Shibata style.

A dojo in Berkeley, California, went through a half dozen teachers after their original sensei died. They were apparently dissatisfied with each one, firing them after a few months. I heard that none of them adequately met expectations for the Berkley New Age — socialist — hippie — Northern California mind set. When I heard Shibata Sensei was the latest hire, I could not stop laughing. I wondered how many seconds his tenure would last. His presence alone, was sure to freak them out. Well, it has been about thirty years, and he is still there. This is truly a mysterious world.

4. Sadateru Arikawa — Mr. Deceptive

HERE was another guy who many students at Hombu avoided. Bruce and Jay fondly called him "Harry." Someone else called him "Dirty Harry." The guys at Hombu loved to mess with new comers like me. "You poor son of a bitch, Harry is looking for fresh meat, and he will find you and break you in half for sure. If you can still walk after he throws you, get up fast to take another fall, or you will piss him off," Jay warned. "When you grab Harry's wrist, get ready to fly. Roll with the punches or you will go down hard." Who was this guy the foreigners called Harry? There was no one on the teaching staff by that name. They were all Japanese names. I decided this time they were just conning me.

There was a wonderful French student I trusted, Daniel Boubault. "Yes, he is real; they refer to Arikawa Sensei as "Harry," and he will strike you the moment you are about to touch him. You must be alert. How is your body? Are you strong?" I told him I was not that strong. "Good, because it is the strong ones who get most of the broken bones. Just stay relaxed and become light. You might be ok." This was not good, because Daniel was a serious guy who did not exaggerate.

At class time, an average sized, slow moving middle aged man with an expressionless face bowed onto the mat, wearing a training uniform that looked two sizes too big. This was the same gentleman I had frequently seen in the dojo office with Ueshiba Sensei, wearing an old suit that also was two sizes two big. What's up, I thought, did this guy shrink? I learned later that he had been seriously ill and lost a lot of weight.

He sort of wandered out onto the middle of the training floor with a demeanor that looked half drunk, and totally bored. He never even looked in our direction to see if anyone was there for class. I relaxed a bit, thinking they may have been just been messing with me. This guy was far from intimidating, he seemed half asleep!

When class began, he immediately looked in my direction, and with a lazy half hearted gesture he motioned me up. He lazily offered me his arm to grab. As I ran up, I recall thinking he was a little strange but not the slightest bit intimidating, with the demeanor of a tired drug store clerk. Half grinning I trotted up to him, thinking how gullible did my friends think I was? I was soon to receive a significant attitude adjustment.

Arikawa Sensei was a master of lulling those who did not know better into a state of complacency, which is the real strategy of aikido. That may be why he liked to demonstrate on all the new idiots, rather than familiar faces who could not be so easily lulled into complacency. He casually offered an opening, drawing me in to grab him. As he did this he slid to my side, putting what felt like his whole body through my face. A loud "smack" reverberated throughout the dojo as my body went airborne across the room. It sounded brutal, and probably looked that way.

It actually was not that bad. Red-faced but uninjured, I popped back up and got blasted a few more times. The brutal smacking sound was actually his open palm forcefully leading me into the fall, a closed fist would have done me in. Then, with just the hint of a bow, he indicated for the class to practice.

Daniel had been correct; I stayed alert and light, and was never injured by Arikawa Sensei. Some of the bigger and stronger guys were. Harry's manner and techniques looked sloppy, and he appeared as if he were totally spaced out. This deceiving demeanor belied masterful skills, with simple but effective movement. I had come to Japan to become stronger, since my first teacher taught only a light, and completely cooperative style of practice. Ironically, it was the ability to be light and cooperative that saved me from injury with Arikawa Sensei and other powerful teachers.

5. Kisshomaru Ueshiba — Subtlety and Dignity

KISSHOMARU Ueshiba Sensei was O'Sensei's son, who was referred to as the Doshu. He was the Master and leader of art during my years at the Hombu, and the person I really came to Japan to study under. He was a small, thin man in his sixties, with quiet dignity. His demeanor was always formal but kind. I attended many of his daily 6:30 a.m. classes, filled with a lot of old Japanese guys in there sixties, seventies, and eighties, some of whom seemed to never miss a class. No old folks home for those guys; if they could get out of bed, they got to the Doshu's class and trained. About these old guys, Terry Dobson used to say, "If they did not show up for training, it was only because the iron lung machine could not fit through the dojo door." Can there be any better role models of what old age can be?

At the time, I did not appreciate how extraordinary it was, and what a profound influence those guys would have on my life as I became older. Occasionally, an old guy died on the mat. He died doing what he loved, and there is absolutely nothing sad about that. I would be pleased to have a tombstone reading something like "Here lies T. Collings — He died in martial arts class taking an excellent fall."

My wife Kimiyo Hamazaki in Kisshomaru's class

Since the Doshu's classes were always very large, it was hard to have a lot of contact with him. The times he threw me and pinned me are etched in my mind and body. He usually used the uchi deshi, the young Japanese professional instructors in training — Seki, Yokota, Miyamoto, and Osawa. Although these guys were really strong, they had amazing sensitivity and could instantly become as light as a feather. This allowed the Doshu to appear soft and graceful, which is how he is remembered.

Actually, the aikido techniques of Kisshomaru Ueshiba were filled with atemi strikes to the head, ribs, and kidneys, executed from masterful angles and dominant positions. He led the attacker's movement into his atemi, drawing them off balance into vulnerable positions. But, to spectators it almost looked like a dance. Just before getting clobbered, the uchi deshi would smoothly throw their head's back, or let their legs slide out from under them to avoid injury.

They would become airborne, as if lifted by some invisible force. Their falls appeared effortless, and their landings nearly silent. It was beautiful, and masterfully deceptive. His subtlety and precision, coupled with the amazing responsiveness and agility of the deshi made brutal techniques appear soft.

The Doshu's art reflected his mission. He presented a fluid, non-confrontational art, which disguised it's devastating capability through subtlety.

When I read the quotes of O'Sensei describing his aikido art as predominantly strikes rather than grappling, throws or pinning, I see it in the practice of Kisshomaru.

I would prefer to forget the first time the Doshu called me up to strike him. The training hall was packed for his class as usual, with many black belts of fifth degree and higher. They all watched, as I ignored his first two invitations to attack him, assuming he was calling someone of higher rank behind me. Finally, realizing he was waiting for me, I leaped to my feet and charged toward him. As I did, my feet became tangled in the pleats of my traditional samurai garb known as the hakama. I stumbled toward him, struggling to regain balance, and felt the suppressed laughter of a large hall full of sixty or seventy martial artists. But the Doshu's steady, dignified manner never registered any of this; his calm, stable presence could even contain the foolishness of a young, hyperactive gaijin. He simply waited until I regained my balance, then executed some wonderful techniques. That incident brought me several weeks of fame at Hombu Dojo back in the 1970s, and provided my friends and sempai with joyful laughter during many late night drinking sessions.

Kisshomaru Ueshiba had a wonderful warm-up and self-massage routine (aiki taiso) that I often use today, which includes the rowing exercise with his father's powerful kotodama chanting sounds. It is a great mental and physical preparation for training, and I am amazed how few dojos still do the full series of these exercises.

Although he is remembered for his unassuming, and dignified manner, few teachers have duplicated Kisshomaru's mastery of position, timing, and angles, from which he slipped in those near invisible strikes. He had martial arts knowledge and combat expertise that many failed to recognize, due to his subtlety.

About a year before he passed away, I returned to Tokyo to visit him. Standing next to him in front of Hombu Dojo, he did not show a hint of illness or weakness. Only his quiet strong presence and dignified manner were evident. That is how I will always remember Kisshomaru Ueshiba.

6. Kisaburo and Hayato Osawa

KISABURO Osawa Sensei was director of training during my years at Hombu Dojo. My clearest memory of him was in the streets of Tokyo. I was walking about a half block behind a fairly young man in a white T-shirt and jeans, who was walking briskly and pulling farther ahead of me. When he turned at a corner and I saw his face I was astounded it was Osawa Sensei. His youthful body movement, the bounce in his step, and the impeccable posture fit a man of half his age. He showed me that sixty-five or seventy does not have to be "old."

When he taught his movements were soft, large, circles. It did not seem to matter how fast people came at him — he would draw them into the same big circles. He was a small man, so it felt strange that he could so easily immobilize us with a simple wrist grab as he wandered around the mat. I have mixed

feelings about him resisting people like that, even though his resistance seemed effortless. Perhaps he was making a point about the nature of strength.

His son, Hayato, was one of the aikido Hombu uchi deshi. The first time I trained with him was a real wakeup call. I figured since his father's style of movement was so soft, practice with Hayato-San would be easy. Big mistake. I can still feel his yokomen side strikes slicing through my raised arm, slamming me in the side of my head for the good part of an hour. Seven years of aikido training, and I had never had that problem before. It spoke volumes about the way aikido is commonly practiced. No other training partner in this art had ever struck me with real intent or focus before. I painfully realized that much of my training had been dishonest and ineffectual.

For a good part of an hour Hayato continued doing the same thing, and I continued doing the same thing — getting slammed in the head each time. Looking back, it is amazing how long it often takes, and how much pain is required to stop making the same mistakes over and over. Somewhere around the thirty or fortieth collision between the side of his hand and my head, I realized that to survive the hour I better try something different. I had been expecting him to be nice, and stop striking with intent and focus. But he had too much integrity for that. It was not a game to him, it was budo.

Why do we so often repeat behaviors in situations so clearly calling out for change. The security of what is familiar dies hard. The alternative is risk taking; venturing into the unknown. Here is where pain becomes our ally. Sometimes it is only pain that provides the energy and motivation to take the leap.

I improved a great deal in the course of that one hour. I had to — with Hayato Osawa there was no other option. If he had been "nicer," I could have maintained my illusion of competence. I could have stayed with what was familiar, and remained in my comfort zone But he was not nice, he was sincere. We need more people like that.

7. Hombu Sempai — Essence of Budo

ᴬFTER Kisshomaru Ueshiba's class I used to watch a senior black belt student do *soji* (dojo cleaning chores) after class. He was one of the old regulars at the 6:30 a.m. class that young guys like me often missed. Most of the "old guys," never missed. Their training was less athletic and acrobatic then mine, but a lot of those old guys had a dedication and life-time commitment that put us young fools to shame. For them, martial arts was not a hobby, or a skill, but a lifestyle. The dojo was not a place to sign up for a year or two, but a permanent fixture in their lives. Through the ups and downs of their lives, they always had the dojo, and their budo training.

The guy I loved to watch exemplified this spirit. I never knew his name, but his face and how he moved remains etched in my mind after all these years. He was somewhere between middle age and old. His smile revealed the simple

joy of being at the dojo, training, and love for the simple things in this life. His belt was an old, grayish bunch of threads, with all the black worn off. His smile was clear and bright. Ueshiba Sensei always acknowledged his presence in class with a smile, maybe a word or two, but rarely interrupted his practice with conversation. He understood that the man came to train.

This sempai (senior) of mine was often the first to the bucket of cleaning rags after class. He would gracefully, but energetically get on all fours, then push the cleaning rag across the wood floor for the entire hundred-foot length of the training hall. Then, turn around and push it back again. He may have been a professional of some kind, a CEO of a corporation, or a shop clerk. None of that mattered. In his mindful movement and humility I witnessed the essence of budo.

The day I asked to take his photo, he smiled but seemed confused why anyone would want his photo? He was not famous, and not on the teaching staff. I have no idea what his rank was. But to me, he was a great teacher, and his photo will always hang on my wall.

I remember watching him leave the dojo, and disappear through the crowded streets of Tokyo each morning. His posture and relaxed flow of movement revealed the positive effects of his morning training. To me, he represented all that is good and pure in the martial arts. May I get old just like him.

8. Nobuyuki Watanabe — Friendly Pain

THERE is a lot of BS and baloney in the world of martial arts. Both aikido and aiki jujutsu have more than their share. I see teachers, once honest and authentic, now performing dramatic demonstrations, implying or even claiming magical powers. They are sad caricatures of the honest martial artists they used to be. While they lose their best students, they retain true believers who see what they want to see, and feel what they hope to feel. The sincerity and trust of these students is exploited, as they become hypnotized to accept what their common sense would otherwise dismiss as foolishness.

It can be hard to separate reality from fantasy in disciplines where "leading the mind" and receiving techniques with sensitivity and responsiveness are part of the legitimate skill set. When I read a recent criticism of the Japanese aikido teacher, Nobuyuki Watanabe, performing "phony, no-touch throws," I understood what people were probably reacting to. Some of what I see him and other senior teachers do today saddens me, but it was not always that way. The memories I hold of

my times with Watanabe are really quite wonderful.

Watanabe Sensei was assigned to teach the weekend classes of Morihiro Saito at the aikido Hombu, after O'Sensei died and Saito stopped coming to Tokyo. I attended a lot of Watanabe's classes, where he continued most of the same basic techniques Saito Sensei taught but did them in the modern aiki kai style which emphasizes flowing graceful movements. He had a serious but relaxed demeanor, which was the same demeanor he presented on stage when performing shakuhachi as one of Japan's very fine bamboo flute masters.

One day he began throwing me around the dojo after class. Getting much individual attention at a huge Japanese Hombu dojo is rare unless you are enrolled for private classes, so I literally jumped at the opportunity to get some personal time with a teacher. The traditional method of mastering Japanese disciplines like judo or jujitsu is to be thrown thousands of times. In fact, being on the receiving end of techniques used to be the only training a student received for the first several years.

True to this tradition, Watanabe Sensei accepted the job of bringing me several thousand falls closer to mastery, and had great fun doing it. He would start throwing me around with the same restrained demeanor he had during class, but after a few minutes, when I really was sucking air, he changed. Was it to distract me from the pain — to keep me relaxed — or was he just having fun? His chuckles gradually gave way to unrestrained belly laughs as he continued putting me through my paces with an element of silliness that softened my pain.

His body movements became smaller and more subtle, until they were no more than slight gestures of the head or shoulders, sending me flying all over the huge training hall. I flew all around the dojo as if carried by some invisible force. To people who knew what was going on, it was probably lots of fun to watch. To those thinking it was some kind of "demonstration" it would have appeared foolish and even "phony."

In between gasping for air I would start laughing too and our laughter would fill the dojo. Eventually, his movements and gestures shrunk to only a finger pointing or moving his eyes in a certain direction, then I would be flying in that direction. As my lungs burned, and my legs turned to rubber, Watanabe's playful spirit somehow kept me moving. It kept me in the game far beyond my usual stamina. He seemed to have great fun wearing me out, but he was also revealing to me a wonderful secret to energy and strength, namely, do not give in to self pity, instead keep the mind light and make friends with your pain.

There was nothing phony about this practice. There was magic — it was how he kept me going long after exhaustion had set in. Looking back on it now, there may have been people watching who thought, "That cannot be real." But, my sweat and pain were very real. The increase in my capacity to fall without injury, even when exhausted, was real, too. Watanabe used the spirit of fun and play to help a young athlete move beyond exhaustion, to reach a new level of mental and physical stamina. He was showing me there is a spirit of play and laughter that can replace the heaviness and self-pity associated with pain. Watanabe Sensei helped me tap into reserves of energy I never knew I had, simply with an attitude adjustment. Watanabe never took himself seriously, or pretended to be doing anything other than working me hard.

Watanabe Sensei reminds me of the Zen master leading one hundred monastics in a three-month, eighteen-hour-a-day, intensive training session I was in. Interrupting the serious, solemn atmosphere, and startling all of us with the admonition, "You all look so grim. This is no good! With this attitude, your practice will never last. Just settle back into the moment in a relaxed and easy way. This is all a big game, please make it playful." He told us to lighten up, and our practice would be stronger. We were even allowed to smile!

9 Moriteru Ueshiba — Sincerity and Humility

IT was a disappointment to find that formal meditation training is as rare and out of place at most dojos in Japan as it is in America. So, while at Hombu, I would disappear into the second floor beginners dojo to do my meditation practice, away from all the noise and people crowding the main third-floor training hall. I always finished before the start of the beginners class taught by Waka Sensei (young master) who was O'Sensei's grandson. He was really good, even though he was only in his twenties and the same age as me.

There seemed to be strict separation between black belts and beginners at Hombu, and I never saw any black belts in the white belt class. In a culture and a traditional institution like a dojo, where protocol is sacred, a black belt entering Waka Sensei's class would be breaking protocol. But, I was still too low on the totem pole to get used much for demonstrations by the head masters. One night over some hot sake, Shibata Sensei looked me in the eye and said in quite good English, "You will not live in Japan forever. Before you return to America you must steal all knowledge you can." Those words had an impact on me. To me it meant that breaking protocol at times in the service of gaining knowledge was a necessary evil.

One day, I just stayed in the second floor dojo after zazen (or maybe fell asleep) and found myself bowing in with the twenty students in Waka Sensei's beginners class. I could have put on a white belt, but Waka Sensei had seen me many times in his father's class, so I could not con him. I did all the warm-ups and falling drills like everyone else, and waited to be politely kicked out of the class.

To this day, I have no idea what Waka Sensei thought, but I am guessing it was something like, "another confused gaijin who still does not know where he is supposed to be." But for some reason, he let me stay. When I kept coming back every other day, he still did not throw me out? In fact, he started throwing me around when demonstrating the techniques in front of class. Maybe he decided it was safer to use me than a beginner, or maybe he was just being nice to me. Whatever his reason, what a thrill it was be tossed around each day by O'Sensei's grandson.

I never told anyone that Shibata was to blame for the obnoxious kid from New York always crashing Waka's class, but not long after I started doing it Shibata resigned from Hombu Dojo and moved to America. Thanks to Shibata, I can someday impress my grandchildren (or drunken aiki friends) by telling them I was young Ueshiba Sensei's main uke for a while at Aiki Central, Tokyo.

Moriteru Ueshiba visiting Iwama

Funny thing is, his only complaint was scolding me occasionally for not throwing the white belt students hard enough. I was being really careful, since I was not even supposed to be there. But, with a big smile he would come up to me and say, "Throw him harder, he is strong student, throw harder please!" So, I would throw them hard and hope no one got injured. They never did.

Moriteru was part of the small group who attended Chiba Sensei's Friday afternoon class. He sat with us waiting for class to begin just like a regular student. He trained with whoever bowed in to him, even me. He showed no hint of self-consciousness regarding his position as the next headmaster of the art. I would start off very nervous, but after a few minutes I forgot who he was, and just enjoyed training with him. What a great training partner. He could have trained as if he had something to prove, but he never did.

I recall Chiba having us work in groups of three, struggling to do a very difficult two-on-one technique. When Moriteru attempted to throw both of us simultaneously, we got tangled up, and all three of us went down in a big, messy pile of arms and legs. As that happened, my body stiffened, afraid we had embarrassed him. ("Great job Thomas — you just embarrassed the next headmaster of the art.") But as we all hit the ground, he exploded with laughter. We had a wonderful time attempting these very old, near impossible techniques on each other. He kept the training joyful, and never let his name or position spoil it. What a role model of humility he was!

Not long ago, on one of my return trips to Hombu, I was sitting on the mat with my friend Jay from New York waiting for a class to begin. A young Japanese black belt sat next to him, and they trained together for an hour. After class, I asked my friend how the training was. "Wonderful, that kid was an awesome training partner." If I had told him he was training with Moriteru's son, the new Waka Sensei, he would have been too nervous to enjoy it.

10. Shoji Seki — Pure Simplicity

WHILE at Hombu, I trained with the uchi deshi Shoji Seki as often as possible. I also followed him and trained in his classes at various dojos around Tokyo, where he was assigned to teach. Among the Hombu uchi deshi being groomed to be professional teachers, who were all great athletes and martial artists, there was something special about Seki. He was powerful in body and spirit, but highly disciplined. There was nothing flashy or even distinctive about his style, just very clean, precise, and unpretentious. His practice and presence had no embellishments, only simplicity and integrity.

When I offered to pay him for private lessons, he reminded me that he was only uchi deshi and not a shihan (master). I expected him to say that, and told him I didn't care about that, but he declined. I was glad I asked, because after that he often threw me around when demonstrating for the class.

Serving the Doshu and honoring his role as uchi deshi was more important to Seki than some extra cash in his pocket, or the prestige of having a private student. Today he is a Master Instructor at the Tokyo Hombu, and they are very fortunate to have him. Seki is the real deal, all heart and class. There must be an ego there somewhere, but I never found it.

11. Hiroshi Tada — Pure Passion

𝒜NOTHER teacher with no discernible ego was Hiroshi Tada. Both Seki and Tada were highly disciplined and completely unpretentious. Like Seki, I saw nothing in Tada's art that was extra, flashy, or designed to impress. Just high energy basic training to purify mind and body. I would go to his class at the big Zen temple in Tokyo, where a big hall was amazingly converted to a matted dojo with the touch of a button. Anyone taking Tada's class or even just observing him sees and feels his strict self discipline and humility.

One year, I was filming the annual All Japan Budo Demonstrations from the balcony of the Budokan in Tokyo. Tada Sensei was on the bill,

as one of the masters people from all over Japan came to see. A few seats away from me, filming every demonstration and constantly exclaiming, "Sugoi! Ah subarashi da yo! (How wonderful! Fantastic!)" was Tada Sensei. When it was time for his demonstration, he briefly disappeared from the audience, then after his demonstration quickly returned to resume filming

others. He was as excited as a kid in a candy shop. Forty years of training and teaching, and he was still that excited; that's passion!

12. Meik Skoss — Classic Budo

MY learning was turbocharged by an amazing martial artist and sempai named Meik Skoss. Meik always seemed more Japanese than American to me. After spending several years in southern Japan at the Shingu dojo of Michio Hikitsuchi, he moved to Tokyo to study at the Aikido Hombu, and study privately with Chiba Sensei. He gave me my first preview of the Shingu focus on position and awareness of your openings. Unlike performance oriented martial art, if your position during real combat is poor, you never get the chance to do your martial art; you get injured or die. Meik never let himself, or his training partners forget that.

We had tatami rooms in the same little house near the dojo, so I saw how he lived and breathed budo. He is a big man, who shook the whole house

when he jogged up the little metal stairway to our second floor rooms. Just like the frequent earthquakes would do, when Meik came home, the whole house shook. Fortunately, our Japanese landlord on the first floor was understanding (or maybe just afraid of him).

In addition to the Aikido Hombu Dojo, Meik studied several kobudo. These are very old combat systems which predate the Meiji Restoration (1868) in Japan. He disappeared on Sundays to some remote area outside Tokyo to study the ancient naginata weapon art with a little old lady who was one of the last living masters. That was Meik; he had no preconceived ideas of who he should learn from. If little old ladies had the knowledge, he sought them out no matter how far. He would go anywhere to learn authentic classical martial art.

I remember him being gone weeks at a time on field trips with the legendary martial arts researcher Don Dreager. Meik returned from one trip to the jungles of Indonesia, and puked his guts out for days. He believed a tribesman had poisoned him. Perhaps they feared outsiders would steal their secret knowledge. That is what you call serious research!

Meik brought with him to the Tokyo Hombu, his not so subtle Shingu style of showing you your openings. The first time I trained with him I got slapped in the face. Was it cruel? I think compared to a closed fist, which it would have been on the street, it was very kind. With Meik, there was no discussion and no criticism, only a quick, unemotional smack to the face or stinging strike to whatever body part was clearly in the line of fire. It was not intended to injure. It was a wake up call, to make you aware of a dangerous flaw in your technique. This style of practice is traditional budo. It wounded the egos of some thin-skinned trainees, including some high-ranking black belt holders absorbed in their illusion of mastery.

Training with Meik was high intensity, high stress, and enormously valuable. After my first hour with him my movement and awareness improved about 200%. He gave no cheap shots, and played no games. He did not resist

being thrown or pinned like a lot of other big guys did. He gave you honest feedback. I heard he was "reprimanded" more than once by Hombu leadership for this "old style" method of practice, and even "expelled" from the dojo at least once. But there was respect for the spirit of sincerity behind all his actions, so he was accepted back.

Jeff was the senior black belt from my first dojo in New York, who visited Tokyo for a week. He was a very strong guy who threw everyone hard. When he bowed into Meik, I remember soon hearing that familiar open hand "smack" in the face. Without emotion, Jeff asked stoically, "Why did you hit me?" Meik replied just as stoically, "That's how we practice here." Then, they simply resumed practice. The casual, totally unemotional tone of the interchange was priceless. Jeff had for years been the biggest fish in a little bowl. He focused exclusively on throwing hard, and little else. He was not concerned with his openings or vulnerable positions. He was very set in his ways, and got a few more smacks before making some adjustments. But, there was no anger, and when the class was over there were no hard feelings. Why is that so rare?

Years later, Jeff recalled those slaps in the face were "nothing," compared to the two broken noses he received as Chiba Sensei's student in America. A few more weeks training with Meik, might have prevented those injuries later on. The moral of that story is — size, strength, or hard throws do not protect you from weak body position. However, only the best training partners are willing to let you feel those openings.

Meik never fit very well into modern martial arts like aikido, where, for many practitioners, ignorance is bliss. Many dojos are ruled by social conventions, with the superficial trappings of "harmony," and deference to rank, pride, and ego. Today Meik is a practitioner and teacher of several systems of kobudo (koryu) as well as a respected writer and martial arts historian.

I met him last year at a seminar; now in his mid-sixties, he is still fit, full of energy and passion, and just as irreverent as ever. He is still full of wit and wisdom. He remains very demanding of himself and partners during training. Meik is a classic, just like the classical Japanese martial systems to which he has dedicated his life.

13.   Paul Sylvain — Too Close for Comfort

PAUL was another of Chiba Sensei's big, strong, students. He was a great athlete and martial arts technician, and my most difficult training partner. He was not brutal, just cold, and intimidating as hell. He projected an absolute indifference to anything you did, thought, or felt. I was told by someone that this was all an act, just a facade. But, it felt real to me. Whether real or imagined, I always felt an attitude of superiority about him, and his need to dominate every encounter. His etiquette was impeccable, and showed great respect for his teachers, but seemed to have little respect for anyone else. I could see that even Meik and Bruce, who were as tough as nails, were not thrilled to train with him. Among the Americans and Brits I knew in Tokyo, he and his wife were referred to as "The Vains." I guess it was not just my impression.

Paul was, in fact, superior to most other students in many ways. He was very strong, smart, and a gifted athlete with outstanding martial arts skill. I suppose he had reason to be vain. He had been in Japan longer than I had, and was in top condition from training every day for years. While he was not a popular training partner with either Japanese or foreigners, I never avoided training with him. The hard fact was, that while I did not enjoy our training,

I benefited from it. I wish there had been no benefit, then I too could have avoided him. Paul made me confront my purpose for being in Japan. It was not recreation, or socializing. It was to learn. I was there to learn, not to have fun.

Training with Paul's wife was often more pressure than training with Paul. She insisted on being thrown and pinned hard. But, Paul was always nearby, giving you the evil eye, a warning of what would happen if she got injured. It was a true Catch-22, damned if you do and damned if you don't!

Paul grabbed strongly and did not fall down easily. I did not take that personally, since handling difficult partners was part of my reason for being in Japan. That method of practice was the preferred training method at traditional dojos like Iwama, but was frowned upon at most aikido dojos, including at Hombu. I recall an uchi deshi, now a high-ranking instructor, really losing it with Paul. More than once, they ended up in a wrestling match, which Paul would always win. He would quickly have the guy hopelessly tangled up and struggling like a bug in a spider web. Then he casually carried him out onto the fire escape. He held the fellow over the railing, several stories above the streets of Tokyo, until he stopped struggling. I guess that is what they call "asserting dominance."

I seemed to be the only one willing to pair up with Paul for the annual All Japan Aikido Demonstrations, where foreign students were expected to give part of the demonstration. Before the demo, he warned me, "There will be a few thousand people watching, so don't try any funny stuff or cheap shots." Was he serious? Does a grizzly bear need to warn a fox not to mess with it? I decided it was just his way of thanking me for partnering up with him. Anyway, we gave a pretty decent demo. I think Paul was happy with it, because he never said anything. I was happy because I survived! A friend taped it, and I take a look every few years to remember our time together.

During one practice, Paul's timing was a little off as I swung a shome-nuchi strike at him. My finger went deeply into his eye. He held his eye as he stumbled off the training floor in obvious distress. I was sure I had blinded him. Always focused on my own safety when training with him, and yet, the first serious injury was to him. I remember feeling fear, but I do not remember whether I was afraid for him or for me — if he ever recovered would he kill me?

After a few minutes, he was able to see again, and we resumed practice. He held no grudge, there was no retribution, and we continued our practice with no problems. That frightening incident reminded me how fragile all our bodies really are, regardless of size, and how easily a smaller person can do great damage to a larger person in any number of vital areas.

Most of the time, Paul seemed bored with his partner's inferior size, strength, and level of skill. Once, while attempting to apply a nikkyo wrist pin on him, his eyes wandered around the room, completely bored, dismissing my meager attempts to apply pain to his big wrist. That overt disrespect was not acceptable. The warrior in me took over. Taking full advantage of the opening he had created I fired a focused atemi strike at his throat with explosive kiai, stopping only after my fist made contact with the skin of his throat. His attention came back to me, and for that moment, he understood. No matter how big or strong you may be, catastrophic injury or death awaits anyone who fails to pay attention during serious budo training. Paying acute attention is also a clear expression of respect for your aite (training partner) and for the art.

At a Chiba Sensei seminar some years after returning to the America, Paul threw me several times off the training mats toward a brick wall. I used the occasion to sharpen my falling skills, but I never demanded he be more careful. Why did I not say anything? After a while, Chiba Sensei noticed and scolded him. In Japan, he would not have intervened, and left it to me to speak up for myself, or accept the abuse. Teachers almost never intervene in Japan; you are on your own. That is the traditional Japanese way. Looking back, I think there were times Paul challenged me to assert myself or play the victim. All of us must make that choice sometimes in our life.

When Paul left Japan, he opened a dojo in Massachusetts. When I visited once, he acted about as excited to see me as he would be watching paint dry. Maybe I was nothing to him, or maybe that cold demeanor was some kind of character armor he was locked into. His students really seemed to love him.

Either he treated his students differently than everyone else, or the responsibility of being their sensei opened doors in him, allowing his students to enter. An old girlfriend of his told me what a wonderful person he really was "on the inside." But I have heard that one too many times before. She continued that he was just very conflicted and self-conscious. I heard from someone else that he suffered from depression.

During our Hombu days, I would fantasize about someday surpassing him in skill, or just age better, so that at some point, we would be training as equals, or maybe I would dominate the encounters. One day, I got word that Paul died in a car accident. His car ran off the road, killing both him and his eight-year-old daughter. My daughter is about that age. There was some conjecture it may have been a suicide, but I do not believe it, not with his little girl in the car.

When I was preparing to travel the three hundred miles to his memorial, a guy who had trained with him was puzzled why I would go. He even joked to people that I was going "just to make sure the bastard is really dead." He had no idea of the significance Paul held in my training history, and no idea that Paul was in some strange way still a part of me. There was little friendship in our relationship, but learning took place, and that had been more important to me than friendship.

There is a strange sequel to this relationship., that occurred years later, when I worked the streets of Brooklyn, dealing with crack heads and parole violators. I would disappear north whenever I had a vacation day to the Green Mountains of Vermont, passing the area where Paul died. It is on the Vermont/Massachusetts border, along Interstate 91, a very beautiful area. There are fields of wild flowers overlooking a river. I would stop there on my way north, to relax and let the stress of the city drain out of me. Just being in nature for a while was so healing, like recharging the batteries. But, it seemed every time I stopped there I had some unexpected strange encounter, suddenly blasting me out of my comfortable spacey state of mind. On one occasion, a perfectly normal looking fellow came walking through the field of wild flowers in my direction, and as he passed, he suddenly reached for my groin. The scene went from wild flowers to battlefield real fast. It could have been bad, since I was so slow to respond — I thought I was in paradise!

On another occasion, while leisurely relieving myself in the woods at a gorgeous rest area, two sleazy characters come barging out of the woods headed right at me. They caught me completely off guard. It is interesting how the human brain is wired with a startle reflex which sends us (our energy) "up tight" and "scared stiff" for the first moment of any unexpected event. Creatures such as wolves and dogs, on the other hand, respond instantly. Someone was watching over me that day, because the morons were unaware my dog Yambo was sniffing grass right behind me. This usually shy and lazy ghetto dog, instantly went ballistic, chasing the dirtbags right back into the woods where they belonged.

What was most upsetting about these incidents was where they took place — at my idyllic spot in nature where I (assumed) could space out and turn off awareness for a while. I don't know....were these incidents Paul's reminders to pay attention, and not get sloppy? He always did force me out of my comfort zone.

Sincere students of martial arts are not looking for a social club; they understand that a dojo is a hot fire that tempers the spirit and challenges our capacity for self-discipline, and our willingness to struggle. A dojo was never meant to be a comfort zone. Although controlled, the danger is real, so we cannot afford to be "casual" on the battlefield of the dojo.

These days, there are several dojos where I have the reputation as a bad guy. I am neither as sociable or cooperative on the training floor as many martial arts students would prefer. I will make you work very hard, and expose all your weaknesses to the best of my ability. I expect no less from you. Many students, including black belts, prefer easy-going martial recreation, therefore they stay far away from my side of the training hall. Black belts who must protect their illusion of mastery avoid me like the plague. Oh my God — this sounds a lot like Paul! I prided myself in being one of the few at Hombu dojo who did not avoid Paul, now I am Paul!

Some of every important training partner we have had, becomes a part of us. It is not good or bad, it just is. Until we train again Paul, thank you. May you rest in peace.

14. Rinjiro Shirata — Aging Powerfully

RINJIRO Shirata had been a student of O'Sensei through every phase of aiki budo development, and was senior to just about every aikido teacher in Japan. In the prewar years he was considered one of O'Sensei's strongest and roughest students. In old photos he looks big for a Japanese. I was there one day when he came to visit Saito Sensei in Iwama. Sensei treated him with such reverence, as if O'Sensei had walked in. Shirata acted like all the fuss and special treatment was unnecessary, he was just very happy to visit. He had a warmth about him which everyone immediately felt. I decided that one day I would try to make my way up north to Yamagata to study with him.

Yamagata is far from other populated areas in Japan. I knew of no martial arts students who had traveled there. The reception visitors receive at some remote dojos is pretty intense; your intentions are suspect, and the simple act of visiting may be seen as a challenge. But, the words of Shibata always came to me when contemplating these things — "Do not waste your precious time here, steal the knowledge any way you can." That spirit made it easy to take risks. I only feared wasting opportunities.

After surviving his service in the military during the war, Shirata became a "salary man," with a full-time job, not a professional martial arts teacher. He never had a dojo, but would travel around teaching at community budo halls in each town. Kind of funny that the highest level instructor in Japan never had his own dojo. His teaching and training took place after work or on weekends. There is something quite wonderful about that.

My first visit to Shirata Sensei came when Chiba Sensei sent us there: Paul, Meik, Bruce, Jay and a few others. The next year I went again with students from Iwama. Shirata's martial arts both sword and empty hand arts were very old and difficult for me to follow. Most of the time, I was confused, but still loved every minute of it. He had the most dazzling smile and genuine joyful spirit. The man was almost seventy, yet his energy seemed boundless. He would lead classes for hours, demonstrating dozens of sword drills that we struggled to follow. He seemed just too full of life to ever get tired. But, he sure wore us out!

Soaking together after class in a big hot communal bath, I remember his big barrel chest did not match his normal size body. Maybe that was his secret, he got more oxygen than we did! He definitely showed us that you can age with great strength and vitality.

His students in Yamagata City were the biggest and strongest boys I trained with in Japan. They were also the most kind and generous. I think everyone who visited there felt that. His students treated every visitor like royalty, regardless of their nationality, rank, or skill level. They undoubtedly got that spirit from their teacher. Along with his knowledge and incredible energy, Rinjiro Shirata's wonderful smile will always be etched in my memory.

Training with Shirata sensei in Yamagata city

15. Michio Hikitsuchi — Mysteries of Time and Space

I wanted to visit O'Sensei's grave in southern Japan, in the area of Wakayama Prefecture, where he was born and raised. In his later years, he frequently returned for brief trips, often teaching at the dojo of the Shinto priest, Hikitsuchi, in the village of Shingu. As a result, his teaching left a strong and lasting influence there. In contrast to his dojo in Iwama, where the technical focus was powerful movement and katai keiko (strong static practice), his focus in Shingu was dynamic execution of techniques with elimination of openings.

Jay and I hitchhiked for three days to get there, but it was not hard to hitchhike in Japan, since so many people wanted to practice their English. Truck drivers, college students and housewives — all saw a hitchhiking foreigner as free tutoring. We could have made it there sooner, but we stopped off

for a day in the ancient village of Nara. Nara was like going back in history three hundred years. It was a serene rural area outside Kyoto, with lots of rice patties, Shinto shrines, small temples, and one of Japan's oldest iconic budo landmarks. We wandered the rural landscape, and everyone we spoke with seemed to point up into the hills, saying "Yagyu no Sato."

We headed up there, getting good and lost among the bamboo

groves. The place had a very strange feeling about it, which I do not know how to describe. It was certainly not a tourist attraction, with few signs of anyone being there for a long time. After a while we found ourselves walking around tall headstones, with shapes and kanji indicating it was some ancient samurai graveyard. We both felt what can only be described as some "otherworldly" feeling. Two rough, tough martial arts black belts, and we both were scared shitless, and had no clue why?

Near the graveyard was a very old, musty smelling wooden dojo. The sliding wood doors were left open? As spooky as the whole place was, we cautiously entered. It was kept immaculately clean, with staffs, bokkens, armor, and a variety of ancient weaponry hanging on the walls, but not a soul around? We wandered around inside for a while, but the place was just too creepy, so we got out of there. At the time, we had no idea what the place was or what the strange feelings were. It was, however, a harbinger of my first encounter with the mysterious side of budo.

Weeks later, when we described the place to our teachers, they explained that Yagyu no Sato was one of the most revered landmarks in samurai history. It was the site of the original Yagyu school, whose headmasters were the teachers to the shoguns. The grave sites were sword masters and fallen samurai of the Yagyu clan. I learned that O'Sensei had studied Yagyu sword and had received a menkyo certification in that sword system. In later years, students of Yagyu headmaster, Nobuharu Yagyu, were to have a profound influence on both my sword and weaponless training.

We eventually made our way to Shingu, where we practiced for several days, and were honored with a private class with Hikitsuchi Sensei. Unlike Yamagata, the Shingu folk seemed suspicious of visitors from Tokyo, and the tension remained throughout our visit. On our first day, one of the instructors grabbed me before class, and offered to throw me around as a warm up before one of Hikitsuchi's classes. I came to accept this informal custom when traveling to rural dojos in Japan. It is a sort of a test, to see if you are a serious student. If you are, then you take your bumps without complaint and show you are not afraid to train hard.

He must have blasted me fifty times in a few minutes. They were not particularly powerful throws, but there were few openings for counter attack which I was used to seeing in most Tokyo black belts. I figured he wanted to see what I was made of, so I bounced back up as fast as I could, no matter how hard he threw me. After a very formal bow, we joined the line of students sitting silently in seiza, waiting for Hikitsuchi Sensei to enter the dojo. I later learned that my welcome practice, was executed by the youngest sixth-degree aikido black belt in Japan. Taking all those falls without complaint was our admission ticket to serious training, and my first glimpse at the Shingu style of budo.

During class these guys were nailing us with shots to the kidneys, as we practiced rear (ushiro) techniques. We never had this problem in New York or in any other dojo in Japan. I tried to nail them, too, but they were never open? This was frustrating as hell. How could these guys at a little dojo in the middle of nowhere, know stuff that wasn't known at the big, world famous headquarters school? Fortunately, a few days training at Shingu forced us to close a lot of openings, and we started to get hit less often. But, my kidneys and lower back were sore for weeks.

Hikitsuchi Sensei had been ill and was very thin, but he still invited us to a private Shinto ceremony, followed by some private training with him. His rank of 10th degree black belt was controversial, apparently received privately from O'Sensei. He was known as one of the finest men with a staff in Japan, but how or why he was given the highest rank remained murky.

I watched as Jay grabbed him a few times, and got thrown with standard aiki throws and pins. He made some comments about O'Sensei and technique which were confirmation of things we had heard before. I think we were a bit jaded, and arrogant, since we came from the big famous Tokyo school, with a half dozen world famous teachers. We were also a bit defensive about our less than warm welcome. Watching him throw Jay around, I saw no great speed, power, or unusual technical skill, in fact, Hikisuchi seemed tired.

Then he motioned for me to attack, so I fired a fast focused blow right into his belly. He moved slowly, much too slowly to avoid my strike. I should have easily hit him. Instead, the knuckles of his right hand suddenly appeared at my eyes, and were not stopping there. My head snapped back to avoid the collision, while my lower body kept moving through the place he had just been standing. The sudden disintegration of balance sent my body careening airborne across the dojo.

I moved very quickly, he moved slowly, and yet, he was way ahead of me? He was not in any defensive posture when I attacked, and did not even seem ready. What happened defied all logic; was he messing with my mind? I got up shocked and confused. I looked over to Jay for a reaction, but there was none. He saw nothing strange, nothing special, and had no idea why I was so shocked. All the way home to Tokyo, I drove poor Jay crazy, insisting he must have seen Hikitsuchi do something bizarre! He had no idea what I was talking about. I remember my attack and fall like it was yesterday, but still have no idea what happened.

Many times the bond between student and teacher is so strong, and the connection so close, that the student is basically hypnotized. This happens quite often in martial arts, and explains why students often fly through the air when the teacher has actually done very little. There are components of expectation, desire to please or not offend — that often make martial arts practice and demonstrations look effortless and magical. But, between me and Hikitsuchi there was no bond, no relationship, and no audience to impress. Whatever happened, it was the real deal. There was some very real and profound principle at work there, which I still struggle to understand forty years later. I left Shingu, and Michio Hikitsuchi with more questions than answers.

A similar mysterious encounter occurred years later during a confrontation at work, with a psychotic man swinging a metal bar, which I describe later as my brief visit from O'Sensei. But, only one other time did someone throw me in a way which defied all logic. In the late 1990s I attacked the aikido teacher Robert Nadeau during a seminar near Detroit, Michigan. He had just admonished me for coming at him with an artificial, performance oriented attack and then taking an acrobatic fall. As I was getting up he moved in close and quietly remarked "Tom, cut the bullshit." I understood; he was giving me permission to get real. I got up, then went at him fast and hard. I was on one side of the room and he was standing in the middle of the room, so I had a chance to build up some powerful momentum, more than enough to knock him on his ass if he made any mistake, or tried any of the foolishness so common in aikido demonstrations.

I was moving too fast and hard for him to redirect my energy much, run me around in circles, or throw backwards. I have knocked a lot of aikido and aiki jujitsu black belts on their butts, attacking with less power than I used against Nadeau. I do not recall any fancy or special technique, but when I got up — I was in the exact spot I had started from. This was not possible, I should have been on the other side or at his feet? It made no sense. It was an easy fall — no head trauma, no concussion. There was no logical explanation.

Just like I had done when drawn into some strange world of disorientation by Hikitsuchi, I insisted the observers tell me what they saw. No one saw anything unusual. How could they not see something unbelievable! There is some dynamic at play here which is not of the physical realm, perhaps it is psychological. It is some sort of disorientation which cannot be observed, only felt. Whereas Hikitsuchi had played with time (or my perception of time) Nadeau was manipulating my perception of space. Many teachers have described similar experiences with O'Sensei.

When I discussed it with Nadeau, he simply made reference to the scroll O'Sensei gave him, which reads, "Do the aikido that cannot be seen." There truly is a budo that cannot be seen. I do not understand it, but I have felt it. I know it exists.

16. Hiroshi Kato — The Phantom

THERE was a man in Ueshiba Sensei's class at Hombu Dojo who I never trained with, I do not know anyone who did. He sat in a far corner of the training hall, training only with the same few students. He was a slim, athletic, middle-aged man with deep, dark eyes. I heard he was a high-ranking student of O'Sensei, higher than most of the teachers. Yet, he only trained, and never taught? Rumors circulated that he was crazy, and too dangerous to be on the teaching staff — why else would he only be practicing at his level? Intimidated by the rumors, and by his mysterious status in the dojo, most of us stayed away from him.

Mindlessly avoiding Hiroshi Kato Sensei for years, because of rumor and his reputation, is my only regret from those early years of study in Japan. Isn't it ironic that I now have a similar reputation in some places. Perhaps, it is my Karma, my karmic connection to Kato.

Years later, during one of my return trips to Japan, there he was. He was still attending Ueshiba Sensei's 6:30 am class. Now 7th or 8th degree black belt, but still training as a student. His eyes were still deep and mysterious. With a dozen more years of martial arts experience, a high rank, years of police training, with more than a hundred students myself — I still felt completely intimidated by this man.

There is a beautiful thing about aging, it is the growing sense of urgency. It cuts through fear and timidity like a very sharp sword. Fear moved through my body as I approached him, but it could not stop me. Before class I slipped in next to him. My mind raced. Tension filled my throat and shoulders. Would he consider my abrupt approach as a challenge? I sat with my heart pounding, as the Doshu stepped on the mat to begin class.

After warm ups, I quickly turned and bowed in to Kato. He smiled and bowed to me, then we trained non stop for an hour. What an hour it was. Training with Kato was different than any martial arts I had experienced before. He practiced at a level which I did not know existed. How to describe it? … painting beside Picasso … jamming with Mozart … hiking with Thoreau. ...or maybe shooting hoops with Michael Jordan. That is the closest I can come.

After training with him I started to curse myself for not having trained with him when I had more chances. But, if I had, I may not have appreciated his level of mastery. I expected strong technique, but this was different. I just kept slightly missing him when I struck, then slightly unbalanced — almost able to stay up but not quite. I felt little or no force.

What a rare and wonderful thing to find someone with this level of mastery, still practicing in class like a student! Or perhaps, his unending practice as a student was his secret of such mastery. The man was not strange, but he certainly was special. How ironic that an individual targeted by the rumor mill, was actually the greatest practice partner there. No one even came close.

Hiroshi Kato recently passed away. A few years ago he did start teaching, and was probably a great teacher. But, his unique gift was his passion for training as a student, long after reaching master level. He showed me what was possible. He is my role model.

17. Kazuo Chiba — Ruthless Awareness

THE grand finale of each week for me in Tokyo was Chiba Sensei's Friday afternoon class. The term "battleground" comes to mind, a battleground of emotion. The emotional intensity, and range of emotions in that class was amazing — terror, fearlessness, vulnerability, and invincibility. He was known for his ferocity, and the extraordinary intensity of those classes; an atmosphere of life and death. In contrast to attendance at most classes at the Hombu, attendance at his was sparse. I felt this group of students to be very special, a small elite group in the sea of martial artists in Tokyo. To most students at Hombu Dojo we were just crazy.

Chiba would approach the training hall slowly and deliberately. He paused at the teacher's entrance to carefully peruse the battlefield before enter-

ing. He sometimes arrived with a bloody rag wrapped around his hand. Not a bandage, just a blood stained rag. I assumed it was from his live blade sword work. That bloody rag set the tone for his class. I think that was intentional. It symbolized the atmosphere of danger, and the acute awareness required. Seeing it was like a molotov cocktail thrown on dry timbers, it ignited something very hot in us. It attracted only those with some deep need to burn hot. Were we moths drawn to a flame?

Sitting seiza in the nervous silence before class, in a huge training hall filled with only a few students. I watched to see if anyone else would show up. No one else ever did. There were about a dozen of us, in a school with an average class of fifty or sixty. But when I looked around I was astonished at the array of talent. Chiba sensei's amazing private students Bookman-Skoss-Sylvain to my left, and on my right sat Waka Sensei — Moriteru Ueshiba, Shibata, uchi deshi Miyamoto and Seki. My only thought sitting there was "it just does not get any better than this." I felt so privileged and honored to be there.

Real and immediate danger was felt by everyone in that room. We trained together in a state of hyper-alertness. It was frightening and exciting at the same time. I have felt it when searching dark apartments for fugitives, and backpacking in southern Alaska's grizzly country. The slightest sound is magnified. The slightest movement nearby is detected. The most subtle smell perceived and instantly identified. Clarity, instant response.

Danger is very uncomfortable, but it heightens our senses. If we channel fear into acute awareness the present moment expands. "Now" becomes immense. Fully alive. I have learned that powerful energy usually feels uncomfortable. A small price to pay.

This feeling of danger created a strange kind of purity, an equality — regardless of size, rank, or level of skill. Everyone felt fear, no one tried to hide it. That shared experience created an amazing level of cohesion. A communion of fear. A level of intimacy difficult to describe.

The group adrenaline burned away pain, weakness, timidity, and all self-consciousness. All that remained was bold action. The battlefield is too hot for ego. There were bumps, bruises, scrapes, and sprains — but no complaining, explaining, or apologizing. None of that was necessary. Incredibly, there were no serious injuries. The intensity of awareness prevented that.

Impressive looking technique held no value here. Success and failure had no meaning. Decisive action was all that mattered. Results were irrelevant. It was pure Zen. Overpowering group energy. Self was swallowed up and lost. At that

shin

ken

sho

bu

Train with "dead earnest"

place — during that hour there was no other way to be. It was wonderful, and exhausting. Once a week was all I could handle. All my other martial arts classes were like a vacation.

I am deeply grateful for being part of something so special. It was not only Chiba Sensei, it was the particular mix of individuals who came together each Friday afternoon. An extraordinary group chemistry was generated. Any intermediate or advanced student was free to attend; you just had to show up. Amazingly, in a student body of perhaps five hundred, only twelve ever came.

The Dojo as a Sacred Place
by T.K. Chiba

♦ ♦ ♦ As long as there is a roof that prevents the rain from coming in, a wall that separates us from the outside world, a floor to protect us in our falling, and a center that reminds us of the Founder's profound concern for the well-being of humanity (his vow and prayer that give us gratitude and appreciation for his achievements, which have been given to us in such an accomplished form as the Way), the Dojo exists.

However, from many points of view, and especially a business one, the Dojo represents an impractical existence. It is not a social club, recreational center or business enterprise, nor even a training hall or school, as it has been treated largely in the West, but it is a sacred place. Not the kind of place that appears instantly when the mats are put down, but one that exists somewhere out there physically, whether or not it is used all the time. It is such a waste, in a business sense, when one considers the size of the space, and such impracticality can be fatal to a dojo in its struggle to survive. I consider that the life of the Dojo is an impractical existence relative to our normal gaining-losing consciousness, and, as such, is of vital importance to it. Normal or abnormal as we are, and we struggle to survive in this competitive and materialistic society, there needs to be a space somewhere that exists for something beyond our sense of practicality.

Our great need for the dojo, which waits out there empty and unused for us to return each day, is what gives it its purpose as a sacred place.

18. Chiba Sensei and Zen Master Hogen

I maintain that your present imperfect state is much much better and more full of grace than the perfect state you intend to achieve in the future. Our lives, as we are practising now, are better than anything we will gain in the future. Therefore, you should switch the centre of your being and your whole attention from your dreams of the future, and instead have your awareness on Here Now.   —HOGEN

I was occasionally invited to Chiba Sensei's private class, a group of gifted athletes preparing for careers as professional martial arts instructors. I felt way out of my league with these people, which motivated me to put out 110 % effort. One day, he announced he was resigning his teaching position and administrative duties at Hombu Dojo in order to be near his Zen master out near Mt. Fuji. His students were devastated. Some left Japan, some even stopped training altogether. Only two asked to go with him. That really surprised me.

It seems they could handle the most severe martial arts training, but meditation was not on their agenda. Why not?

While they were devastated, I was excited. It could be the opportunity I had always dreamed of. Martial arts in a monastic setting, where deep meditation was practiced, like at the ancient Shoalin Temple in China. I had

creation   Hogen   present moment

found no place in America or Japan where both disciplines were practiced intensively. I would do anything to be part of it.

Before he left, I stopped Chiba in the dojo stairwell, and asked to go with him. He stared long and hard at me before responding. He said he would think about it. A week later, he said no. He had checked my attendance at Hombu dojo for the past year, and it showed only four training days each week. He did not consider that the training schedule of a serious student. I had to gather up all notes, maps and records of the other places I trained each week and brought it to him. I did not know how he would react to all the other dojos I trained at, in addition to the aikido headquarters where he taught. To my relief, he was actually pleased to see all the other places I had trained. He said yes.

A week later, I left my English teaching job, my girlfriend, and gave up my Tokyo apartment. I rode the train for three hours out to the small village of

Kannami, near Mount Fuji. My life as a monk would now begin.

I had done some Zen practice before coming to Japan, and it sparked a lifelong quest to discover who I was, and how to manage this thing called "mind." I had trained briefly with the Zen Master, Sasaki Roshi, who dismissed every one of my responses to his questions with a gesture of disgust (egotistical bullshit)! I remember his last words to me as his eyes cut through me:

> "Zen practice is not to believe in God,
> Zen practice is to **realize** God.
> How do you realize God through Zen practice?"

I did not try to answer, thank God. That would have been more clever ego bullshit. All answers would have been wrong, because it was not a question. It was a challenge. Going to Asia, learning and living whatever wisdom I found, that is my response.

茶 茶 茶 茶

Chogen-Ji Zen Temple was very old, and very hard to find. It was hidden on the other side of the hills, from Kannami Village. It was next to a beautiful bamboo grove, which surrounded the village graveyard. Even many people in the village who I asked did not know how to get there. When Hogen finished his years as a wandering monk, studying with Zen masters around Japan, he found this little temple in the hills, long abandoned. He received permission from his Soto Zen sect to reopen it, and serve as the village priest. He was a married priest, and was raising three small children at the temple.

Hogen and his wife Keiko both welcomed me warmly. Although middle aged, he had a youthful appearance and was always full of energy. In some ways he was the polar opposite of Chiba Sensei — soft spoken, gentle, and always smiling. There was no fierce, commanding "Zen Master" like presence. He was easy going and natural, with a quiet strength, the kind Terry Dobson called "soft power." I found Hogen and Chiba to be the perfect combination of teachers — I had found the best of both worlds!

When I met Chiba Sensei at the temple, he immediately began searching for something under the temple crawl spaces. Hogen said it was "a treasure" he had left there many years ago when practicing with O'Sensei. When he finally found what he was looking for, it was wrapped in old dusty burlap. He carefully unwrapped the burlap to reveal an old tanren ken; a long, thick, wooden sword used for striking bundles of bamboo. Tanren uchi practice had been one of O'Sensei's favorite training methods.

Sensei disappeared into the bamboo grove, returning a few minutes later with thick bamboo for the supports and a big bundle of thinner bamboo for the striking target. Then he disappeared again under the temple, returning this time with an enormous old wooden sledge hammer. With no discussion, he handed me the monster sledge hammer, held one of the support stakes with both hands, and said, "Drive the stakes into the ground, hard!" He appeared to have little concern for his hands being smashed — which would happen if just one of my strikes was slightly off the mark. And I knew he would not tolerate even one cautious, halfhearted strike.

How many thoughts can pass through a racing mind in one moment? That stake would take fifteen or twenty strikes to drive into the hard ground, and there were two stakes to be driven in....and the odds of being slightly off the mark just once were high...and...then...slam!! — the sound of my first full-force strike blew all thoughts away. Only feint, fleeting background thoughts lingered, and the weight of the heavy sledge hammer came down again and again driving them away. Somewhere in the total attention to that one spot — the head of the stake — all thoughts disappeared. Only that one point in the universe existed — only the hammer smashing down again and again — only breath, sound, and sweat.

When the stakes were both driven deep, he said, "good." I was soaked in sweat, more from the intense concentration than the physical exertion. He had not shown the slightest concern about his hands. I would not trust my best friend to do what he had just let me do. He had that much confidence in me? I do not have that much confidence in anyone. Was it some kind of test? Perhaps it was his confidence in the power that danger and risk have, to create a laser-focused mind.

For a moment, my mind flashed to a man in a business suit, who translated for the elderly Zen master, at a Zen temple I attended in Tokyo. "No fire," he told me. He was a middle-aged man with an impeccably strong sitting

posture, a warrior's presence and powerful stillness that I lacked. I had asked him why we had to sit so uncomfortably straight, and why not on comfortable chairs? "No fire," he said, his eyes filled with compassion and appreciation for my struggle with discomfort, "no fire." He was right, sometimes we need fire.

After he tied the supports and the bamboo bundle on top, sensei took his big sword and exploded with a ferocious flurry of strikes. He cut through several of the bamboo, even with a wooden sword. But in his hands, it seemed to be sharp. When he finished, he gazed lovingly at the old sword, then handed it to me. "Let's see what you can do." Still vibrating from my last task, I took the heavy bokken and felt the fear of crushing my teacher's hands change to fear of embarrassing myself. But again, fear, became the engine of focus and power. I struck over and over, as fast and hard as I could, feeling and hearing the smashing of oak against bamboo. I would show him I have potential as a student! I gave it all I had and more.

On my last exhausted strike, there was loud "crack!" To my horror, sensei's treasured sword cracked in three places. I froze. He stared at three splintered pieces of wood, that moments ago was a treasured bokken. Two pieces were on the ground, and I still held one tightly in both hands. He kept looking at the pieces without speaking, it seemed like an hour. The silence was worse than if he was yelling, or pounding me. All I could do was stare at the damage, no words came. What do you say when your first act at the temple is to destroy your teacher's prized possession?

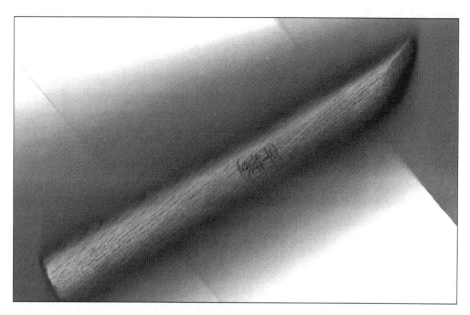

After a long and painful silence, he slowly picked up the broken pieces. One had his family crest burned into the wood. Staring at the family crest, he said, "These will make good training knives." There was no anger, no blame. How could he move on so seamlessly?

After several weeks of sanding, shaping, oiling, and polishing, those broken pieces of wood did indeed become beautiful tanto (training knives.) When I presented them to him, he ran his hands up and down the beautiful, polished, old wood. Then he handed them both back to me, and with a halfsmile said, "These are good tanto, they are yours now."

Sensei's teacher, Hogen, was a recognized Zen master in Japan, formally known as "Hogen Yamahata Roshi," but he would only let us call him by his first name, or Osho-San (monk). The demeanors of Hogen and Chiba were as different as night and day, but their different qualities complemented each other. Chiba was intense and imposing — "The Last Samurai," Saito Sensei would call him.

Hogen led us in two hours of Zen meditation and yoga every morning and evening, culminating with a twenty-minute run up into the hills. When we ran back down, he never turned around, he just started running backwards all the way down. How we ran backward down that steep, winding mountain road without breaking our necks, I will never know. We were athletes in our twenties, and he was approaching middle age, but he laughed and laughed as we struggled to keep up. On a return visit a few years later I asked why we ran down the mountain backwards. His reply was "Now we run up backwards, too." You cannot get a more Zen response than that.

Hogen was rarely what people expected him to be. Behind the great Buddha statue in the temple, he had a stereo set up which played classical music during our Zen practice. He rarely lectured or gave Dharma talks, and had none of the usual formal Zen question/answer sessions. I did not understand much of his book, *The Open Way*, but he said that was not important, "just practice." After sitting, he would often stand on his head for a half hour. I never asked why. He usually wore a jogging suit, except when he went into Kannami Village to perform Buddhist ceremonies and other priestly duties. He usually looked more like our coach, than our Zen master, which is just how he thought of himself.

The only time I remember him totally embracing the Zen master image, with all the traditional clothing and custom, was a few years later when I got married at Chogen-ji. That day he became the perfect image of the regal, dignified Zen master. That day, in front of friends and family, he wore the most magnificent robes and offered the look and demeanor of a great Buddhist master. He did that for me. I saw he could really play the part if he needed to, but except for that day, and a few funeral services, I never saw him take his position or title seriously.

Before the wedding, he gave me a long scroll written in Japanese, to read during the ceremony. It was very old Japanese, and I could hardly understand any of it. When I asked him to help me translate it, he said, "Scroll means promise. Marriage is promise. That is all."

Chiba Sensei would come at odd times to teach us, and sometimes

Hogen would join the class. Hogen had spent one month with O'Sensei in Iwama but that was his only martial arts experience. You could throw him hard, and he would have a big smile on his face, he actually seemed to enjoy pain. He was not a skilled martial artist, but he enjoyed it, even his mistakes.

His mistakes did not seem to bother him or dampen his enjoyment. I was jealous, and wished I could do that. He was always teaching us without trying to teach. Practicing martial arts with a Zen master is highly recommended, if you want to witness someone laughing and having fun with their mistakes.

Chiba Sensei would sometimes teach a live blade *iaido* sword class, which a few villagers attended. I remember one of those guys repeating the same mistake, again and again, after sensei had corrected him. Finally, sensei sprang from across the room, slicing the air at lightning speed, and stopping the blade a hair's width from the guy's temple. "Like this!" Everyone froze in shock for a few seconds, then resumed training. About a minute later, I saw the blood begin to drip from the guy's temple. The blade had actually touched the surface of his skin. With a highly sharpened Japanese katana blade, a touch is all it takes.

Sensei quietly asked Hogen for a raw egg, while the rest of us continued to train. He sat next to the bleeding guy and calmly broke the egg into a small bowl. I was so intrigued by what he was doing that I stopped training to study his every action. He scraped the membrane from the inside of the shell, then placed it across the cut. It quickly dried, pulling the wound closed. He told the guy there would be no scar. Then we all went back to training. Just another day of training at Chogen-ji.

Demetri was a Greek student at Chogen-ji who lived with his girlfriend. They argued often, and on two occasions he hit her. When sensei learned about it, he was brutal with the guy during class. After class he ordered him out of Japan, "Now!" Hogen tried to intervene and reconcile the situation, but that behavior warranted no second chances with Chiba Sensei. It was the only time I saw Hogen upset. After the incident, I watched him pace nervously all evening. It blew my whole image of what a Zen master was. They are supposed to be calm and cool as a cucumber at all times, completely detached from all concerns, right? Bullshit. That was my childish fantasy. It was a superficial and erroneous understanding of Zen. Hogen was deeply affected by the pain and suffering of others. It is the compassion of the Buddha.

Watching Hogen's concern reminded me of the rare times my mother was anxious and worried. It was only when someone else was in trouble that she got anxious, she never seemed to worry about her own issues. Call it Christian love or compassion of the Buddha, but real masters hurt when others hurt, because they are open to the pain of others. Hogen's pacing was not the typical, "poor me" worry, he was searching for an answer to help this guy, and I watched him struggle for days to find a resolution. In a few days he was back to his usual self, and I assumed Demitri left Japan. But, about a year later when I visited Iwama there he was, studying under Saito Sensei. Hogen had undoubtedly made those arrangements. Saito and Demetri really bonded well, and he became one of Saito sensei's favorite students.

Sensei taught a kids' class with Hogen's three kids and a few village kids. I remember him pushing one of Hogen's kids, Motomichi, quite hard. He was only around six or seven, and he cried a lot in class, but he always stayed. I had a lot of respect for that little guy. It seemed like they had higher expectations for that kid. When I returned to visit Hogen many years later, I saw him from far away sitting with his unmistakably erect and relaxed posture but, he looked years younger than I remembered? It was not Hogen, it was Motomichi. He had become a Zen monk, and ran the temple in his father's absence.

Chogen-Ji only had adequate living quarters for Hogen and his family, so only overnight guests stayed there. The rest of us had small tatami rooms over the hills in the village of Kannami. My trek up through the bamboo groves into those hills each day at sunrise, and again at sunset, was quite wonderful. On the ridges high up in the hills above the temple, the farmers grew the huge Japanese radish named after Zen master Takuan. From it is made my favorite sushi — oshinko maki. Most days, just after sunrise, the enormous outline of Mount Fuji would be staring down at me, as I rounded the last turn to take the mountain road down to Chogen-ji. The last one hundred yards went through the bamboo grove, with gravestones all around. Villagers often came up there leaving jewelry and expensive bottles of sake, for their departed relatives. There were no fences or security guards, but no one ever disturbed those items.

One morning, the other two students had gone to Tokyo to renew their visas. When sensei came, I was the only one sitting there, waiting for class. I expected when he saw only me, he would cancel class. Perhaps I would visit the local hot, sulfur baths outside of town to boil away the aches and pains. But that was not to be. When sensei came and saw only me, he bowed in exactly as he did every day. Then we trained one-on-one. I gave it everything I had, and just shy of an hour, just before I passed out, he bowed, saying "You are becoming supple." It does not get any better than that.

Before lunch, we would rake the big open area in front of the temple. There was not much to rake, it was mostly bare ground, but raking is part of Zen practice. It is moving Zen, like the tea ceremony, sword training, or conscious walking. Raking practice is like kinhin, Zen walking, which is feeling each step touching the ground. It is treating each movement, each breath, as a sacred act. Really feeling each body movement puts the mind right here, right now.

Before the year was out, Chiba Sensei announced that he was moving to America, and would take over a dojo in southern California. I was disappointed, but not shocked; these were his restless years. He encouraged me to stay at Chogen-Ji, and continue my training with Hogen. That is what I did.

Sensei's leaving was part of the momentary nature of this life. Things come, and things go. People come and go, opportunities come and go. Grab opportunities when they arise, and take full advantage of them because they will not last. Nothing lasts. Hands together in front of the heart in *gassho*. *Deep Gratitude.*

The way we are born

The way we live

We are alive now

This is busshin, the awakened mind

Somewhere in the ever-lasting stream

of life of the great Buddha,

we are gifted with a glimpse of it.

In appreciation and awe of this fact,

we put our hands together.

19. Koichi Tohei — Relax!

$\mathcal{A}$FTER training at Chogen-ji for a few more months, I returned to Tokyo to resume studying under Kisshomaru and Moriteru Ueshiba, but I continued visiting other dojos. On Fridays, I filled the void left by Chiba Sensei's "clash of the titans," by attending the Ki No Kenkyu Kai dojo of Koichi Tohei. While very different and not as intense as Chiba, Tohei had his own commanding presence. He projected an absolute confidence in the power of complete relaxation. There was little martial intensity to his class, where he would relentlessly repeat "You must relax more, feel your weight." He said it so often I would joke to friends "Tohei is like a broken record," but I kept attending every Friday. Although I never got excited by his class, I never forgot what Chiba said about Tohei; "No one could touch him." His method of movement was that good.

I wished I could have trained with him in the 1950s and '60s, when his strange but dynamic hopping/prancing style of movement blasted people around like they were rag dolls. Tohei's own invention, it did not look martial or resemble O'Sensei, but it sure got the job done. Appearances can be so deceptive. Tohei was the aikido instructor who left Japan for Hawaii, and traveled around the United States, accepting challenges from all comers. He represented O'Sensei well, proving the power of blending, leading, nonresistance, and moving from the lower body. He referred to it as "the power of ki." It did not hurt any that Tohei was a powerfully built man, with a strong judo background.

Tohei Sensei had a distinctively "non-Japanese" personality, outgoing and outspoken. The Japanese way is to reserve all but the most subtle criticism of others, for late night drinking sessions. In the morning, all is forgiven. Tohei, however, expressed his opinions all the time, and without reservation. At our first meeting, after asking where I was from, he proceeded to criticize my New York teachers, pointing out their weaknesses and shortcomings. They had been Tohei's students, and he never forgave them for not following him when he left the Ueshiba organization to start his Ki Society. The feeling of giving so much, but not receiving proper recognition, is something we have all felt at one time or another. He was hurt and resentful.

Tohei's fall from prominence and influence in the martial arts world was due both to politics and his own abrasive manner. Perhaps it takes a huge ego to break from traditional forms and create something new. His form of aiki martial art was truly unique. When I grabbed him, I would not feel much power, then his relaxed dead weight would come crashing down on me like a ton of bricks. He demonstrated levels of relaxed power I had never felt before. Years later, when I had a "Tohei Day" at my dojo the first exercise was getting students to prance and skip across the room, like they did as kids. The purpose was to release tension and tightness, and free up lower body movement. Predictably, prancing around the dojo was less than macho, to put it mildly, and embarrassing for some. They only made a half-heartedly effort, and did not take the exercise seriously. But when they did not give the exercise (Tohei) the respect it deserved, I threw them all full bore, Tohei style. Several of them got the wind knocked out of them.

Politics and ego aside, Koichi Tohei Sensei took O'Sensei's esoteric concepts and simplified them, which popularized and expanded the art of aikido. He also enriched it with his own genius. His simple concepts and explanations were more accessible to modern students. Takemusu aiki became "relax completely and extend ki." The contributions Tohei made to martial arts were huge. I continue to practice and benefit from many of his early training exercises.

After a brief period of study with him, I shelved Tohei's "aikido with ki/relaxation is everything" style martial art for many years, concentrating on more sword based roots of budo. Most of Koichi Tohei's teachings, have now faded from the martial arts scene. But, thank God, some of those neat tricks of his have come back to me, when I needed them! (see "Mean Streets of New York.")

20. Kazuo Kato — The Unforgiving Sword

𝕴 believe it was the Thai meditation master, Ajahn Chah, who directed a friend of mine dissatisfied with the quality of his meditation, to sit on the edge of the deep well in the monastery courtyard. That edge is the boundary between life and death. No margin for error. No excuses.

Jack's struggle to liberate himself from his wandering monkey mind — lost in past and future — worry and fantasy — was assisted in dramatic fashion by that deep, dark well. Dangerous? Yes. Reckless? Perhaps. Some things are worth the risk. During visits to the Grand Canyon, I remember Jack and sit a bit closer to the edge than is comfortable. Near the edge is enough for me. Is it fear of falling, or fear of liberation? Maybe liberation is just a nice idea that can wait until later.

My path requires risk. Not legs dangling over the canyon edge, a bit further from death than that. Room for error, but with a price to pay. Dangerous enough to energize awareness, providing the fire for purification. A nasty and immediate sting the moment presence of mind is lost. Kazuo Kato and the blade of a very sharp sword offered such a path.

Old bikers like me love to make sure new riders know what they are getting into by telling them, "Listen guy, there are only two kinds of motorcycle riders

— those who have gone down leaving skin on the pavement, and those who have not gone down yet." The same is true for live blade practice. There are those who have been cut, and those who have not been cut yet. When this is understood, the sword becomes a powerful tool of Zen practice. It is the ruthless — unforgiving nature of the sword, the razor sharp edge which opens any part of the human body with just a touch — that gives it the power to cut through our hyperactive monkey mind.

My respect for the sword is rooted in fear. A healthy fear. Just a touch, the slightest contact between skin and blade is all it takes. At work I had a knife catch my forearm. I felt almost nothing, and yet looking down — tissues and muscle had parted like the Red Sea. Offering a clear view of the bone. This is why the katana has such power to keep the mind here and now. Totally present. It elicits something deep, something primal. Both powerful and frightening. An hour of iaido (*batto jutsu*) practice is the highest quality of mind in my day. It has to be. It is "extreme Zen".

Kazuo Kato Sensei was my teacher of Seigo Ryu Batto Jutsu, from the Yagyu Shinkage Ryu sword school. It is the budo of drawing the sword and cutting from the formal seiza (kneeling) position. After completing the cut, the "noto," returning of the sword to its scabbard, offers further opportunity for injury. For just as in police firearms training, one never looks down when returning the weapon to its holster or scabbard. The mind (field of vision) must remain on the battlefield, unrestricted at all times.

Kato Sensei and his brother studied with the twenty-first generation headmaster Yagyu Nobu-haru Toshimichi, for ten years in Nagoya. Yagyu Shin Kage-Ryu is a very old sword school, still very combative in form. There are few embellishments, few stylistic additions of more modern sword styles. Kato Sensei's brother went on to become a Japanese national champion in the sport of Kendo, but Kazuo continued traditional Yagyu budo practice.

There is no flash or acrobatics in Kato's technique. Just smooth, efficient movement. He makes rising, moving, and cutting cleanly from the kneeling position — with complete stability and postural integrity — look easy. But, it is not easy. It is one of the most difficult activities to do well I have ever attempted. Only tremendous lower body strength allows the upper body to move with such stability and undisturbed alignment. You must activate muscles you did not know you had in your toes, feet, ankles, hips, thighs, groin, and many core muscles. Some muscles used in this practice have never been used before. The wakeup call can be painful, but I have found nothing as powerful for keeping the knees and entire lower body strong and flexible.

Batto and iaido are internal Asian disciplines like chi gong. An observer cannot see, but the adversaries are real and immediate. Distraction can instantly inflict grave injury. A wandering thought, self judgement, analysis — all can instantly cut you.

Kato Sensei is ruthless in keeping his upper body erect and relaxed, allowing power to pour from the unified movement of his core and lower body. His arms allow the sword to glide to its destination. No excess force. Constant vigilance is required to keep the arms and shoulders relaxed, for they compete with the lower body to dominate action. There is a quiet struggle all serious martial artists experience, as we trade familiar and trusted upper body strength for the lower realm — where power, although vastly greater, is subtle and less easily felt. The process involves risk, and faith that the legs, hips and waist will take over once the shoulders relax. It takes courage and great patience, but a new strength is eventually felt, and with it a new way of being.

Most students do not use a real sword, and this is understandable. The iaito or bladeless sword is safe. I practiced many years before using a live blade sword. Even after all that practice and preparation, I was still cut. Those moments are indelibly etched in my mind. Injuries do not just happen, there is always a reason. Forgo blame, and an injury becomes a pivotal opportunity to learn. The moment is often wasted with — excuses, denial or blame.

My first injury occurred due to greed. After several years practice, I was captured by the thought, "I should be moving faster now. I should be more dynamic." I reacted to an "image" of how I should be. The live blade does not forgive such sins. It demands truth. Get ahead of who you are, and you are cut!

During my firearms instructor days, I studied films of the world's fastest combat shooter. He was a big, fat fellow, and used an old cowboy six-gun.

With that old thing he effortlessly beat challengers who used modern semi-automatic hand guns. It should not have been possible? His hand speed almost defied belief. When asked how he got so fast, he replied, "I don't practice for fast, I practice for smooth. Smooth is fast." His movement was so fast it was hard to see that he moved as smooth as silk. Now I practice for smooth, rather than for speed. It is probably better training, and definitely safer. I usually learn the hard way.

My sword punished me again a few years later. I had been studying films of a master Yagyu swordsman. While practicing, I visualized his movement — and was instantly cut. This mistake was more subtle than the first.

No hurrying, no inattention. But, I was not really present. Even the image of smooth, precise movement is distraction. Any image is not true presence. The sword's razor edge demands presence! No room for images — only direct experience. Only movement — posture — breath. The sword cries out — "come to your senses" — feel — hear — see. Images of reality have no place here.

Kazuo Kato is not a famous sword master. Actually, very few teachers of the Yagyu sword school possess the menkyo kaiden license to officially teach. Yet, he is an excellent teacher. He gave me enough to work on for many years to come. Through his generosity some of the four hundred year lineage of the Yagyu School continues to evolve in me.

I place my sword down in front of me, and bow to begin practice. I bow to the sword which is my teacher now. I bow to Kato Sensei, for faithfully preserving and sharing this wonderful budo.

21. Steven Seagal — Gaijin with Outrageous Dreams

I first heard the name Steve Seagal in the 1970s, while finishing an ice cold Sapporo beer after some brutally hot training in southern Japan. There is probably no place on earth in July, more "mushi atsui" (humid-hot) than Wakayama Prefecture, near O'Sensei's birth place. When I hung my training gi outside to dry, it never dried. It just slowly turned green, as algae grew on it. The guy I was staying with received a letter from a fellow Californian named Steve, who was training in Osaka. We had a big laugh as he read Steve's request for help writing a movie about himself, which he believed would make him a famous martial arts movie star. Who is this jerk, and why would anyone want to see a movie about him?

It was an excellent shot across the room into the waste basket, as Steve's letter was filed under "trash." We had a good laugh about this tall skinny guy, just another martial arts bum like us wandering around Japan. Like us, but with crazy dreams.

His name meant nothing to me at the time, but it came up again three years later when I was an "uchi deshi" (live in student) at O'Sensei's old Iwama dojo. An American studying aikido in Osaka visited Iwama for a few days. As usual, Saito Sensei gave us detailed instruction about being good hosts. We set him up with a futon, cooked for him, and gave him the history and orientation in the ways of Iwama. I even showed him O'Sensei's sword, staff, and spear still hanging on the wall of the dojo.

I do not remember exactly what he did, or failed to do, but by the second day he had really pissed off the senior Japanese sempai. They blamed his sloppy conduct on me because he was an American, and I was the resident American at the dojo then. End of story. I was responsible. His ignorance of basic dojo etiquette reflected poor guidance on my part. The fact he ignored everything I told him, was no excuse. I was responsible. He was a temporary guest, and guests are forgiven for most mistakes. The sempai stayed pissed at me long after the guy returned to Osaka.

The visitor was no beginner; he was a fairly high level black belt who had been in Japan for a while, and yet seemed to be ignorant of the most basic Japan etiquette? When the jerk was leaving, I asked who his teacher was in Osaka, and he mentioned some guy named "Steve." That gave me a bad attitude toward this guy Steve.

A few months later was the Taisai, the big annual event in which officials and senior aiki teachers from all over Japan came to Iwama for the O'Sensei memorial. The small Iwama dojo suddenly swelled from a usual dozen students, to hundreds. Saito Sensei was always the perfect host, pushing himself and his deshi to clean, polish and prepare everything days in advance. After the religious ceremonies in the aiki temple across the street from the dojo, the big banquet began in the field next to the dojo, There was a sea of old Japanese martial arts masters and dignitaries from all over Japan. They were all short Asian men in conservative dark suits, all except one — a tall foreigner with a pony tail, wearing a bright white suit.

Somehow, I just knew who this guy was. To me, he looked not just out of place, he looked ridiculous. Here was another foolish American, sure to bring heat down on me by doing something stupid (like crashing a banquet for Japanese dignitaries in a white suit !) I prepared to catch hell for any other dumb things he did. I remember thinking — Who cares if he is big, maybe I could call him over, and when no one was looking — bounce his butt right out of town!

I was surprised to see that Saito Sensei did not mind him being there. He was treated with the same warm hospitality as everyone else. Damn, now I would not be able to get rid of him! But, I was pleasantly surprised by his polite behavior, and his appropriate socializing with all the old masters, who were twice his age. His Japanese was excellent, much better than mine.

My only memory of Steven Seagal is a tall guy in the white suit, who did not get me in trouble. A few years after returning to America, I went to a martial arts movie, and there he was on the big screen. The silly fellow with crazy dreams, who had the audacity to wear a white suit in a sea of black. He ignored all the guys like me who thought he was an obnoxious idiot. Maybe he was, but he held firmly to his dreams. However unrealistic or outrageous those dreams were, he did not let them die. He stayed focused, and committed to making his dreams come true. That is the lesson I learned from Steven Seagal.

III.

SEARCHING FOR O'SENSEI IN IWAMA

1. Morihiro Saito — A Vow of Service

𝕴WAMA is a small village a few hours outside Tokyo, on the opposite side of Tokyo from Mount Fuji and Chogen-ji. It is in a valley below the mountain, Tago-San. I never saw any horses in Iwama, but you could have described it accurately as "a one horse town." In the 1970s and 80s there were a few noodle shops, a grocery, a small train station, and a dojo. It was the dojo where O'Sensei created the martial art of aikido.

Iwama was a town where a lot of trains did not stop, or even slow down. If you were lucky enough to get a train that did stop there, you found yourself on the station platform, wondering why they ever built a station there. But it's lucky for Morihiro Saito they did, because he got a job with the railroad there, which supported a martial arts study of twenty three years with O'Sensei.

Entrance leading to the Iwama dojo, Ibaragi Prefecture

It is not hard to see why O'Sensei chose Iwama to seclude himself from the insanity of the imperial war machine, after resigning his high-profile teaching positions at military academies and budo organizations. He called it "retirement," but it was in truth more of a refuge from the death and destruction he felt a part of. From the fields and forests of Iwama, he would have seen the waves of B-17 bombers fillings the skies, and raining death down upon Ibaraki Prefecture. He must have wondered how "yamato-damashii" (Japanese spirit and destiny) could have gone so wrong. How could a culture so rich, and so shaped by codes of conduct and civility, have become so brutal and uncivilized?

By 1942 Ueshiba knew the war effort was doomed, and could see the fate of his beloved nation. He agonized over the corruption of Japanese society by militarists, and the ugly exploitation of budo. A lifetime devoted to budo, to what end? It made him sick emotionally, spiritually, and physically. His health deteriorated, and he became physically ill for months.

In Iwama, he rose each morning at 4 a.m., immersing himself in prayer, meditation, chanting, and farming. He began to heal both physically and spiritually, rebuilding his strength through his rigorous shugyo self purification practices, and the rugged simplicity of farm life. Although he was sixty years old, Iwama villagers reported that his legendary strength returned, and he was soon back to doing the work of several men.

Before long, he had thrown himself back into budo training. He had to, it was in his blood. But, this budo would be different, it would be reborn as something new, with a new purity. He needed to build something with a greater moral and ethical foundation, a foundation not easily subverted and distorted. It would be a discipline that cleanses a man's soul — a true change from bujutsu to budo.

During the war years most of his old students were conscripted into the military, and many did not survive the war. Survival on the home front was a struggle, so few villagers could train with him. A young university student named Tadashi Abe was one of his few students, the uncle of my teacher Yoshimitsu Yamada. But during the war years, O'Sensei often trained alone.

In 1946 a local boy named Morihiro, heard about the crazy old man doing strange new budo at the edge of town. He became the old man's student, and devoted the rest of his life to serving O'Sensei, and O'Sensei's vision of a new Aiki Budo. Comfortably secluded from the speed and distractions of modern urban life, Ueshiba rarely left the isolation of Iwama until later years. More villagers began training with him, including a local boy named Isoyama who enrolled in 1949.

About that time old students who survived the war such as Shirata, Tohei and Shioda began teaching in urban areas, as did O'Sensei's son Kisshomaru. But, few students other than those living in Iwama received much direct instruction from O'Sensei until his elderly years when he often traveled. Most had contact only through demonstrations or brief visits. It is easy to understand why so few students or teachers ventured out to Iwama to train with the Master. In Iwama you give up most of the modern comforts and conveniences of city life. You leave a relaxed recreational practice, for harsh discipline and a harder old style practice. At Iwama, students could also not escape O'Sensei's relentless, long and painful periods of self-purification.

When I first visited Iwama I was struck by how few students were there, less than a dozen compared to a thousand or more in Tokyo alone. There were nine students in Saito Sensei's class, and of those nine, three were — his son, his son-in-law, and his brother-in-law.

I was warned in Tokyo, against going to Iwama: "It is in the middle of nowhere....and there is nothing to do there other than train....they broke a guy's arm who visited there.....Saito dislikes outsiders, especially people from Tokyo.....he has a terrible temper.....you have to sleep on the dojo floor...... there are no toilets, only an outhouse....." No wonder so few came.

The part about the outhouse was true; it had the largest spiders I have ever seen. About that temper, yes, I think Saito Sensei got that from O'Sensei. Making a mistake in Iwama was acceptable, but heaven help you if the mistake was due to laziness or sloppiness. That is because Tokyo and Iwama were two different worlds, in fact, Iwama and all of modern Japan were two different worlds. My decision to study with Saito Sensei in Iwama, I would soon discover, was a journey far back in time, back to old Japan.

One day my house mate in Tokyo, Meik, said he was going to "aikido Mecca." He would visit his friend who was a student there, Stan Pranin, and take classes with Morihiro Saito. "What do you mean Mecca?" I asked. "Iwama is where O'Sensei lived for twenty years after the war, and where he created aikido. Saito is obsessed with keeping things exactly as it was when O'Sensei ran things there a few years ago. Chiba Sensei calls it a 'wax museum,' because O'Sensei's weapons are still on the wall, his books are piled on his desk, and Saito only teaches using direct quotes from O'Sensei. Not a thing has changed there, but someday it will, so you better go now."

Meik had been in Japan for many years, so I respected his opinion. "Just don't do anything stupid. Saito is very strict, and you do not want to piss

O'Sensei's room at the Iwama dojo

him off." Both Meik and Stan were experienced black belts, and very knowl-
edgeable about Japanese custom and culture. I would be in good hands.

We met Stan at the Dojo, and he took us to meet Saito Sensei at his
house, next to the dojo. He was gracious and friendly, and said something to
Stan about providing accommodations for us, but my Japanese was not good
enough to understand everything said. Later, we took his aikido class, and it
was great. It was very intense, very strict, but none of the brutality they talked
about in Tokyo. The training was highly structured, with very detailed instructions, and everyone expected to practice the same way. There was less individual expression and artistry than in most dojos, but also less confusion and more
clarity. It was very strong and precise training, which I liked very much.

Saito Sensei at the Aiki jinja

Meik was right about Saito's obsession with doing exactly what O'Sensei did — I could feel his presence there. Saito spoke little English, but his
ability to communicate technical points with crystal clarity was astounding. If
there was any hint of confusion by anyone during class, he noticed it immediately. He would stop the class, and then use the student's problem as the focus

of the class, later expanding his focus to include related concepts. He transformed a complex, esoteric martial art into a simple and logical set of skills, insisting it was easily learned if O'Sensei's training sequence was followed: strong-static practice first, and later fluid-dynamic practice. This was very different from anything I had learned before, and it made a lot of sense.

After class we went back to the little house Stan rented near the dojo. He showed us old grainy 8mm films of O'Sensei. I kept annoying them with continuous comments about the class, I was so exited about the training I could not contain myself. Stan suggested we stay with him, since his place was more comfortable than the dojo. "Sure, sounds good," we said. Big mistake.

Following more wonderful training the next day, we were invited to join Sensei and all his students in the shokudo. That was the long, warehouse-like building next to the dojo. It was where the resident students cooked and ate meals, and where Sensei came to socialize with students, sharing stories of life with O'Sensei. As we approached the entrance, I could hear the laughter and partying. This was great, we were being treated like honored guests with a big party! But, as we entered, all sounds of laughter abruptly ended.

Sensei's demeanor abruptly created absolute silence. Tension filled the big room. Everyone's eyes were downcast, and even the senior black belts slowly and nervously put down their glasses. Everyone's posture straightened, as they stared down at the table. Saito Sensei politely summoned us next to the table. He did not offer us seats.

My dad had a pretty good temper, but I had never before witnessed the eruption of a human volcano. It began gradually with short bursts of angry words I struggled to understand. Then, increasing to full blown rage until it felt like the whole building shook. At the pinnacle of his rage, his meaty fist slammed down on the long, heavy, oak table, bouncing it off the ground and spilling drinks. I could swear that several of the light fixtures started to flicker. Stories of wise and kindly O'Sensei occasionally exploding in anger, had seemed remote and hard to fathom, until that moment. Short bursts of reprimand became louder, longer, and more furious. My limited Japanese struggled to decipher bits and pieces: "…disrespect…O'Sensei's home…lack of appreciation…protocol…Tokyo people…attitudes…sloppy…casual…no respect…O'Sensei's home…!! His language was interspersed with many loud "DA-ME!" (NO GOOD!)

From the depth of their bows, which Stan and Meik maintained the whole time, I assumed Sensei's language must have been even worse than I could decipher. We remained with heads bowed low, and eyes fixed on the floor. We knew enough to offer no excuses.

It seemed at that moment, we represented every careless, sloppy, casual "city" person that Sensei had been obligated to host — People with little understanding of where they were, and what proper conduct was at this sacred place. The fact that Meik and Stan were senior black belts with knowledge of budo and Japanese culture, made their indiscretions worse. O'Sensei was famous for a thunderous temper, but then, his anger would disappear as suddenly as it came. This human volcano just kept erupting. Sensei even attacked himself — for being too lenient with students, and letting O'Sensei down. I was sure when we finally came up from our seemingly endless bow, Saito's big arm would be pointing the way back to Tokyo.

After a few minutes, which felt like hours, sensei's wife, Oku-San came in. If you spent any time in Iwama, you know there has to be a special place in heaven reserved for her. She heard Sensei's rage from her house 100+ yards away, and when it did not dissipate she responded. I came to know her as "the angel of mercy." It seemed she possessed the only power on earth that could calm Sensei down when he got really pissed off.

Gradually, the intensity lessened, and his attention returned to the students sitting around the table. He motioned for them to pick up their drinks, then explained in a quiet voice about the importance of following protocol here at "O'Sensei's dojo." Ignoring us, he quietly told them that knowing the right way to behave was an important part of budo. Then he directed a senior student to show us where we were to sleep in the dojo. We apparently were not being thrown out.

My futon was placed in O'Sensei's old room, connected to the dojo by a short hallway. Sensei had intended for me to have O'Sensei's room on my first night at the dojo, that was one reason he flipped out. It was a great honor to bestow on someone, but I never showed up. The room was amazing — many of O'Sensei's personal effects were still there. There were photos of him and his wife, all his books — hundreds of books. I felt his strong presence there, it was a little spooky.

Iwama dojo

The next morning Sensei met us at the dojo entrance just before class. I prepared myself for further scolding, but he was pleasant. "Did you sleep well? Good, that's fine. What would you like to practice this morning?" He smiled and nodded when I said, "basics please." As we entered he said "Gambate kudasai." (please train hard) It was another amazing class.

To Morihiro Saito Iwama was a sacred place where anyone could visit, but staying there was a privilege. That demanded a higher level of conduct than the outside world. Iwama was old Japan, with a code of honor approaching samurai bushido. Sensei was responsible for preserving not only the physical facilities and training style, but the frame of mind and lifestyle of O'Sensei. Manners and protocol were to be strictly followed. Students were expected to understand that Iwama was not the modern world; it was O'Sensei's world!

Impressed by Saito Sensei's earnest sense of mission, and phenomenal teaching ability, I began returning to Iwama frequently, and fell in love with the place. For my last eighteen months in Japan, I trained there seven days a week. Occasionally receiving Sensei's wrath was small price to pay for all the knowledge shared. And those giant spiders in the outhouse — we became friends.

There was a sense of urgency to Sensei's teaching, and the passion he expressed for O'Sensei's budo was contagious; "We must master O'Sensei's budo before we get too old, and you must all learn it well before you leave Japan." The ethic expressed at most dojos in Japan was a relaxed, long term commitment — budo as lifestyle. That attitude has great value, but the urgency instilled at Iwama was pure excitement.

At 4:00 p.m. sharp every day I would jog through the mass of humanity on Tokyo streets to the nearest Yamanote line train connection that loops around Tokyo. Then, arriving at big Ueno Station I would slip through the crowds just in time to make a 5:15 p.m. Joban train that stopped at Iwama. At 6:46 p.m I hit the Iwama station platform at full sprint, taking a shortcut through a hole in the rail yard fence, and sprinting the half mile to make the evening class. If my timing was just right, I met Sensei walking toward the dojo — stopped to give a bow, and changed into gi and hakama as I ran. I would be in my place on the mat at 6:59 p.m. sharp, just before Sensei bowed in to start class.

Weekends were a great time to train at Iwama, because there were often college clubs visiting, and Sensei would teach all day Saturday and Sunday. When there were no visiting groups, I would grab the one uchi deshi who was always ready to do extra training after class — an old (back then fifty was old) New Zealander, Keith Hartley. He had practiced every style of aiki martial arts for twenty years before finding what he called "the bloody real thing." We practiced for hours all afternoon, reviewing all the sword and staff exercises, and all the forms Sensei had taught that week. Most uchi deshi seemed to disappear after morning classes on the weekends, but that tough, old kiwi was always ready for more training. More than twice the age of the other students, surely the oldest uchi deshi in Japan, his spirit shined the brightest. Instead of resting, Keith used those powerful hands at every opportunity to massage Sensei's stiff, aging knees, which helped a lot.

I was puzzled by the sharp contrast between the martial art at Iwama, and the aikido in the rest of Japan — training exercises, techniques, concepts, and spirit of the practice was radically different from what I learned in Tokyo, or in America? For months, Sensei would interrupt class to have me demonstrate my techniques — then visibly frustrated, he would insist that teachers in New York and Tokyo "are not teaching O'Sensei's budo!" He would show in great detail why "O'Sensei did not do this...because..." and then explain why my technique would never work in a "real" situation. He frequently came up to me during training to remind me "Thomas, embu janai, budo da kara," which meant, "aikido is not a dance, it is serious martial art!" His most common critique of modern aikido training was "koshi shinda" (lit. "dead hips") which meant a lack of hip and lower body movement, resulting in over-reliance on arm strength if you were held strongly.

I accepted what Saito said, but for years was confused by the extreme difference between the budo of O'Sensei in Iwama, and the aikido outside of Iwama. It was only after listening to old timers in Japan, and reading a portion of Kisshomaru Ueshiba's book, A Life in Aikido, that I understood. Describing his return to Tokyo from Iwama after the war, Kisshomaru wrote:

> "The move to Iwama had allowed us to practice freely and openly....In Tokyo, we would have to be very circumspect to avoid trouble with the American occupation forces who were suspicious of anything connected with budo. Our application to the Ministry of Education (to practice outside Iwama) bore the name Aikikai Foundation...it reflected the circumstances of the time... (defining aikido) as an activity combining the study of health with the arts of 'kagaru mai,'

ritual dance offered as prayer. Once the application gains official approval, the former Hombu Dojo in Wakamatsu-cho will offer training that meets the needs of the times....On February 2, 1948, the much awaited authorization for the Aikikai Foundation was granted...In 1953, O'Sensei told us it suited him to train in Iwama, but we should work from Tokyo in whatever way we thought best to achieve the growth of Aikido there...My vision was that this (Aikikai Hombu) would be the main shrine of Aikido, its outlook on the world, while Iwama would be Aikido's innermost sanctuary, the Oku-no-in."

Kisshomaru confirms what Saito Sensei and other budo teachers have reported — that O'Sensei chose to stay secluded in Iwama in the post war years, to practice and teach his old style aiki budo unaffected by the prohibitions and restrictions of the US occupation. He permitted Kisshomaru, Tohei, and others to modify his art in order to conform with the authorities. General MacArthur's oversight of postwar Japan included a ban on martial arts and weapons training, and a new pacifist constitution. The high profile of activities in Tokyo, and other urban areas therefore required the removal of many key elements of Ueshiba's aiki budo, including: weapons training, kiai shouts, aggressive initiating movements,"katai keiko" (strong attacks and full power grabs.)

Call it modification or evolution, but out of necessity, O'Sensei's martial art was transformed into a significantly softer, easier, and less martial art outside of Iwama. There are numerous accounts of O'Sensei expressing dissatisfaction or ambivalence at these changes, when he observed training in his travels. Yet, he did lend support to his son and old students as they established schools (and livelihoods) by visiting, and performing demonstrations which emphasized the spiritual principles of the art, consistent with the modern aikido. While he remained the figure head of Kisshomaru's Aiki Kai organization, throughout the 1950s and 1960s he mostly trained and taught at his home and small dojo in Iwama.

Training at this "Oku no in," innermost sanctuary, was not just about studying O'Sensei's old style budo, it was about assisting Saito Sensei in caring for the old dojo and the Aiki-Jinja, the small temple O'Sensei had built nearby. I raked the grounds each morning in front of the Aiki-Jinja, just as I

The author and sempai Bruce Klickstein in a rare informal moment, receiving instruction from Saito Sensei

had at Chogen-ji, the difference was that Sensei would watch us like a hawk, to ensure we were raking properly. Every chore had a proper technique, and raking was no exception. Correct raking ensured we would not damage the brittle old straw rakes, which were decades old. "Be careful, those are O'Sensei's rakes."

Iwama life was raking, cleaning, caring for visitors, and a lot of sword

— staff — and hard weaponless training. Work would often be interrupted by Sensei instructing us in O'Sensei's method of tanren uchi striking exercises with the extra heavy bokkens, or how to throw the ancient Japanese shuriken darts, using tatami mats as targets. On the weekends after training, he would show off his culinary talents, like making soba and udon noodles from his secret recipes. Since it is Japan, there were many obligatory after hours drinking parties (but missing training due to a hangover was unacceptable!)

When Saito Sensei got married, his honeymoon was staying close to home to address the needs of O'Sensei. Oka-San accepted that her life was also dedicated to O'Sensei, and taking care of his legacy which was Iwama. They did not have an easy life, and had zero privacy. It was not uncommon for them to drop everything, to prepare for a last minute visit from one of O'Sensei's old students or a member of the Ueshiba family.

Although little about this big — hard drinking — loud and opinionated — country farmer appeared to be very "spiritual," his vow of service to O'Sensei was absolute. It was karma yoga, the path of service. Allowing us to share that service was a rare and wonderful privilege. In my last letter to Morihiro Saito I tried to express some of this:

Dear Sensei,

You were so gracious and hospitable when I first visited Iwama, as you were to all visitors coming to O'Sensei's dojo. But when you accepted me as your student, you put me through hell, for my casual attitude, my "dead hips," and neglect of basic skills. You scolded harshly, and corrected relentlessly during those first months, never expecting me to stay. I stayed because I understand that you were obligated to pass on two decades of detailed instruction from the Founder. You were committed to every student, even foreigners, learning exactly as O'Sensei taught you. It was your sworn obligation.

You taught us much more than martial art, much more than techniques. You hit the roof when you saw sloppy etiquette or improper protocol, and there were right and wrong flowers to be placed on the dojo altar, and a special broom to be used for the tokonoma — heaven help the student who screwed that one up. Raking the grounds of the Aiki Jinja — all Iwama deshi know your response to someone raking with improper technique. After all, you were "just a farmer, not a rich Tokyo sensei," and "rakes cost money, so they must be used correctly and carefully."

But, it was not about the money, it was about treating each movement, each moment with a warrior's attention and precision. You required no less of us than O'Sensei required of you. Your simple country farmer ethic of not being wasteful, and caring for your tools, was a very practical lesson. I have no doubt those rakes will last another hundred years, if there is anyone to demand the same care and precision when raking that you did.

Each night, I would replay every moment of your class in my mind, filling notebooks with diagrams and the quotes from O'Sensei you stressed that day. That is how exciting your classes were — you were giving away all O'Sensei shared with you — all your secrets! So much detail poured out of you, and you held nothing back. It was pure love.

After more than a year at the dojo, I would still ask permission to do certain things, because it was O'Sensei's way, it was courtesy. I remember the day a high-ranking Japanese black belt visited Iwama, perhaps because of his rank, he was rather casual about some of his actions, and took some liberties without asking your permission. You did not hesitate to admonish him severely. You looked at me, and told him "Tom-San has been doing that for over a year, but he always observes the courtesy, and asks permission. He is not Japanese, but, he understands budo. You should learn budo like that."

Thank you for giving so much, demanding so much of us, and caring so much. You remain in my heart.

Your student,

Thomas

My last letter from Saito Sensei:

Dear Thomas,

I am sorry for taking long to answer your last letter. My new books have been published, so I asked the publisher to send some to you. How is training going at your dojo? O'Sensei's Iwama budo is now being born outside Japan in many places. You are an Iwama sempai, and you are preserving what O'Sensei created here. Please give it your very best effort.

On March 31, I will be another year older, and I do not have a lot of time left to master O'Sensei's martial art, so I am training hard, and I am busy teaching what he taught me....Please give my best wishes to your family and your students.

Regards,
Morihiro Saito

2. Upside Down & Backwards in Iwama

Cold January night in the Iwama Dojo. Nemoto sempai is helping me stay warm, bouncing me on the tatami training mats with powerful shihonage throws. My palm repeatedly slams the old mats, echoing off the aging wooden walls. It is no nonsense budo at its best, strong and precise. Whirling, swirling energy — piercing kiai shouts — bodies flying all around. Breath — sweat — danger — thrilling!

Sensei demonstrates a dangerous variation, ordering "shizuka ni" (practice it carefully.) My assumption is Nemoto will slow down. Serious mistake. It does not mean slow — it means throw according to your partner's ability. My erroneous expectation puts me one step behind, so I pay with a nasty wake up "zing" in my wrist. Just a brief bolt of lightning to the wrist highlighting my sloppy thinking. This is no place for assumptions, or expectations. "Budo da kara!" — it is budo! Stay alert and respond. It is that simple.

With any one else I might be annoyed, the ego always trying to place blame when there is pain. But blame is not possible with Nemoto — not with that smile. A huge smile of pure joy which never leaves that big round face. You just can not get angry at that smile, it is too genuine.

Now, back with the program — airborne and deep inside the technique. Spinning about four feet off the ground as Nemoto cuts down on my arm as if slicing with a sword. Upside down, I catch a glimpse of foot prints on the ceiling. They only looked like vague stains and smudges up there before; the marks where old sempai claim O'sensei sometimes walked at midnight. I never believed it, but upside down in the air — they damn well did look like foot steps. Could it be?

There is no heat in the Iwama Dojo, so I can see my breath. Even with a sweat soaked training uniform I cannot feel my feet, they are numb from the cold mats. As I am getting up from a fall someone is thrown on my foot, but I don't feel a thing. We continue training, but my balance feels weird. I cannot figure out why. Nemoto looks down at my feet, and for the first time in two years his blazing smile has vanished. Gone. Why has Nemoto lost his essence?

I look down too, and it is a bizarre and grotesque sight. My big toe is backwards and upside down. It is pointing back at me, like some cruel joke.

But, my feet are so cold I can not feel a thing. For now. Sensei sees it, and stops the class just long enough for the two biggest sempai to drag me off the mat. Even Sensei seems a little shaken up. He directs them to take me to the dojo doctor immediately. Someone mentions that it is almost 8 PM, the clinic closing time, but Sensei will call to "make sure" the doctor waits for us.

As we pull up to a little clinic on the edge of town, I cannot read the kanji on the sign, but sempai assures me, "the doctor gives special care to students of Iwama Dojo. He was a friend of O'Sensei." I don't think I met one person in this village who did not say they were a friend or student of O'Sensei. Everyone from shop keepers, to farmers, to the town drunk.

Lucky they kept the clinic open, because the feeling is returning to my feet and starting to hurt like hell. Half the bones in the front of my foot must be broken. I hobble in with a sempai on each arm, and sit next to another patient in the waiting room. One of the guys goes in to see the doctor, then returns announcing "the doctor will see you next." Feeling like a real VIP, I try to apologize to the other guy waiting, but one look at my mangled foot and he waves his hand, "Ok, ok." It looks really gross.

As we enter the examining room the doctor is finishing with another patient, and has his back to me. A nurse passes me to help the other patient out of the office — the patient is a cat! A cat !!

It takes the doctor — I mean veterinarian, a long time to turn around because he is about ninety five years old! My body tightens as I glare at the sempai tightly clutching my arms. "He is a very good doctor, do not worry," they insist. They are struggling to hide their grins. "Really, very good." This is not funny, I want out of here!

It could not get any worse, right? As the old man slowly crosses the room, shuffling in my general direction, he ends up in front of one of the guys holding me. He is redirected to where I am — because he is blind! Blind as a bat! He sees nothing! Nada! As they direct him to where I am standing they have to repeat their words loudly — he is apparently deaf too! This was the special "doctor" for Sensei's students. A blind — deaf — veterinarian, about thirty years past retirement age.

The throbbing pain in my foot is now replaced with terror! Get me out of here! They hold on tight repeating their lame assurances. "He is really, very good, very good." The old guy works his way, one inch at a time, down my body eventually finding my foot. Then he spends what seems like an hour just touching, touching all around what was left of my big toe. Not doing anything but touching, as I suffer. The minutes pass as he mumbles incoherently to himself. His fingers wandering aimlessly around my foot. One sempai asks a question, but gets no reply. They are still holding me tight, but maybe I can throw them. Then escape!

They are beginning to crack up — to them the whole scene is hysterical. Like they have seen this before. What is so funny about a student probably crippled for life? In between the stabbing pains I have thoughts like: How about x-rays? Medication? Surgery? How about....a REAL doctor! and.... what a stupid idea to train in Japan!

I am sure the old guy has become lost in some senile fixation with my foot. Maybe thinking it was his late wife's hand, or some old toy from his childhood. Suddenly the pain goes from intense — to excruciating! On a scale of one to ten — it is FIFTEEN! Like being stabbed in the foot with a large kitchen knife! Then.....nothing. All pain is gone. Just a dull ache.

I look down at the disgusting mess that had been a mangled toe to find a normal looking foot. Unbelievably, it had been a severe dislocation. No broken bones. This centenarian — veterinarian learned everything an x-ray and MRI would have shown — just by taking a long time to feel around very carefully. His sense of touch was extraordinary. He held my foot a certain way, and at exactly the right angle he yanked and twisted it — popping the whole mess back into its socket. Then he smeared some foul smelling black tar all over it, and wrapped it up. "Tell gaijin boy it will swell twice its normal size for 3 days, then be fine in one week." He put on his hat and coat, grabbed his cane, then disappeared into the cold night.

Exactly one week later I was back at training. When Saito Sensei saw me in class he grinned, announcing loudly in Japanese, "Our doctor for Iwama Dojo students is the best, right Thomas-San?

3. O'Sensei's Iron Kettle

IT was the early 1980s, and I had been living in Japan for a long time. I could have easily stayed for five or ten more years; it felt that natural living there. The Asahi Shinbun newspaper had a picture of the American president, Jimmy Carter, a very intelligent, spiritual, and principled man from everything I had read. For some reason most Americans seemed to dislike him. That old actor Ronald Reagan talked tough like in his movies, and rattled his saber much louder than Carter. It looked like Reagan would be the next American president. He did speak well and look very presidential; he was a very good actor.

I decided to treat myself to one souvenir before leaving Japan. My sword, staff, and a few scars did not count as souvenirs. Harajuku was the place to go. It is the section of Tokyo with lots of fancy coffee shops, many pretty young ladies, and a big antique warehouse. I wandered around the warehouse for hours, so much cool stuff — very old tea sets, samurai armor, ancient calligraphy, a beautiful old bamboo flute, a rusted and blood-stained samurai tanto knife. Then I saw it — a small iron kettle with an unusual shape and texture. It was a half-foot wide and half-foot high, old and a little rusted, with a detachable iron handle. With all the cool stuff there, why was I attracted to a kettle? But, it was not expensive, and the heavy iron could definitely handle the banging around in my pack during my travels.

I have had that old kettle for more than thirty years now, and it must have been twenty years before I spotted it in a grainy old film of O'Sensei, from 1961. He is sitting by the tokonoma, in front of class supervising training, as Saito Sensei teaches. In his late seventies, he sits in impeccably erect seiza, like a mountain dressed in a formal attire. His eyes remind me of the eyes of eagles, perched high in the trees which followed my every move in the back-woods of Alaska. His eyes scan the room, following the movement of every person, roving eyes that miss nothing, and stick to nothing. He has overwhelming presence — totally alert, totally still. Still, except for those wild eyes.

There is water boiling next to him, with steam pouring from the spout of a rust colored iron kettle. It is my kettle, not a similar kettle, the same one. That fact drew my attention away momentarily from an easily missed, bizarre element of the film. Overshadowed by his regal and intimidating presence, his left hand is calmly resting against the side of the steaming kettle. His face is expressionless, his body motionless. Only his eyes move — darting about the room, not missing a thing. The total stillness of his body reflects deep meditation.

I once burned my hand on the handle of that kettle when water was boiling. The body of the kettle where O'Sensei was touching had to be several hundred degrees hotter. How was he doing that? Why was he doing it? To impress, to teach something…? To show there is some dimension where it is possible, perhaps? When I had asked Saito Sensei if he ever saw O'Sensei perform any kind of magic he said no, with a tone that clearly indicated he thought it was a really dumb question. He was with him for twenty three years, and he saw no magic — so what was his hand doing against a hot iron kettle? I am as intrigued by WHY he did it, as I am by HOW. Was he showing off his power? But this guy had nothing left to prove, he was at the top of his game. By then he only cared about God.

Why do I care about this? No one I know who has seen the film seems that interested. At age sixty-two, part of Thomas is still a kid, excited by the magical and mystical. So what do I want from the Asian disciplines — internal powers? Mystical experience? Is it about being "special?" Old guy Thomas seems to have some of the same wide eyed fantasies of little Tommy, only wrapped in more sophisticated language. This is not bad, just a part of who I am. All childhood dreams and wonder need not die.

I do love that old kettle. I have no immediate plans to lay my hand on it, as it pours its steam into the room. I still wonder why that kettle attracted me so, long before I saw it in that film. Did I see it in the dojo or in O'Sensei's room? I am sure I did not. I still wonder why O'Sensei placed his hand on it for us to see. Perhaps just because he could.

4. Masao Umezawa — Zen Priest, Healer, Iwama Sempai

MASAO Umezawa was born in Kamakura, Japan, in the shadow of the great Daibutsu. It is the enormous forty foot high statue of the sitting Buddha. In the 1960s, at age eighteen, Masao moved to Tokyo to attend college, and also began aikido training. After four years at the big Hombu dojo, he had an opportunity to speak with O'Sensei, a conversation which changed the course of his life. In a moment of apparent frustration, O'Sensei turned to him and said, "Umezawa, the aikido practiced here in Tokyo, is for exercise — my aikido is for the battlefield." When he asked O'Sensei how he could learn his aikido, O'Sensei told him "You go to my dojo in Iwama, you train with Saito."

So, following O'Sensei's advice he left his friends in Tokyo, and family in nearby Kamakura to become an uchideshi in Iwama. Eventually Masao became close with Saito Sensei's daughter, and they were married. As Saito did with several family members, he set up his daughter and new son-in-law with a small restaurant to support themselves. But, Umezawa would frequently return to Kamakura to pursue his dream of becoming both a healer and Zen priest. This did not please his father-in-law.

In spite of Saito's disapproval, Umezawa pursued his study of healing and Zen for many years, in addition to martial arts. He eventually became both an ordained Zen priest, and a doctor of Chinese medicine. When Saito Sensei passed away in 2002, it was Umezawa who conducted his funeral ceremony.

After the death of Saito Sensei, the Tokyo based Aikikai Foundation, took over management of the Iwama Dojo, changing staff and curriculum to be more consistent with modern aikido. The dojo which faithfully preserved O'Sensei's traditional style of practice, became a historical relic, used primarily for banquets and Aikikai demonstrations. Aikikai publications and web sites omit references to O'Sensei's traditional form of practice at Iwama, as well as the enormous contributions of Morihiro Saito. Why the roots of an art, which form its foundation would be considered unimportant is bewildering?

Several Iwama sempai, including Umezawa undertook to preserve O'Sensei's traditional form of aiki martial art by building their own dojos in or near Iwama. Among them are Hitohiro Saito, Nemoto Sempai, and Umezawa. The beautiful Genshin Dojo was built by Umezawa, which is a large dojo — zendo, where he continues his daily training in both Zen and Iwama style aikido. At 5:00 a.m. each day, you can hear the same powerful chanting, and see the same concentrated meditation practice, as when O'Sensei was there. Umezawa continues O'Sensei's tradition of daily shugyo, sword and staff.

With unshakable commitment, Umezawa continues his daily practice with relatively few students. But this, too, follows the tradition of O'Sensei, who preferred the isolation and seclusion of Iwama, and company of a few serious students, to the notoriety and fame afforded him in the outside world. It is ironic, that most martial arts teachers strive for notoriety and large numbers of students, while O'Sensei preferred the opposite.

When I recently visited the Genshin Dojo, I was coping with a serious illness. I trained with Umezawa in the morning, then each afternoon he would treat me at his clinic. The payment for this medical care was "only what you can afford." On my last day with him, we sat in stillness for a long time;

the wonderful silence filling the beautiful dojo, and the smell of immaculately clean tatami mats filling each breath. In his limited English he said; "Tom-San, I build dojo and zendo for service. O'Sensei budo service. All people who come this place, we give a good feeling. Maybe help cover bad feeling. For this I build dojo. Please use aikido for service."

The English translation of the word samurai is "to serve." Masao Umezawa is a true samurai. He is part of O'Sensei's living legacy in Iwama, Japan.

IV.

SEARCHING IN CIIINA

1. Ajahn Jumnean — Dharma Cop of The Thai Jungle

*A*JAHN Jumnean began meditation practice at the age of six, then he was ordained as a Theravada Buddhist monk at twenty. I met him during his travels when, he was the middle-aged abbot of several jungle monasteries in southern Thailand, living in a cave in the mountains of Krabi. His sense of humor captivated me from our first encounter, when he handed me a laminated business card with his jungle cave address on it. I guess when you live in a damp cave, it is wise to laminate your business card.

Even with a shaved head and monk's robe, he did not look much like any monk I had seen before. He had a thick neck, and big muscular legs, definitely not your average monk. He is a famous meditation master and Dharma teacher who travels the jungle paths between monasteries and villages, teaching and settling disputes between villagers. He carries the same begging bowl

as other monks, which villagers fill with rice and other scraps of food. But, as the abbot of the monasteries he wears a special robe when he travels, on which villagers attach beads, jewels, or other ornaments to express gratitude and respect. When I met him the robe weighed nearly seventy pounds! This made his routine treks through the jungle heat quite difficult. Removing any ornaments was not an option, since everything attached to the robe is considered sacred.

Out of desperation, he consulted his grandparents, who are of Chinese decent. He knew they practiced the Chinese yoga of qigong, and was told it might help him. They taught him a short set of exercises which they said would strengthen and balance the flow of chi through his body, and give him vast energy. They also told him he would not get any older. After practicing each day, he found he was much better able to walk the long distances through the jungle wearing the heavy robe. Now he teaches the exercises to his monks, along with sitting meditation. He told me "You practice, and you no get old." Seeing he looked twenty years younger than his age, I took his advice and continue his practice:

> There are four simple movements, performed with a relaxed, erect posture, with knees slightly bend, and long, soft breathing nose to belly:
>
> 1) *Slowly open the arms and palms to the sides, "taking in the energy of the world."*
> 2) *Right hand squeezes into a fist, "taking in energy through the right hand."*
> 3) *Left hand forms a fist, "taking in energy through the left hand."*
> 4) *The hands slowly rise up in front of the body palms up, then push upward above the head, "holding the world."*

Learning about Ajahn Jumnean's amazing life lent credence to his teaching and fueled my commitment to practice what he taught. As he walked the jungle trails between monasteries, his success in settling disputes between villagers, and success in dealing with bandits, came to the attention of provincial government officials. They needed to address the problem of bandits accosting villagers on remote jungle trails, but the provincial police refused to patrol those areas. So, they asked AJ to become the Regional Peace Officer for the areas of the Thai jungle he routinely traveled.

This was a very unusual request, indeed, to a Buddhist monk with a vow of nonviolence. But he agreed without hesitation, because he could help prevent bandits from accruing the negative karma, which results from harming others. He accepted the job, but he would not carry a gun, or use any force that caused serious injury. From then on, a Buddhist monk became the only cop patrolling a large jungle area of southern Thailand. He was "the Dharma cop." I called him the "DPO" — Dharma Peace Officer.

Wearing that heavy robe all day gave AJ a powerful body, which did not hurt any when dealing with bad guys. But he did not have to rely much on physical strength, since his main tool was what you might call "tactical Dharma." He was a master of persuasion, befriending bandits and usually convincing them to come out of the jungle with him. They sometimes became monks at his monasteries. "What if they refused to surrender?" I would ask. "Power of the Dharma," he would say. "But what about the violent fellows?" I persisted. "Those guys need tough love." (My translation) "What if tough love does not work?" I pressed him further. "Dharma powder," he replied, with a mischievous smile. Dharma "power" or Dharma "powder"? I was confused, and so was the monk translating. He finally made a motion of holding, and blowing through a tube. After more discussion, I understood. He mainly relied on "Dharma power," but his backup tool was his "Dharma powder." Yes, AJ carried his own homemade pepper spray.

He periodically made stops at the ant hills of fire ants, just about the nastiest creatures in the jungle. Careful not to step on "anyone," he would gather the bodies of the dead ants, chant prayers for their well being, then grind them into a fine powder. He poured the powder into a short bamboo reed which he carried in his belt. If the bad guy was too crazy to talk, or came at him with a weapon, he would simply give him one puff. That powder would end the altercation fast. He would then bind the bad guy's hands with the nearest vine, and lovingly wash the powder out of their eyes. They were a captive audience for his Dharma talks on the long journey out of the jungle. Some bandits became his friends, some became his students, some followed him out of the jungle, and surrendered to authorities. He was supposed to bring the bad guys to justice, but it sounded like he took more guys to his monastery than to jail.

Years later, across the globe in Brooklyn, New York, I am reminding ex-convict Martinez about the conditions of his parole, which include no weapons. With pleading eyes, he replies, "So, how do I get home at night? I've already been robbed twice this month. Collings, you walk this neighborhood with a gun and bulletproof vest, I got nothing?" He is a small guy with an anguished look. He may have done hard time upstate for burglary, but he is not a violent guy, and not an imposing figure on the street. He is an easy mark for the predators of Bushwick and East New York. He vents his frustration, openly questions the rules. I respect that; his openness and honesty are refreshing, since most parolees never challenge me on the rules, they just ignore them.

We brainstorm together how Martinez can negotiate the nasty streets of this neighborhood to make it home without getting robbed or killed. I cannot remember if Achan Jumnean ever came up in our conversations, but a few weeks later, Martinez came in with a big grin on his face. "Collings, I solved my little problem." My eyes instinctively focused on the hand in his pocket. "No weapon, Collings. Go ahead and search me, but all you gonna find is a little sand. Sand is legal, right?" I pat him down, and all I find is sand in his pockets. "Two days ago, one of the same sons of bitches who jumped me last month came at me again. I told him OK, and reached in my pocket like I was giving him my cash again. When I saw that cocky look on his face, I knew I had him. Before he knew what hit him, the sand was already in his face, and he could not see a thing. The son of a bitch was helpless. Before I took off, I planted a real good kick into his family jewels. Like you told me, I even called the cops to have him locked up."

I congratulated Martinez on his creativity, and assured him his use of sand was fine, as long as it was defensive. I thought of Ajahn Jumnean, and jokingly asked Martinez if he was a Buddhist. Of course he had no idea what I was talking about.

Too bad the only monastery we have for bad guys in New York City is Rikers Island. It would be wonderful to give guys the option that Ajahn Jumnean did. We could use a lot of Dharma cops like him around here.

2. Ping Lu — Incorrigible Jailhouse Master

MY favorite qigong ("chi gong") practice was learned from a real trouble maker — a Chinese Taoist teacher named Ping Lu. He was a child prodigy in traditional Chinese medicine, and came to the attention of government officials as a young boy. He was sent to medical school in his teens to learn modern medicine, then conscripted into the Red Army for several years as a military physician. After military service he became a Professor of Medicine at Beijing University.

At the top of his profession, he used his influence as a platform to criticize government censorship and repression. His stature must have had an impact. It was very embarrassing to the government, so after repeated warnings he was sent to prison. When he refused to sign a confession he was threatened with execution, and kept incarcerated for several extra years. He was eventually released without a confession. Thus began the long and unsuccessful struggle by the Chinese government to silence Ping Lu.

The problem for the government has been that Ping Lu is a deeply spiritual man who is not attached to position or material comforts. Therefore, he is not easily intimidated or silenced. Worse yet for the government, he does not have the normal fear of imprisonment. He seems to have little difficulty adapting to prison life. From his prison cell he becomes engrossed in his sitting — standing — moving qigong meditation practices, more deeply immersed than is possible in his busy life out of prison. Qigong, like all internal disciplines, can be practiced anywhere; in a beautiful forest setting, or in a cell behind a locked door. The beautiful thing about Asian disciplines is they only require a little space, a bit of air to breathe — and you're in business!

For Ping Lu, entering and leaving prison became his life style. After serving a prison term he would return to his medical practice, but also to his dissident activities. For spiritual warriors like Ping Lu, the solitude of prison is a refuge, similar to a monastery. Repressive governments always have trouble with powerfully spiritual individuals like this; Gandhi, King, Mandela. These guys do not have the usual fear of simplicity and solitude. They are the most powerful of warriors. They are the purist examples of what Sir Thomas Moore called "a man for all seasons." Even killing them does not silence them, for in death, their message and spirit exponentially expands, like ripples on a pond, emanating far beyond the place and time of their death.

I met Ping Lu during a hiatus between his incarcerations. His light-hearted, playful manner was captivating. He looked far too youthful, healthy, and joyful to be a middle-aged dissident, with years of prison under his belt. The set of qigong exercises he taught was so simple, not like an Asian master instructing an esoteric discipline — but play, pure fooling around fun. I have learned very few things in my life that were so simple and yet so powerful. After more than fifteen years I still practice it regularly.

> * BEWARE * Like most qigong, this practice is so simple —
> so easily learned that there is a great danger of dismissing it's
> value and power:
>
> 1) *Stand erect and relaxed, with knees slightly bent. The body softly turns from the waist, one way, and then the other, with arms gently swinging and following the hip turn. Long, soft breaths flow through the nose to the abdomen.*
>
> 2) *After a few minutes, keeping the erect posture, add a dip in the hips with a knee bend, which swings the arms up and around the body — one hand tapping the lower back and the other tapping midway between shoulder and neck. This becomes quite aerobic if continued more than a minute or two. Breath is allowed to be full and open. The body areas being tapped and simulated are acupressure points.*
>
> 3) *Finally, leave out the turn and continue dipping the hips, bending the knees, and swinging the arms. The arms are now swinging freely above the head, then down and behind the body. Your shoulders become like well-oiled hinges, and all tension in the upper body drains away.*
>
> 4) *After a few minutes, the body returns to an erect, and deeply relaxed posture with breath flowing softly and unrestricted. You may feel the body vibrate. Lightly bounce on the heals, letting everything jiggle a bit, releasing any hidden tension.*

This exercise is a wonderful preparation for meditation, martial arts training, or any physical exercise. It is also a great practice by itself. It is one of my secrets for training hard and wearing out people half my age (Oh no — my secret is out!) I call it an "invisible" practice, because many who learned it from Ping Lu with me have long since stopped practicing — it just seemed too simple to have profound benefits. Perhaps I never let go of the practice because I get so much inspiration from Ping Lu's life.

After I studied with him, Dr. Lu was in a serious car accident. I lost touch with him after that. But, it seems that he bounced back from his injuries. Not long ago, I did a web search and found a Dr. Ping Lu teaching at a school of traditional Chinese medicine near Beijing. He is probably still a royal pain in the ass to those poor government boys, who try so damn hard to keep everybody in line.

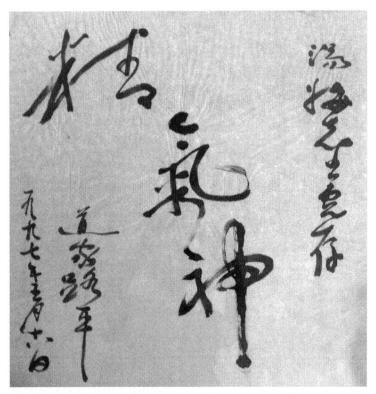

"Jing Chi Sheng" Essence –Life Energy –Spirit
Taoist Ping Lu

3. Radical Monk — Tamo Bodhidharma

TRAVELING through China I sought out temples where the legendary figure Tamo Bodhidharma visited and taught. Just as Jesus, Mohammed, and the Buddha seem far more alike to me than different, so O'Sensei and Bodhidharma seemed to be of one mind. I followed the epic journey of this great Buddhist master, from a warrior class in India, as he traveled to monasteries and Buddhist temples causing a ruckus, and upsetting the status quo. After Tamo, things in China were never quite the same.

At the Shaolin temple, he found monks steeped in idol worship, and lifeless ritual. There was apparently lots of religious ceremony, but little spiritual practice. He considered most of what they did to be foolish distraction.

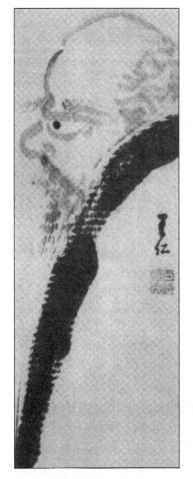

They were so outraged that the head monks banished him from the temple. He disappeared into a mountain cave, content to pursue intensive practice without distraction, much like O'Sensei did in Iwama. Like all the greatest teachers, he demanded more of himself than others, and thrived on isolation. After a momentary lapse from his ferocious presence of mind, he cut off his eyelids to enhance his alertness. He was that ruthless in his commitment to liberation.

The legend is that after seven years, the monks realized the truth of his observations, and begged him to return. Tamo agreed and shared the Buddha's practice of training the mind, being totally present, and freeing oneself from the chains of attachment. He admonished them not to worship the Buddha, but to become the Buddha, and to live as a Buddha. When the monks of Shaolin were on the right track, he resumed his wanderings throughout China. Wherever he went, he challenged monks to practice and live out their Buddha natures, with less focus on the afterlife, and more focus on this moment. This approach came to be known in China as Chan Buddhism, and later in Japan as Zen. Even today, throughout China, there are many temples small and large with sculptures, paintings, and calligraphy reflecting Tamo's travels and teaching.

Tamo not only presented new ideas, but offered the monks new tools

of practice. He likely brought yoga to China, as well as the ancient Theravada Buddhist mindfulness traditions of sitting — standing — and walking meditation. Chinese monks would have integrated these into their native Taoist traditions creating a variety of powerful disciplines such as qigong, tai chi and kung fu. The monks developed extremely efficient and powerful body movement, as well as enhanced balance and coordination from these mind-body exercises, resulting in amazing protective skills. Stillness and deep relaxation releases significant upper body tension. This lowers the center of gravity and allows for unimpeded lower body power for pushing, pulling or striking.

Bodidharma's influence integrated physical exercise and spiritual practice, both internal and external training. Unfortunately, the integration of stillness and movement has become rare today, with most Zen and Buddhist practice being largely sedentary, while most martial arts are strictly physical exercise. Sadly, few martial artists have a serious and committed meditation practice as part of their training routine.

I have never had much luck getting fellow martial artists to do regular meditation training with me. My friend David is a great swordsman. He has excellent focus and technique, but my efforts at recruiting him as a meditation training partner always failed. Who was I to give advice to David ? After all, he is a student of Nobuharu Yagyu, the great master of the Yagyu Shinkage Ryu Sword school in Japan. But, after he returned from his last period of study with Yagyu Sensei he called me: "I should not tell you this. When I was leaving Yagyu Sensei last week, he commented on my training. He said my technique was good, but to get any better I needed to do Zazen."

The human mind has not changed much in the 1400 years since Bodhidharma traveled to China. It takes vision, inspiration, and effort to integrate the discipline of stillness into one' martial arts training. This is why the legend of Tamo Bodhidharma is of such significance, and why Morihei Ueshiba is such an inspiring link to this great lineage. Their examples shine bright, and light the path for us. We can travel that path with them if we choose to.

4. The Treasures of Shamian Park

MANY parks in China are great treasures; with a vast array of mind-body disciplines to see and learn. There are young and old, individuals and groups, focused on their particular Chinese yoga (qiqong) or martial arts forms. The parks are more pure and exciting than any schools or academies could ever be, filled with wonderfully ordinary people doing their daily practice among the trees and meadows. You see individuals creating amazing energy together. Some are moving very slowly, some very fast, some explosively, and some are still — completely motionless for an hour or more. The panorama of different ages, shapes, sizes, postures, and styles of practice is too beautiful to adequately describe.

One of the best parks is in Guangzhou, which used to be called Canton. Every morning, I would get there just after sunrise, as the park began to fill with life. It is called Shamian Park, an oasis of ancient Chinese culture and

Everyday training in Shamian Park

wisdom, in the midst of modern China. Shamian is located on a river next to the classy, old White Swan Hotel. It is a testament to the depth of their focus, that few people are bothered by me hanging around, transfixed as I study their practice. On rare occasions, I am an unwelcome distraction, which folks are not shy about letting me know, but most people kindly just pretend I am not there, too deep into their practice to care. Slight smiles betray some people's pleasure seeing the intent interest on this foreigner's face.

Author's daughter Lien Bi Wang, training hard in Shamian Park

I am mesmerized by an old woman standing in complete stillness, by the same tree for over an hour each morning. She becomes part of the tree, and like the tree her roots seem to go deep into the earth. I would watch for movement, but the only movement was her clothing rippling in the breeze. One day I continued watching for a long time, but I never saw her move — and yet, by the end of the hour her position had changed? She had been moving all the time, but so slowly it was imperceptible. It was invisible movement!

I can never forget the three individuals doing their kung fu forms together, an old man, a middle-aged man, and a young boy. It looked like three generations of the same family, each moving according to their stage of life, with a rhythm and flow of energy just right for who they were.

Two of the best practitioners were a middle-aged couple, who always did their tai chi forms together. I would observe them from a distance at first, but be drawn gradually closer, as if their energy was pulling me to them. When they took a break, they would motion for me to show them my practice. It was

painfully embarrassing, since they were both light years beyond my level. But, a little embarrassment was a small price to pay for their putting up with me each morning, so I would do my best. It was not just a polite gesture on their part, they had a genuine excitement about seeing what a foreigner practiced. With big smiles they would give a thumbs up, or applaud, always enthusiastic and encouraging. Such excitement and curiosity seems to be a common thread among masterful practitioners. That spirit was their great gift to me.

There are still many places in China like Shamian Park. These days, when I get stressed out, I take a mental journey for a few minutes back to the parks of China for some peace and inspiration. We all need places like that to go, sometimes.

V.

BACK IN AMERICA — LIVING BUDO

1. A Brief Visit from O'Sensei

WE all need a vision. Not dreamy fantasy or illusion, but a vision of what is possible. Vision inspires our practice, and no lifelong commitment with passion can be sustained without it. There are transcendent moments in this life, when grace shines on us; when that vision is realized.

I have been asked if I ever met Morihei Ueshiba O'Sensei, and I say no. I respond by saying I studied with his son, Kisshomaru, and his grandson, Moriteru. But, denying I was ever with O'Sensei is not entirely true. The deeper truth is, I did meet him. It was a powerful encounter, both intimate and confusing. He entered a room and showed me what aikido was.

It was 1984, shortly after returning to New York from my journeys in Asia. I was working at a hospital in New York, as a psychiatric social worker on a locked mental ward. Four cops brought in a big, twenty five year old skinhead. He had swastikas tattooed on both arms. He had lots of scars, and was bleeding from his fight with the officers. Screaming at the top of his lungs, he challenged them to remove the cuffs, so he could kill all four of them. They removed the handcuffs, then quickly slipped out the heavy steel door. I remember the loud slamming of the door as it locked behind them.

The patient immediately began pacing like a caged lion. He threatened to rip off the heads of the first nurse and doctor who attempted to approach him. They backed off fast. Giving patients in crisis space and time usually helps de-escalate anxiety and rage. But this guy's rage was off the scale, and just kept escalating.

He started tossing chairs down the hall trying to knock down staff. He was threatening to kill us all if he was not immediately released. The standoff got louder and scarier. A dozen staff — nurses, doctors, attendants, and security guys at one end of the hall, and this human inferno at the other.

Continuing his threats to kill the first one who approached him, he ripped a clock and bulletin board off the wall, smashing both. Any words spoken to him just inflamed him more, as it usually does when someone becomes irrational. He continued pacing his end of the hall, and finding more things to destroy. With all my years of martial arts, all my psychiatric training, and all my degrees — I was as scared shitless as everyone else. Adrenaline poured in — heart pounding, palms sweating, throat dry, body vibrating, mind racing.

Suddenly, he ran into an unlocked observation room by the nursing station, which had a big glass window. Through the window we watched him busting up all the equipment in the room. Then he pushed all the desks and chairs in there up against the door, and piled furniture and medical equipment on top. The big barricade blocking the door actually made us feel safer, separated from him.

Then he found a heavy metal IV pole, using it to smash anything in the room that was glass. Soon there was broken glass all over the floor in that room. For now, he could not get to us, and we could not get to him. We felt a little better. Let him do his damage in there away from us.

Seeing all that broken glass in there, I realized how easy it would be for him to cut his wrists or neck. Homicide and suicide are different sides of the same coin; it can change in an instant. We would not be able to stop him if he began cutting himself. My fear *of* him suddenly turned into fear *for* him. That is when everything changed.

For the next few minutes I was there, but not involved. I just watched. I had neither the courage, nor the skill to do what happened next. I just watched in awe:

O'Sensei slipped through the crowd of staff people almost unnoticed, then he slammed his body against the door. It had such force that the big barricade of desks, file cabinets and furniture came crashing down. As he moved through the door he seemed to know everything the crazed man would do — what he would shout — where he would move — how he would move — and when. Like it was all prearranged.

The patient ran to the exact spot he was supposed to go, then raised his metal pole just the way he was supposed to. O'Sensei silently told him what to do, and he followed each directive perfectly!

He challenged O'Sensei — exactly following the script, screaming "Come on mother fucker, now I'm gonna crack your head open." Why was he being so compliant? His position, his focus, even his grip on the metal pole was exactly the way it was supposed to be, the way O'Sensei needed it to be.

O'Sensei walked directly to him, directly into an inferno of violent rage — without the slightest hesitation or preparation. No martial arts. No blocking, dodging, throwing.

No hurrying, and no uncertainty. He just walked to him, allowing the guy to play his scripted part. It was so simple and natural. Like it was nothing special. The crazed man was drawn in to something, as if by a magnet. The metal pole came at O'Sensei's head precisely when — and how he requested, but he just ignored it. Then two bodies entered some kind of winding — spiraling thing. It was impossible to see just what the thing was. I did see O'Sensei's hand protecting the man's head as they went down.

The fall knocked the wind out of the guy. He was stunned but uninjured. I was sitting on the floor right where it had just occurred, firmly holding the guy's head. Attendants and security ran in, and held the fellow's arms, while a nurse gave him medication. But he was not fighting anymore. It was like he woke up from a very bad dream. Where did all that violent rage go?

I was almost as stunned as the patient. What the hell just happened? I had no idea. Kathleen, the head nurse was angry. She scolded me for recklessly entering the room alone; "You would have been killed, if he had not tripped on something and fallen down! You are a professional, you know better. Don't ever do that again."

I wanted to tell her I only came in at the end. I wanted to tell her about O'Sensei. That there was never anything to worry about. That it was not me. But I just apologized, and agreed I was very lucky. Then I left for a while, taking a long walk around the hospital grounds. Later, I sat in the hospital coffee shop a long time, just staring blankly at my cup. What the hell just happened? What was that? It was not martial arts. But it was not a hallucination. I was confused, elated, and a little frightened by what had just occurred. But mostly confused.

Ten people watching that day saw nothing but the patient swing a metal pole at Tom's head — then "probably" trip on something and fall down. I pressed them for more detail, but I only got puzzled looks. "That is all that happened" they said, and added, "and you were really lucky." When I asked

how I pushed the door open myself and what I did after entering the room —
not one of them could remember.

I left work that day with many questions. No answers. My biggest
question is whether O'Sensei will ever come again? Perhaps he has, but not
with such drama. I figure maybe he needed to give a cynical little bastard like
me, a few wondrous moments with him. Just to show what's possible.

NO SELF DEFENSE

He explodes....I accept such power

Guiding him to earth....assisting him

Assisting his fall...No one throws

Mind silent....like before dawn

Before birds speak....before dawn breeze

The mind of ancient hills... stable and still....

Stillness in motion...silent as before time

The Open Way.... stops nothing

No defenses...defenses are fences...

Self-defense...miss-leads

Perfect timing....but whose timing...

Whose timing...?

There are moments of Great Faith...

Great Trust....when Vision is realized ....

And I was there...somewhere

2. Peace Officer on New York's Mean Streets

𝕴N the mid-1980s, I left my job working on a locked psych ward for an even crazier place — the ghetto streets of New York City. The ad for street parole officers sounded like crazy fun.

The civil service announcement stated:

> *"Applicants must be over twenty-five years of age, college graduates with at least three years counseling experience. Officers assist ex-convicts with living a law abiding life, provide counseling and guidance, perform unannounced residence inspections, curfew checks, and surveillance, apprehend and arrest parole violators. You must deal with individuals who have openly hostile attitudes toward you. You must attend the state law enforcement academy to learn lawful arrest procedures and become proficient in the use of firearms. Starting salary $34,500, excellent medical and death benefits."*

Strange job, I thought — social worker with a gun? What kind of weird individual would be attracted to a job like that? It was a sort of "warrior-priest," like the boys at the Shaolin Temple. I could get to play both sides, soft and hard. The job was a $500 a year increase for me; a lot in those days. And don't forget the death benefit ! (I had never realized there were benefits to being dead).

After a few months of police training, I was thrown onto the streets of South Jamaica, Queens. It was not that far from where I was born, but a totally different world from the 1950s New York City I was born into. My precinct was the 103 Pct., ground zero of New Jack City. There were drug lords and drug gangs fighting for turf, with serious weaponry, and a level of violence comparable to scenes from third world countries. These were the crack cocaine wars of the 1980s, with gangster craziness hard to imagine today.

Someone said I was a replacement for Officer Brian Rooney. He had been murdered the year before by the notorious "Fat Cat" Lorenzo Nichols gang, as payback for Rooney violating Fat Cat's parole. "Don't get crazy like Rooney, and get yourself killed," said my tired looking boss. By crazy, he meant caring too much about the job, and not enough about yourself. I never forgot that advice.

When Nichols was caught with drugs and weapons, Rooney used his parole officer authority to put a no bail remand hold on him. Then, all his drug money could not bail him out. That so infuriated Nichols that he had a

Parole Officer Brian Rooney

contract put out on Rooney. While gathering evidence, Rooney was ambushed in a city park. He lost the firefight reaching for the gun in his ankle holster. That is a bad place to keep your gun. Rooney taught me that. The street is an unforgiving teacher.

It seemed the Nichols's crew was everywhere, including inside the parole department. There were secretaries inside New York State parole offices who were Fat Cat's relatives, and it seemed Nichols could get to anyone. It was war in New York City, and the gangsters were winning.

On a Friday evening, when I was still a rookie, some of the sickest of Nichols' sickos, the Pappy Mason crew, snuck up on the squad car of an unsuspecting rookie cop named Eddie Byrne. While one guy knocked on the window to distract him, the others fired five shots at his head. He was killed near the same corner I had been on the day before, visiting parolees. Byrne was stationed in front of the house of a witness, who had been threatened but he had no concept of the war zone he was in. It was no assignment for a rookie, and he should never have been posted there alone.

Those fallen heroes were my teachers, and I studied every detail of their deaths, determined to make no fatal mistakes. Back then, the good guys were definitely out-gunned. We were not authorized to carry either automatic or semiautomatic weapons. Only little revolvers. So we carried lots of them. Some officers carried a pistol in every pocket. There is always a way to get around the rules, if your life is at stake. I learned early that agencies care first about image and liability; your life is a distant third or fourth priority. Those who follow policy to the letter, may die by that policy.

I was amazed to discover that even in this war zone, parole officers usually worked alone. A kind of crazy tradition that set New York parole officers apart from other law enforcement. The state claimed they could only afford one parole officer per caseload. I could call on my partner if something especially dangerous came up, or if it was "hit day" — twice a month when we grabbed a handful of parole violation arrest warrants, and went hunting for fugitives. But most of the job checking convicts in their homes, work sites, and in the street was done alone.

Working alone means you are responsible for your own safety. So, after reading the details of the Byrne murder, I went directly to the library, reading every book they had on military firearms until I found the nastiest pistol made at the time. It was an ugly, black plastic thing made in Austria by an engineer named Gaston Glock. Made for the Austrian military, it held 18 bullets, and carrying a few extra magazines gave me some serious firepower. If you practiced enough with it, the strange trigger on this thing allowed you to fire eighteen bullets at almost the rate of a machine gun. So Gaston's little plastic monster became my heavy-duty backup artillery.

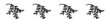

I was well aware, however, that firepower alone would not keep you safe. The mind is your most effective weapon, or your most deadly enemy. The most important attribute of a warrior is not courage, it is decisiveness. The two are related, but not the same. A frightening example of this is when a parolee I was watching like a hawk got into a shootout with two NYPD housing cops. I had just made a "home visit," as the agency insisted we call our unannounced house searches. Feeling this guy Bradley was particularly dangerous, I asked my partner, Richie, to come along. During the check, I spotted an owner's manual for a 9mm pistol on his dresser, so we cuffed him, and did a full search of his place. But, we could not find the gun. We had to release him with a warning. A few weeks later, Bradley opened fire on the two cops with a MAC-10 machine gun.

The shootout happened in the courtyard of his Brooklyn Housing Project, with him spraying gunfire all through the bushes the cops had jumped behind. The officers' revolvers quickly ran out of ammo, so one

pulled his backup gun and kept firing. The other cop fumbled frantically, attempting to reload, dropping bullets all over the ground. Unfortunately, fine motor coordination goes out the window when bullets are whizzing by your head and you are filled with adrenaline.

I later asked the second cop why he did not grab his backup gun like his partner, he said "I started to, but then put it back; I was afraid of getting in trouble, because it is against NYPD policy." He only survived be-

Police Officer Eddie Byrne

cause his partner took a deep breath, focused — tuning out all the chaos, put one bullet in the bad guy's chest with his back up. Otherwise, they both would have died that day following agency policy. That day I decided there would never be a plaque on my tombstone reading: "PO Collings died heroically, following agency policy."

🎋 🎋 🎋 🎋

It keeps coming back to decisiveness. Like when I escorted a female officer on a "routine" investigation of a proposed residence, for a guy who did twenty years for manslaughter. With our shields out, we knocked on the door of the sixth-floor apartment, at the notorious Cypress Hills Housing Project, in East New York. Light knocks, then loud knocks. No answer, so we left a card, and turned to leave. We took one step, then the door flew open with an old lady brandishing a ten-inch kitchen knife, and a crazed look on her face. I leaped back, drawing my gun and screaming "Police, don't move!" To my shock, the other officer had not moved but froze in place, right in front of the knife! I grabbed her collar and yanked her back toward me as I backed away. Feeling my index finger contact the trigger I screamed one last time "drop the knife!!" No response to my commands. I was about to shoot my first little old lady.

We continued backing away from her, ready to open fire if she so much as shifted her weight to take a step. The craziest things go through your mind at times like this; "All the big bad guys I had dealt with, how embarrassing to die at the hands of a little old lady." Someone is about to die, but my mind is concerned with embarrassment? As we exited into the stairwell, she was still in her doorway, and still holding the knife, like a stone statue.

Was this abnormal behavior? Not really, not when you are seventy years old, and stuck in the Cypress Hills Project, with gangsters and crack heads all around you. She had probably been robbed more times than she could count. But, I would make damn sure no other parole officer ever had to visit that apartment again. A few days later, I saw the neatly typed "Community Preparation Investigation" report the other PO wrote, sitting on my bosses desk. I did not bother to read it, I just wrote across the front page in thick black magic marker; "PROPOSED RESIDENCE NOT APPROVED."

Why did a good officer freeze? The unexpected, that is what steals our presence of mind. A routine job, a simple knock on a door, and suddenly someone is about to kill you! A little old lady? That is not supposed to happen! It's not what you plan for, and the last thing you would expect. How to prepare for the unexpected? That is my koan, the warrior's mantra.

🌲 🌲 🌲 🌲

In 1989, I joined the SOU, that is the Special Offender Unit. What a luxury to go from a caseload of sixty convicts, to only twenty! With that number, I could actually keep track of these guys. They were the high-risk, or high-profile felons, a very interesting bunch. I had one drug dealer who was the son (partner?) of a city politician. Another fellow was a paranoid schizophrenic who was back on parole, after serving a few more years for carrying a loaded handgun to every meeting with his parole officer. Someone he pissed off snitched on him, or he might have eventually used it on his PO.

You see, convictions for weapons, robbery or murder, are not considered reasonable justification for a parole officer to search convicts without "probable cause." So I needed a wife, girl-friend, or someone else to tell me someone was carrying or hiding a gun, before I could legally search them or their room. Insane? Absolutely, so I just assumed every guy I dealt with was armed. Sometimes I was right, sometimes was wrong, but that was always my attitude.

Then there was a little man twice convicted of kidnapping and child molestation. He had served fifteen years for each conviction, and was just paroled again. What was his name? Fomer, Flommer, Fromer? I stuck to this guy like white on rice, following him around Manhattan all night as he did his phone company job, emptying coins from pay phones. If he so much as spit on the sidewalk, I would lock him up again. This was personal — no kid would get hurt by this guy on my watch. I watched, and waited, one screw up and I would pounce.

I have to admit his work ethic was impeccable; never late, never skipping one stop. I watched him pick up every coin he ever dropped, never putting one in his own pocket. It was not because he was being observed — I was very good at tailing people without ever getting close enough for them to see me. He was allowed no side trips, just work — shop — home. When I made unannounced checks at his home, I was impressed with how clean he kept his place, and how well he cared for his dog and cat. I wanted to hate this guy, but it was hard, and I was angry at myself for not disliking him more.

One day we caught him with a little pen knife, a tiny thing people carry on their key chains. That little mistake sent him back to prison for about five years. SOU was no joke, our mission was clear; find — any — lawful reason to get the guy off the street, and if you did not find a reason, you were not looking closely enough!

I respected many of the guys trying to start a new life after prison, and went the extra mile to support all their positive efforts. I liked some of these guys, but, you can like a guy and still not hesitate to lock him up. They would often say, "Collings, why are you violating me?" I would respond " I can't violate your parole, only you can violate your parole, I just slap the cuffs on, and do the paperwork. It was all under your control." That is the truth. But, the standard jail house mythology still exists about the bonus a PO gets for each violation. If that were true, I would be a rich man.

I spent a lot of time tailing a union racketeer, we will call him Carmine Molino (don't want the sleaze to sue me) who was responsible for the $600 cost to exhibitors, if they wanted their lamp plugged into a wall socket at the city Convention Center. He was a very pleasant businessman type fellow, with a very nice family. I would tail him all around the city, trying to catch him going to the center, which was off limits to him. He would make dozens of stops all around the city, probably doing worse things than his union racketeering, but I never found out what they were. My job was just nailing him if he ever set foot again in the center, but he never did on my watch.

I cannot forget my first encounter with a convict we will call Werner. Two hundred twenty pounds of pure mean. He was on parole for brutally assaulting several prostitutes, and suspected of murdering several more. The day he was paroled, and walked into my Brooklyn parole office, I could tell in his eyes he had no use for parole, or a parole officer. As he sat there hearing me review the conditions for his parole, which he signed to get paroled, he had a look of complete disgust. There was also a rage inside this guy, which was way beyond the normal criminal. My partner, Leon, glanced over from his desk with a look that said, "You got a real winner here."

When I reminded Werner about his required sex offender counseling, his reaction was predictable. "Fuck that, I'm not doing that bullshit. I don't need

Leon Flanagan

that." I took a long breath, relaxed, and put my social worker hat on. The next five minutes of my quiet obligatory counseling was wasted breath. To some convicts, civility equals weakness. This guy was secure in his macho defiance.

When I glanced in Leon's direction, he was up in a flash. A good partner is a beautiful thing. We had Werner pinned against the wall in three seconds, and cuffed before he knew what hit him. Timing is everything if you are to avoid a knock down, drag out fight. O'Sensei called it "irimi".

Down the hall I went to my supervisor Big John, for a warrant. In thirty minutes Mr. Werner was secured behind bars at Rikers Island. Job well done — I thought. The next week was his preliminary court hearing, to show reasonable cause for my arresting him. I explained to the judge why I locked him up, and thus began one of the most bizarre dialogues I have had:

> **Judge:** Officer, is it true you locked up this man before he failed to go to required sex offender counseling?
>
> **PO Collings:** Yes, sir, he refused to go.
>
> **Judge:** But officer, you never gave him the opportunity not to go?
>
> **PO Collings:** Yes, sir, that's right.
>
> **Judge:** Officer, you have to let him not go, before you can lock him up.
>
> Legally, you must allow him to not go. You failed to let him not go.
>
> **PO Collings:** Your Honor, my job is protecting the commu-

nity. He said he would not go.

He indicated a clear intention to violate the conditions of his parole. He should not be on the street.

Judge: That is not for you to decide, officer. That is for this court to decide.

PO Collings: Yes Sir, that is why we are here.

Judge: I understand that, but you did not give this man a chance. You must let him violate his parole, then you can arrest him for violating. You failed to do that. Warrant is vacated. Mr. Werner, you are released. I suggest you do the right thing.

Werner gloated at his victory, but I would not let him enjoy it for long. At 6 a.m. the next morning I was banging on his door for a curfew check. When he saw me, his eyes were filled with pure hate. There was no discussion, it was only a curfew check and he was there. So I backed away, and left. I never turned my back on that guy.

I may have "violated" his rights by locking him up quickly, but now he knew I was not playing. He began attending the counseling, with a minimal level of compliance to avoid violation. All my contacts with Werner were low key and serious, none of the usual joking around and small talk I do with most convicts. I would be lying if I said I never felt fear around this guy, but I never let him see that. You cannot function if you let anyone intimidate you. In situations of danger fear is healthy, fear is my ally. It kept me on point every moment with this predator. With Werner I kept an ice cold presence, with no openings, and no mistakes.

You try to keep close tabs on the really bad guys, but you cannot watch them 24/7. A few months after he was paroled, I got a call from a detective reporting that he had locked up Werner as the main suspect in four homicides. It seems that on the days his brother loaned him his van to look for work, Werner drove around Long Island City, Queens, picking up hookers and having a good time by beating them to death. They found one body, and he pled out that case getting twenty years to life. In about twenty years another lucky PO will get to deal with this guy.

❦ ❦ ❦ ❦

One really cold February, around 3:00 a.m., I was doing a surveillance in downtown Manhattan, trying to feel my fingers as I opened my second thermos of coffee. There was a movie theater across the street with a huge flashing sign: *Above the Law* with Steven Seagal. That name? Where do I know that name from? Then it came to me. That was the jerk back in Japan, the white suit, the guy who tried to recruit my friend to help write the movie that would make him famous — the letter my friend tossed in the trash can. There he was, making millions of dollars pretending to be a cop, pretending to arrest people, and pretending to be in harm's way. Here I was, freezing my balls off on a real stakeout, risking my life, dealing with real bad guys, and barely making a living! I would never be rich or famous doing the real thing, but Seagal was earning millions pretending — fake guns, fake bad guys, fake danger — making millions!

Then, I began to hear the voice of my teachers; "Cut the crap Collings, and stop your bitching and moaning! You wanted to be a warrior, a real warrior. Well, you got what you wanted." It was true. I liked what I was doing. It got my juices flowing, and pretending could never do that for me. The idea of big money is nice, but I am really a monk at heart. In truth, I am not interested in doing the things required for big money. I made that decision a long time ago.

Looking up again at Seagal's name in lights, the irony of it — the cosmic absurdity of the whole thing really cracked me up. I broke into hysterical laughter, one of those great laughs you just cannot stop. I spilled coffee all over the car seat, my notes, and my jeans. Good thing the coffee was cold. I gave him a quick wave as I drove away from that theatre, good for you Steve.

3. More Mean Streets and Modern Budo

FOR a few years I was assigned to East New York, Brooklyn, which is the seventy fifth precinct. The homicide capitol of New York City in the 1980s and 90s. The "All News" New York radio station, 1010 Wins, would blast all day; "You give us twenty-two minutes, we'll give you the world," so a cynical cop made a bunch of sweat shirts proudly advertising our precinct: "75 Pct. Brooklyn — You Give Us Twenty-Two Minutes, We'll Give You A Homicide." The bosses were not happy about that, but the shirts sold like hotcakes. They could prohibit wearing the shirts on the job, but the 2,300 homicides in the city that year were a little hard to hide.

One morning I was cruising down Sutter Avenue with partners Richie Basso and Jack Ray. Jack was a big guy from upstate, who I heard had been a lumber jack. I had those guys with me because I was on the lookout for a crazy, young gangster named Darrell. Word on the street was, Darrell was an enforcer for an East New York drug gang. I made this neighborhood off limits to him, and told him it would be a violation of his parole if I saw him there. But, I expected him to ignore the warning, since it would interfere with business.

As we drove down Sutter, Darrell drove right past us from the other direction. We turned around and caught up to him within a few blocks. We did a car stop on Georgia Avenue, in the Unity Plaza Housing Project. Stopping him there was a big mistake, since he came from that project and knew everybody there. Arresting him within shouting distance of his family and all his homeboys turned bad fast. We cut Darrell off, jumped out of our car, and I snapped the first cuff on him as he was exiting his car. Then all hell broke loose.

On TV, it's click, click, and off to jail they go. But in the real world, getting the first handcuff on someone is often like pushing the insanity button. Ask any cop who has worked the streets a while, and they will give you several of their "I got one cuff on and then…" horror stories. Screaming at the top of his lungs, "Why you doin' this! Why you doin' this!" The struggle began, with a totally berserk Darrell pinned up against the car, with his free hand clamped on his belt buckle in front of him. With all my adrenaline, police tactics, martial arts, pressure points knowledge, and equipment, I was getting nowhere. Even big Jack could not get that damn second arm behind his back. My radio came out, and just before cracking him on the head with it, I looked behind me to see a dozen homeboys and family members cheering him on, and chanting, "Police brutality!" I called a "10-85 Forthwith," and kept struggling.

It was scary to see even Jack soaked with sweat, and tiring just like me. Richie could not jump into the fray since he was busy covering our backs; keeping the swelling crowd back. They were now chanting "Kill the Five-0, Kill the Five-0." (Brooklynese for police). Our badges meant nothing to these folks; all they cared about was that we were messing with their homeboy! When cops describe their job as "ninety-nine percent boredom" and one percent "wouldn't do it for all the money in the world," they are talking about nasty moments like this.

Left to right. Officers Richie Basso, Jack Ray, author, Leon Flanagan

I believe the only reasons the mob did not charge us, was my decision not to crack Darrell in the head with my radio. Richie's calm demeanor, and the big silver Colt .45 cal. he held probably helped. Mixed in with survival re-lated observations, and sensory overload, were utterly useless thoughts like; It's ten a.m., don't any of these people have jobs?.... How can an obnoxious jerk like Darrell have all these friends?....

The struggle proceeded into its fourth or fifth sweaty minute, with no backup units in sight. The crowd got bigger, and we were getting weaker. Dar-rell was young, fit, and energized by the special brand of nitro fueled adren-aline that comes when your freedom is at stake. We were losing, and in this business, you cannot lose.

Perhaps out of desperation, or just exhaustion, Tohei Sensei's old an-noying refrain started ringing in my ears: " relax...relax completely...weight underside...relax...weight...." I looked at Jack and yelled, "going down!" He knew what I meant and shook his head, reminding me the ground is a very dan-gerous place to be in the street. But with not much fight left in me, I dropped to my knees and took both of them with me. One hundred seventy pounds is a lot of weight to hold up from an awkward position, so the arm I was holding and the body attached to it dropped with me. Jack came crashing down, too.

Fortunately we ended up on top. I guess the fall stunned Darrell, be-cause he momentarily lost his focus, just enough time to finally get that second hand cuffed. Bless you Mr. Tohei! As usual, backup arrived after we needed them. We hustled Darrell into the car and got the hell out of their. Happy to be alive.

Darrell's parole was revoked, and he returned to prison for a year. When he got out he was no longer on parole. Free to run wild without my interference; within a few months he was dead. He had entered a Brooklyn barber shop to do his enforcer job, but got his head blown off. The mean streets of East New York, and the life he chose, finally caught up with him. On the brighter side, our nasty little street battle which ended in his arrest, bought him an extra year of life.

🌿 🌿 🌿 🌿

Jimmy was a New York City ironworker used to walking on narrow beams thirty stories above Manhattan streets, like it was child's play. He was also built like a tank. Unfortunately, he was on parole for a bunch of crack cocaine-induced assaults, and several DWIs. Some of the assaults were on cops, and the DWI's usually included resisting arrest. A pleasant enough fellow when sober, when he drank and smoked crack, he got mean and crazy. After getting a call about him relapsing, and violating a stay-away order from his ex-wife, I headed out to look for him. I was definitely not looking forward to this one.

The precinct sent a lot of units to meet me, since Jimmy's reputation was well known. We searched his ex-wife's house, then cruised the neighborhood but could not find him. When a neighbor said she saw him behind a house, we called for K-9 units. The dogs took us all around the neighborhood, but kept returning to this tall oak tree, but we did not see him. This continued for a while before we realized he was in fact up there — way up there at the very top of the tree. With the dogs going crazy, and cops all around, he yelled down, "You stupid bastards, I am an ironworker, and you will never catch me. In a little while I'll jump and take a bunch of you assholes with me!"

The standoff continued for an hour, with special units, and high ranking bosses being called. The dogs kept making a terrible racket, giving me a big headache. I stood there watching the show, as Jimmy got crazier, the dogs got louder, and everyone got more pissed off. Now when he threatened to jump, several cops replied "go ahead and jump you crazy fucker." Someone else yelled "We ought to shoot you down, asshole."

I thought of friend and teacher Terry Dobson, who would have loved this scene. I wondered what crazy conflict resolution trick Terry might try. I guessed it would be a softer approach. With things going nowhere, and darkness near, I asked the boss on scene to pull back the swat guys and k-9 units, to let me try a dialogue with Jimmy. My timing was good, because the first hour he would have said "no way," but by the second hour he was tired and frustrated. He ordered everyone to pull back. Finally, my ears stopped ringing from all the damn barking. I felt better already.

"Hey, Jimmy, you got cigarettes up there?" I yelled up to him. "Collings, is that you? You come to join the party, with all those assholes down there? I plan to kill a few of them today...." I just let him go on for a while until he got tired of talking. Finally, he said, "I don't have smokes up here, you got any?" I replied "Sure I do, how do I get them to you?" The boss was rolling his eyes at me, but was wise enough to let our conversation continue. Fortunately he knew the first rule of high stakes negotiation; slow things down, and take your time.

It ended with Jimmy agreeing to come down after smoking two cigarettes up there. I would be the only one to hand cuff him when he came down. Like any good ironworker, he had brought a long rope up there with him, which he lowered to pull up the cigarettes. Now a lot of officers were rolling their eyes at me and mumbling things like "why don't you send him flowers, too." I didn't care. My way, nobody gets hurt.

About ten minutes later, he climbed down. Even drunk, this guy had no trouble effortlessly climbing all the way down. When he saw only me there, he turned around and put his hands behind his back, just like he promised he would. Those were not just cigarettes I gave him. They were a small bit of respect and power, in a world where he felt worthless and powerless. Soft power was tested on this battlefield, and proved its effectiveness again.

Thank you, Terry Dobson.

O'Sensei's principle of "takemusu aiki" requires that we tap into all parts of ourself. All that is within us must be accessible — both the soft and the hard. Within every human being resides: the still and stable element of EARTH — the soft and resilient element that is AIR — and the explosive intensity of FIRE. When a wildly impulsive supervisor once sent my partner and me into harms way, I believe it was takemusu aiki that got us through it. Late one night shortly before heading home (it always happens then) my partner Leon and I were ordered to follow two drug dealers down into the Brooklyn subway. What is the plan? Where is our backup? "Just follow them, go!" When the boss of the elite New York State Special Offender Unit orders two rookies to do something stupid, they usually do it.

Down through the winding tunnels of the Flatbush Avenue subway station we went, winding our way underground to the Schermerhorn Street Station. They spotted us tailing them down the long narrow tunnel, just as crazy Al came over the radio blasting "Take 'em, take 'em now!" In the middle of a 200-foot tunnel, no cover, no backup, and now — no element of surprise! Worst possible scenario.

As they turned to confront us, I heard Leon, who is usually stone faced and unemotional, blurt out "oh shit". They had the next move — would they run, or pull weapons and open fire? As we moved toward them, guns in hand I could feel how totally vulnerable we were. I knew that a gun fight in this narrow corridor, with no cover — would end very badly.

In the next moment something poured out of me that I had never seen before — it began with a deafening sound which bounced off the tunnel walls stunning all four of us. An ear piercing sound reverberating off the walls "On the wall now or I Blow Your Fucking Heads Off! Now! God Damn it! Now!"

Searching for a parole violator in his usual East New York, Brooklyn hangout

This lunatic had the demeanor of a crazed maniac — Insane, blood thirsty, and totally irrational. It was not just the voice — it was the body language and the glazed eyes — this crazy-man looked really anxious to shoot someone. This explosion of unrestrained rage was coming out of me!

They responded without hesitation. They spread eagle on the subway wall, staring straight forward, nose to the cold concrete wall. They did not move a muscle. They did not even breath. They may have been tough Brooklyn dope dealers, but at that moment they were just two guys afraid for their lives. They were afraid of a crazy man, crazier than they were. They chose not to fight. We took them into custody, and nobody got hurt.

It took a day or two for me to completely recover from what came out of me. That "pure violence" part of me had never been allowed out before. It was not pretty. An ugly thing to see, and ugly to feel. Yet, it may have saved our lives. It was a part of what O'Sensei referred to as the "Fire Element" within us. Afterwards I felt emotionally exhausted, like a battery that was completely drained in a few seconds.

Leon and I had not been partners long, and for a while there, he thought I had really lost it. But, a potential disaster turned out all right. Tired, and happy to finally be heading home, as he passed me his usually stoic face broke into a smile. "Collings, I like your style."

I think that was the night he decided that this white boy from the suburbs, might not be such a bad partner after all.

One of the most dangerous individuals I ever dealt with was a thin, eighteen-year-old Hispanic girl. By age thirteen, Nicole was a hardened veteran of New York's awful foster "care" system. It is the prime breeding ground for mental illness and criminality. By fifteen, she had already committed several armed robberies in her Bushwick, Brooklyn neighborhood. By eighteen, she was on parole for shooting drug dealers to get their crack cocaine.

She was probably at one time an attractive girl, and actually resembled actress Angelina Jolie. But, her thin emaciated face from years of crack addiction, along with her crew cut and leather jacket, gave her the appearance of a skinny teenage boy. Although we never spoke of it, I know she had been sexually abused in foster homes — you don't get that mean any other way. I saw it in her face; she did not care if she lived or died. She lived only to get high, and if she had to kill to get it, or die trying, no problem.

The detectives I worked with suspected her in several homicides, but there was insufficient evidence since the victims were drug dealers. I had locked her up before when she relapsed. They gave her the usual sentence for nonviolent violations; three months — then right back on parole. She was one more "Revoke and Restore" which meant back to the streets, and back to me. Lucky me.

She had been attending counseling, and seemed to be doing better when the call came. I could hear the panic in her brother's voice. She had relapsed, and was demanding money from him to buy more crack. She just put a .32-caliber pistol to his head, and went into a rage when he had no money to give her. She stormed out, promising to blow off his head if he did not get the money in an hour. I told him to get out of there, then called the precinct to have units meet me there.

When I arrived, backup had not arrived. I called again and the same lame desk Sgt. claimed "units are on route." We waited a while, but no units came — he was definitely jerking me around. I was tempted to make a radio call for "10-85 or 10-13" for emergency assist, but I did not know if Nicole was in there. After some loud cursing, PO Stewart and I climbed the long stairway of the ratty two-floor apartment building. We listened at the door. Only silence. I hoped the door would be locked, and nobody would answer. But it was not locked. It was not even closed all the way.

I silently pushed the door the rest of the way open, and scanned the room. Sitting on a bed in the one room apartment was Nicole, staring at me. She sat upright, with jacket covering her hands. "Let me see your hands! Now!" No response. She just kept staring right through me. I yelled the command again but she just kept her eyes fixed on me, with a vacant, emotionless 10,000-mile stare.

We were trained to assume a weapon is present whenever someone fails to show their hands as directed. Training dictates the use of deadly physical force if your life or the life of another person is in immediate danger. If the split second decision to use deadly force is made, there is no attempt to wound or limit the injuries; you fire — and continue firing. You do not stop until "the threat is neutralized." It is a monumental decision, and you cannot take it back.

I hugged the door frame for cover, her chest targeted in my sights. Ready to open fire the moment she raised her arm. I realized from the position of her hands, she did not have to raise her arm to kill me. She could fire from her lap, no movement required.

With sweat pouring down my face, I yelled again to see her hands — and again she would not comply. I felt my finger contact the trigger and begin a slow steady squeeze. It was the longest moment of my life.

My mind raced. Was this suicide by cop? Or was I about to hear a barrage of bullets coming at me? I expected to hear PO Stewart's gun begin to fire any second, and hoped he would be the first to fire. My finger passed the first stage of the Glock trigger. Now, the slightest pressure would send +P+ 9mm hollow-point bullets exploding into this girl's chest. I remember gripping the door frame hard, bracing myself in case I was hit. "Last time. Show! Your! Hands!"

After a long pause, she removed her hands from under her jacket. She placed them on her lap. There was no gun. Her face remained expressionless. Stewart covered me as I moved in to handcuff and search her. Drenched in sweat, with my heart pounding out of my chest, we walked her down the stairs to our car. On the way to jail, no one said a word. Adrenaline surged through me all day. I did not sleep for two days.

I wish I felt good about not shooting that day, but things are not that simple. By not shooting her that day, I got someone else killed. You see, after doing another few months in jail, Nicole went right back to the street and killed someone. I never checked the details of who she killed. Sometimes at night, I wonder if it was a drug dealer, or some innocent person she robbed, or got in her way? What would their mother or widow think about my sparing her life that day. I try to forget about that. But, it is baggage I will always carry from the job.

4. Sifu Sheng Yen — My Refuge From The Streets

𝕴 am sitting straight and still, at the Chan Meditation Temple where a pretty Chinese nun leads midday practice. There are only a few of us in the second floor meditation hall, but the group energy is strong. Stillness and sweet cedar incense fills each breath. It could easily be Chen Village or the Shaolin Temple in China, but the muffled sounds of the big city outside remind me I am back in New York. It is my lunch hour, and I am in Corona, Queens.

Fully engaged in the ancient battle, the one we all fight — mind clutter. The relentless waves of thoughts, images, fantasies....I engage them with

awareness — most dissolve into my breath. As any veteran of Dharma battles knows — your breath is where these battles are won. It takes only a moment for a ninja thought to creep in, unnoticed. It silently captures the mind, carrying it away on a long chain of association: Did I turn off my police radio? Will a harsh blast of static destroy the silence? What if....Emotions follow thoughts. Fear moves through my shoulders and throat. A presence of mind settles the feelings, and again there is peace.

Sheng Yen would say, "Excellent sit," filled with many thoughts and feelings to notice. "Sit strong, stable, undisturbed by the flow of 10,000 things. They come and go in the vast space of Big Mind." In stillness the "wanting mind" flutters from one thing to another, like a butterfly moving innocently among the flowers. Then dissolves into breath.

Her light touch on the bell ends our sitting. I ride the vibrations far into the next minute without movement. Then, rise very slowly — do not trust your legs yet, for they have fallen asleep. Move slowly so that all those toys under your jacket — handcuffs, baton, flashlight, pepper spray, etc., do not jingle and jangle in this sacred place.

Another lunch break well spent at the Chan Buddhist Temple, my refuge from the wild and crazy streets of New York. The Master has been absent for a while, back in China this month at his big monastery. He created this sanctuary in Queens for wayward warriors like me, who need to clear and quiet their minds. My fondest memories of Sheng Yen are strangely not his wise words and scholarly lectures, but his joyful spirit, especially around the lunch table. "Eat more! Yes, please eat more. Good, very good!"

I never disappointed the man. I was not his brightest student, nor his most dedicated. But, I definitely was his best eater.

"Relentless" by Sheng Yen

Your method of practice is like a long,
slippery rope in a dark, deep ocean.

It is difficult to find it. Once you find it,
grab it.

Start climbing, hand over hand,
unceasingly.

If you rest or stop, you may slip backward.

Worse, you may forget you're even climbing
a rope and slip off entirely or let go.

If you do that, you may not find the rope
again, so be alert and determined.

How far must you climb?

Do not think about that, just climb.
At one point, you will disappear, and when
you do, so will the rope.

Shortly before he passed away Sheng Yen wrote these words:

Busy with nothing, growing old.

Within emptiness, weeping, laughing.

Intrinsically, there is no "I."

Life and death, thus cast aside.

NAME 姓名 Thomas Collings		SEX 性別 M
DHARMA NAME 法名	常乘 Chang cheng	
DATE RECEIVED THE THREE REFUGES 皈依日期	YEAR 2003 年 MONTH 5 月 DAY 18 日	
TRANSMITTING THE THREE REFUGES: MASTER SHENG-YEN 傳授三皈本師：聖 嚴 和 尚		

5. The Master of Canarsie Pier

IT is the mid 1990s, and I am assigned to the sixty-ninth precinct in Canarsie, Brooklyn. Canarsie runs along the southeastern shore of New York City, where the sky and ocean begin their escape from the noise and smog of the city. Air and water begin to clear, as they meet the one hundred mile Long Island where I live.

My business takes place in the maze of big housing project buildings. The projects are filled mostly with black and Hispanic working-class people, the working poor, classy elderly folks, and welfare mothers with beautiful little kids. There are also crackheads, dope dealers, and high school dropouts in search of fragile street dreams — quick cash, gold chains, and $300 sneakers. Some carry shiny little hand guns. The latter often inhabit the lobbies, elevators, and stairwells.

I check on parolees living there, convicted felons who are the sons, brothers, fathers, and husbands of project tenants. My day starts at the precinct detective squad. I get the latest intel: recent shootings, gang turf wars,

some of my really bad boy parolees

hot street corners, and the high-risk buildings. The squad mentions that the "A-Team," from the Cypress Hills Project, two miles north, is moving into the Canarsie Projects. It is no contest; the A-Team is tightly organized, and equipped with nasty AK-47 assault rifles.

My mind re-visits my diving for cover last month. I dove behind a tree at the sound of "crack–crack–crack," in the huge open courtyard of the Cypress Hills Project. I was lucky that day, it was only target practice up on the roof tops. But, it got my heart racing pretty good. As I thank the squad for the info and head out to work, the sergeant reminds me I am nuts for entering the projects alone. As usual, I grin and reply "you're right."

I head for the ninth floor of a building near the Cararsie Pier. I am looking for Duane, a nineteen-year-old knucklehead who has been absent from his drug counseling program. I referred him there after two drug tests I gave him were dirty for weed and heroin. He violated last year, and did three months at Rikers Island. Now, he was screwing up again. Is this all a joke to him?

I am wearing my cop hat for him this morning, he gets no social worker today. PO Collings has become quite good at ignoring his own fear, and putting the fear of God in young gangsters, addicts, and dope dealers. If I get the wrong answers this morning, Duane is getting locked up when he reports to me downtown next week. If he fails to come in, I add him to the "hit list," and track him down with my warrant team.

Having a partner with me would be nice this morning, but Richie has a lot of work of his own today. Got to have eyes in the back of my head; need to cover my own back. Three little knocks on the door….then, three big bangs with my baton. I am used to no answer. Most guys know my knock, and won't answer if they are screwing up. Duane's mother finally calls out "Just a second, I am getting dressed." If this were not a ninth-floor apartment, it would mean she was buying him time to go out the back. On the ninth-floor, I believe her.

She answers the door in her nightgown. I forgot how young Duane's mother was. She is very attractive, and very stoned. She says Duane did not come home last night, but I check his room to verify he is not there. I see a box cutter is next to his bed. When I confiscate it, she insists it is hers. She left it in his room by mistake. "Is he in trouble," she asks. She tells me I am the best PO Duane has had, and asks me to stay for coffee.

Wanting to protect her son — and being stoned — means it is party time with the PO! This is definitely Satan coaxing me to pull up a chair and stay a while. Against her protests, I get out of there fast.

The court would say there is no "proof" the razor is Duane's, so I will just add it to my large box cutter collection. Walking down the long hallways, I am careful to avoid the puddles of piss, which are gifts left by the junkies and crackheads who frequent the building. From high up on the ninth floor I see beautiful Canarsie Pier, far below. I will meet the Master there soon, for my mid-morning training.

As I trot down the stairwell, I am captured by an erotic fantasy — there is a hot stoned lady with a beautiful, inviting smile....a see-through night gown... slim hips.... Suddenly I slip on a wet step! I go flying down half a dozen concrete steps. "Ouch, God damn it!" My yell echoes through the 8th floor stairwell. Someone scurries out of the stairwell, on the floor below. I get up, and wipe myself off, angry at myself for spacing out. Day dreaming and fantasy is a luxury no warrior can afford. But, it was a nice fall. Just a bruised knee and bruised ego. Bravo for ukemi — the wonderful falling skills we learn in martial arts.

Limping out of the stairwell onto the 7th floor, to give myself the luxury of an elevator ride down, which I usually avoid. In the stairwell, I have room to maneuver. You can go up or down if I do not like what you see — or hear — or smell (smoke from a crack pipe). Elevators, however, are closed boxes, dead ends, with no room to maneuver, no cover. Another reason I usually avoid project elevators, they often have the largest puddles of urine.

I told a rookie who once asked me for advice "Do not wear those old sneakers again, or you will be going home from this job in wet, yellow socks. That's my only advice." I laugh at that memory, because right behind it, is the memory of my sempai, Meik, giving me a tip years ago in Japan. "I have been training here a long time, and have one piece of advice for you," (I waited for some profound Asian wisdom) "Feet — take care of your feet." What kind of deep insight was that? I dismissed this as silly. And suffered for it later. Meik was right. Curious how nitty-gritty truth sometimes comes disguised as trivia. Got to take care of those feet.

The elevator stops — it is empty, so I get in and ride down. When it stops a few floors down, I am prepared for the worst. Think one step ahead — do not let things just "happen" to you. Police trainers call it "If/Then Thinking." It derives from the old military adage, the "6Ps": Proper Planning Prevents Piss Poor Performance. It is preparation for the next moment in situations of potential danger. Tactical planning replaces the usual alternatives — paranoia or denial:

> *"IF — You do not like who gets on the elevator —*
> *THEN you will get off.*
> *IF — they block my path —*
> *THEN you will instantly make the first move.*
> *IF — You don't like what you see in the lobby,*
> *when the doors open —*
> *THEN you will not get off there.*

You might think it is a tense and stressful way of thinking, but it actually becomes a rather relaxed mental habit.

So, when the elevator doors open my hands are resting in my jacket pockets. I do not look imposing or threatening. Predators, however, receive a clear message — "This guy may have his hand on a gun. Do not fuck with him." This is why the preferred weapon for those who work the projects is not the big semi-auto handguns. It is the small, 2" barrel hammerless revolver.

A grandmother and a child get on, followed by two young men. They all assume I am either the elevator repair guy, or some kind of cop; few other white people come here. Grandma and child get off on the second floor; I decide its ok to stay on with these guys. Joking about the Yankees' lousy game last night helps me feel them out. They respond easily, with little tension. I study their demeanor, watch their hands, and look for eye contact between them — that would signal trouble. Now they know I am not the elevator guy. The doors open at the lobby, and I let them get off first. Nobody in the projects is allowed behind me.

A few more stops before break time, but I cannot be late for my 11:00 a.m. appointment on the Canarsie Pier. On my walk to the next building, three young men on bikes enter the courtyard in my direction. "Hey, hey, look there — that's my PO! That's my PO over there! Collings, how you doing, man? You come to see me?" "This cannot be, Jerry" I reply, "Because Jerry is at his GED program now, right?" I give him the evil eye. "I am on my way now, PO Collings, you caught me on my way there." Leaving his buddies, he zooms down the street in the direction of the program. As his voice fades I hear…. "I'm going there Collings… I'm doin' good….you don't have to worry about me…"

Break time, and I head onto Canarsie Pier. There are guys fishing off the pier, a guy selling hot dogs and coffee, and others just enjoying the view. We all feel a million miles from the city here. My eyes scan the pier, then I see it — the long, black limousine. I sip a coffee, feel the lovely breeze, and hear seagulls screeching. My teacher is still sitting in the back seat, reading the morning paper, and sipping his coffee. I am transported way back, to somewhere in China.

He exits the limo at his usual time. He is a short, middle-aged Asian man in a dark business suit. He removes his jacket, tossing it in the back seat. By the sea, next to his car, he begins a wonderful routine of movement and breathing. His movements are clean, smooth, and natural. His posture is strong and stable, yet relaxed. There is a stillness to his movements. He is some kind of master.

I study everything: his demeanor, posture, motion, rhythm, breathing. After a few minutes, he turns and smiles in my direction. "Do chi gong" he says, as he slowly gets in the big limo and drives away. I will bet you it is the only English he knows. He could be a rich business executive, or the limo driver. Don't know, don't care. I do his practice routine, and follow his form as best I can. Gradually I make it my own.

Breathing salty air on Canarsie Pier

Shoulders soften and settle

Presence of black limo master lingers

Loud Brooklyn sea gulls play with the sky

Salty breath is long and deep

All is perfect on Canarsie Pier

6. Toughest Day On The Job!

IT was a hectic report day at the downtown Brooklyn Parole Office. Several hundred convicts making their mandatory reports to their PO's. My partner, Leon, had transferred out of Brooklyn, after a dispute with the boss, so I had partnered up with Richie Basso. These two guys were different as night and day - Leon was African American, serious, often moody, and like me pretty much a loner. Richie was white, Italian, easy going, and the most sociable guy on the planet. Two totally different individuals, and yet both were great partners. I could trust them implicitly in all situations. That is a huge part of law enforcement work — trust.

We had a lot of lock ups that day — failed drug tests, weapons found in pockets, and tips received about parolee criminal activities. Why guys show up to see their parole officer carrying weapons, I will never know. Or with illegal drugs in their system when they know they will be tested. Some guys believe they can talk their way out of anything. Some mistake the respectful way I treat them as weakness. That is a mistake.

Richie had a bunch of guys waiting, so when someone asked me to assist with an arrest I went without him. "This guy is ok, he will not be a problem." These are famous last words I had heard before. A red flag should have gone up. I got sloppy; I should have waited for Richie. When you arrest a lot of people, it can become "just another arrest." Falling into a casual attitude like that is very dangerous.

As the officer escorted the guy into the office from the waiting room, I looked up at the biggest black man I had seen in a long time; almost a foot taller, and a foot wider than me. Announcing he was under arrest, I put his arm behind his back — and was immediately swung around the room like a rag doll, slamming into the wall. Somehow, I managed to stay locked on his arm, but I felt like a piece of seaweed stuck to a battleship. He could not shake me, and I got one handcuff on him, but there was no way I was getting that second handcuff on. Another of those "oh shit" situations.

The sound of a body banging into the wall sent a half dozen officers down the hall to assist. Unfortunately the officer who grabbed the other arm had no more success getting the second cuff on than I did. With arms locked at his sides, he was like a big growling stone statue. I clamped on a wrist lock, applying some serious torque — nothing! He just looked down at me with a blank stare — absolutely no reaction. I remember thinking — "oh shit, I'm tangling with fucking Godzilla!"

This is where officers usually pile on. At the first sign of resistance, we overwhelm the perp before they can access a weapon and do any serious damage. Custody situations are not a game, or a sport; it cannot be a fair fight. We have to win. I waited for others to tackle him. And waited— and waited. No one moved? I tried a pressure point — nothing. Finally, I slipped behind him with a move known as irimi, dropping my weight, which drew him backwards off balance temporarily. For the moment he could not hurt anyone, but he was still too strong and resistant to get that damn second handcuff on. These are the times you wish you were anywhere else (I should have stayed in school and gotten that damn PhD!)

Glancing up, I saw the other officers standing there, just watching the action. The biggest officer, Darryl Washington just stood there repeating "take it easy" 'take it easy." I first assumed he was trying to calm the prisoner. But, to my astonishment he was ignoring Godzilla, and focusing on me! The other officers appeared to take their cue from Washington; hanging back, and doing absolutely nothing! The worst moment was seeing the same blank stare in their eyes, that I got from the prisoner when the wrist lock failed. In that moment, it was not seven officers and one resistive convict — it was seven black men and one white guy. That was terrifying. Was I being set up?

Racial issues impact every job, but until then I never felt any racial conflict between me and other officers. Most New York City Parole Officers are black and Hispanic, which makes sense since most convicts are too. Richie and I were the only two white males on our floor, but that never seemed to be an issue before. We all did the same dangerous job, and covered each others' backs. I had apparently been blind to an undercurrent of racial tension, and simmering resentments which were now surfacing in the most horrific way.

Recent shootings and abuse of black men in New York City by white NYPD officers — i.e. Amadou Diallo, Abner Louima, and others, impacted the psyche of many black officers. In retrospect, I should have seen it. Following the infamous O.J. Simpson trial, when he was acquitted — every black person I asked "knew" O.J. was innocent; just another black man being rail-roaded in a racist system. I do not recall one white person who did not "know" he was a guilty as sin, who beat the case due to an incompetent prosecution. That same racial divide was just as dramatic among law enforcement officers.

Was this the white guy Collings being too aggressive with a black prisoner? Was it black officers hesitating to escalate the use of force against a fellow black man? Was it the hot shot, black belt Collings left on his own to humble him? Or just a bunch of cowards terrified to tangle with a very large convict? I will never know. What I do know is that I never felt such a mix of terror — rage — and total isolation. After holding this guy off balance, alone, for what seemed like an eternity, I could not handle the stalemate any longer. I shoved him away from me hard, then pushed through the crowd of vacant black faces. Cursing loudly as I stormed out of the room. I paced the hall like a caged lion.

Ten minutes later Richie came up to me, reporting that the prisoner had finally been "talked down," and stopped resisting. He then unknowingly lit the fuse of a powder keg that was smoldering inside me. I had recently bought a very expensive knife for my wife, who worked in a florist shop. She spent all day cutting the stems of plants, going through a ridiculous number of cheap knives. I bought her an incredibly sharp knife, made out of the finest steel. It cut through almost anything like butter. Now, Richie was holding up the very same knife in front of me. "Good thing he did not have a chance to go for his knife, he was carrying this." At that point, I lost it — if he had gotten to that knife, I might have been killed!

Washington was now back at his desk. I got in his face, yelling at the top of my lungs, "You worthless piece of shit! — You God damn coward! — You incompetent asshole...etc...etc." I felt like slugging him. I felt like slugging every one of them. I took a few steps out of his office, spun around, and put my fist through his wall. Hearing the commotion, our boss came running. He ordered me out of the office, and I left for the day. When I returned the next day, the chief was charging me with:

Attempted Assault On A Peace Officer / Threatening The Safety of a Peace Officer / Excessive Force With A Prisoner / Destruction of Government Property (the wall)

No apologies, no explanations for those officers' failure to assist, and no charges against anyone else. They had apparently circled the wagons, covered their tracks, and chosen a strategy of "the best defense is a good offense." For the moment it worked. The reception I received upon returning ignited all the anger from the previous day. Standing in front my boss, I was fuming, but thank God I kept my mouth shut. Taking some long, slow breaths, not saying a word. I walked out of his office in shock.

Taking a few days off was a very good decision. I ran several miles a day, flushing out all the excess adrenaline from my system, which takes several days after any critical incident. Extra martial arts training and some deep meditation helped release a heavy load of mental toxins — rage, self pity, paranoia. When I felt reasonably balanced, I wrote a carefully worded proposal to the chief. It offered him two options. One, suggested we all "forgive and forget." The other would be "War" — I would obtain legal representation, aggressively fight all charges against me, while filing charges of Dereliction of Duty and Cowardice against six of the officers. When I returned to the job I left it on his desk.

My plan was to work the streets, and come to the office as little as possible for the next few weeks. I did not want to see any of those officers for a while, especially Washington. He might come after me, or I might go after him. It could get ugly. But, on my way out of the office who was coming the other way? You guessed it, Washington. As we met in the hall — a strange and amazing thing happened. To my total amazement, I apologized to him. Part of me could not believe what I was doing — I have no idea where that came from. Washington looked stunned. Then, with a smile on his face he gave me a big friendly bear hug, saying "We're good man, no problem."

I will never know if it was that impulsive gesture of reconciliation, or my intention to aggressively defend myself. Maybe it was both. But, when I finally did venture back into the office the whole incident had been buried. It officially never happened. I did not even have to pay for the wall (I just hung a picture over the hole.) The incident made me a lot more mindful of the complex racial issues on the job, and the role conflict a lot of minority officers struggle with.

It also strengthened my capacity to let go of anger. Resentment festers. It infects us if not released as soon as possible. The peacemaking with Washington reinforced my confidence in the power of initiating reconciliation. It is often a skillful alternative to battle, since battle always has a high cost. Offering "pre-emptive" apologies have defused interpersonal conflicts on several occasions. Even when I believed "they" were wrong. Sometimes difficult to do, it has always produced good results. Warriors fight hard when they must, but you choose peace whenever you can.

7. The Incredible Eric Marshall

ERIC Marshall is one of a kind. A unique martial artist, and one of the best cops in the history of the NYPD. When I last met with him, he was serving as a bodyguard for a high profile individual, who would probably not appreciate him in the spotlight. So, I have used a pseudonym.

He is intense, and passionate about everything he does, and like others touched by genius, can be temperamental as hell. He has moments of excruciating honesty, a destroyer of the dreams — fantasies — mythologies that do harm. It was my great fortune to cross paths with him.

An Olympic-caliber tae kwon do practitioner, Eric left karate to immerse himself in years of soft Yang style tai chi, winning form tournaments for his mesmerizing grace and beauty. Then, drawn to the soft/hard roots of tai chi, he focused on the original Chen style tai chi, with its alternation of soft and blindingly fast, explosive strikes. Fascinated by the relationship between soft and hard, stillness and explosive power, he would disappear from street cop duties on his lunch hours to train at the Shaolin Temple in Queens, studying with Ren Guang Yee, from Chen Village, China. I would watch them train in their deep, low stances, and see how they got such massive thigh and hip muscles.

I have trained with great martial artists, but never felt the power that Eric has harnessed through this sustained study of both soft and hard, internal and external power. Training with him, I sustained my only serious martial arts injury. Such power is hard to describe. He was disqualified from Chinese push hands competitions for "excessive power." I tried to interest him in a pro boxing career (he would have been my only successful investment), but he had by then, lost interest in competition.

How a man of average size could generate such power amazed me. Chen masters call this soft hard generation of energy "steel wrapped in cotton." The Chinese word for this instantaneous explosion of "steel" energy from deep relaxation is "fajing." This power served Eric well on the streets, but like all serious power, it has its dark side as well.

After making detective, he pounced on each case like an angry pit bull. He was relentless in catching New York's bad guys. Time stood still when he was on a case. His wife and kids would sometimes not see him for days at a time. It must have been exhausting working with him, especially for the partner Eric referred to as "the big fat lazy bastard." Perhaps the boss thought the partnership would mellow him out a little, and perhaps his work ethic would rub off on the big guy. Unfortunately, it proved to be a disaster.

One day, it came to a head. Disgusted with being called lazy by this "hyper-active prima donna" of a partner, the big guy exploded in rage. He bolted from his desk in the squad room, ranting that he would "beat the shit" out of Eric. He did not know who his partner was; since smart cops keep their martial skills private.

Just before reaching the target of his rage, the big fellow met the full force of fajing. He was only struck once. But, he went down hard. Most of the bones on one side of his face had to be wired together, during many hours of surgery. He was out on sick leave for a long time. Thus ended one of the worst partnerships in the history of NYPD. Eric was nearly fired. It was only his amazing record and reputation that got him through. That one strike ended any chances of rapid career advancement he had so tirelessly earned. Power like that, has a high cost attached to it.

But, career advancement was never Eric's priority, he just loved doing the job. He was already somewhat of a legend among NYPD detectives, when a job we worked on together cemented his name in NYPD history. It also made him a lot of enemies.

A female prosecutor from the district attorney's office was carjacked at knifepoint. She gave police a good description of the bad guy, and the case got top priority in the city. A suspect was quickly apprehended, and after the victim made a positive ID, he was convicted and sent to prison in record time. Eric only had a minor role in that investigation, so, commenting that "Another dirt bag bites the dust," he quickly moved on to the next case. But, after a while little things about the case started eating at him. He could not let it go. Even at the risk of humiliating the top detectives in the city, the district attorney and police commissioner. He still could not let it go. That is Eric.

Little things kept bothering him about the case, and he began bitching and ruminating about details that seemed trivial. His boss preferred he not piss everyone off by second-guessing the lead detectives and prosecutor, or questioning the validity of the "positive ID" made by the high-profile victim. But guys like Eric live for pissing people off. The detail that bugged him the most was the music on the car radio. When they recovered the highjacked car, the radio was set to a reggae station. "So, the bad guy liked reggae music; now he can listen to it in his cell for the next twenty years," I told him. With a look of irritation Eric said, "I asked around about the guy they convicted, and he likes jazz. He only listens to jazz." So, you are going to open a big can of worms, pissing off and embarrassing a truckload of people a lot higher on the food chain than you, because of some music?

At first, that little detail sounded as crazy to me, as it did to Eric's boss. But as I thought about it, it brought back memories of some cases of my own. I have seen cops, detectives, prosecutors, and judges screw up big time. Like this parolee, Gonzalez, I supervised, who was on parole for vehicular homicide. A much loved elderly couple was killed in a multi-vehicle accident on Flatlands Avenue in Brooklyn. Gonzalez claimed the only evidence against him was a statement he made at the scene that he had a glass of wine with dinner the night before. That has to be a load of BS, I thought. To get the real facts, I ordered the court transcript. When I read it, I was stunned. He was 100% right, there was no evidence of reckless or drunk driving, nor any alcohol in his blood — only that statement.

It was a terrible accident. The district attorney decided someone had to pay, so an ambitious prosecutor made sure someone did. Her opening statement to the jury was, "Drunk driving is an epidemic in our city, and you people on this jury must be the ones to say no more! The defendant admitted to drinking the night before — that decision killed two innocent victims!" The defense attorney objected, and the judge told the jury to "disregard" the prosecutor's inflammatory statement. But, they heard it, and found him guilty. He served three years in prison, then 2 years on parole, with 8 pm curfew checks and mandatory drug treatment, before the conviction was finally overturned. The criminal justice system is full of "junk justice" like this, especially for those who cannot afford high priced law firms.

So, Eric's "crazy" hunch did not seem that crazy to me. His boss gave him a few days to (quietly) investigate other possible suspects. When he found a guy on parole with the same MO, a similar face, a history of armed robbery, who was Jamaican — I jumped on the case with him. My partner Richie and I joined Eric in tracking the guy to a girlfriend's Brooklyn apartment building, then did surveillance. I don't think I mentioned to Richie that getting this guy would embarrass both NYPD brass and the District Attorney.

After another unsuccessful all night surveillance, Richie and I took a breakfast break, while Eric and his partner headed back to their Queens office. You may not believe what happened next — driving through Queens, our suspect pulled right up next to Eric at a red light!

Both stunned and delighted, Eric followed him to a bodega. As the guy bought his Jamaican beer at the counter, he paid no attention to the scuzzy looking white guy in the black leather jacket busy grabbing groceries off the shelves. When he turned to leave he was slammed across the store, and through several display cases. As he hit the ground he pulled a big knife from his coat. It was the same knife he used in the carjacking. But, as the shiny knife came out, Eric's Glock 9mm was already pressing against his temple.

DAILY◼NEWS

COP GOES EXTRA MILE FOR JUSTICE

BY PETE DONOHUE / NEW YORK DAILY NEWS / Wednesday, May 5, 1999, 12:00 AM

After 13 years of putting bad guys behind bars, a Queens detective worked around the clock - even through his wedding anniversary to help free an innocent man. The case against Gregory Ford seemed rock-solid. After all, a Manhattan prosecutor identified Ford as the thug who carjacked and kidnapped her at knifepoint in Queens. But Ford maintained his innocence, and 115th Precinct Detective ▆▆▆ ▆▆▆▆▆ had a hunch he was telling the truth. That hunch paid off late last month when ▆▆▆▆▆ nabbed the real culprit, who confessed to the carjacking and said he used the prosecutor's stolen shield to rob drug dealers to feed his drug habit, authorities said. Charges against Ford were dropped. "Detective ▆▆▆▆ is to be commended for the thoroughness of his investigation," District Attorney Richard Brown said yesterday. ▆▆▆▆▆ deflected such praise, saying he was able to catch the right guy because his boss, Sgt. Jim Carroll, allowed him to continue the probe. The Manhattan prosecutor had just parked her car April 17 in an underground garage in Corona when a man put a knife to her side, forced her back into the vehicle and sped off. He demanded money and kept her captive for a harrowing five minutes before she managed to jump from the car when the thief got stuck in traffic, authorities said. After reviewing photographs from prior arrests, the prosecutor picked out Ford's photo, and later picked Ford in a police lineup, authorities said. ▆▆▆▆▆ however, was troubled by Ford's seemingly heartfelt claims of innocence, and launched an all-out effort to prove it going so far as to postpone anniversary dinner plans with his wife of eight years to work late on the case. Meanwhile, cops recovered the prosecutor's car in the Rockaways on April 20, arresting one man found in the car. Another escaped. The trail led to Preston Ravenell, 32, of the Rockaways. Ravenell who strongly resembles Ford was arrested April 23, authorities said. He had the prosecutor's shield in his pocket, authorities said. He was charged with kidnapping, robbery and possession of stolen property.

According to Eric, as he handcuffed the guy, the fellow actually laughed and told him, "You are really good, man." He was right.

I never asked how much it hurt his career, to humiliate those senior detectives who collared the wrong guy, the victim who "positively" identified the wrong guy, and the prosecutor who convicted the wrong guy. They all deserved humiliation for doing a half-assed job. Eric's motivation was an old fashioned desire to get things right. Embarrassing highly paid incompetents, was just icing on the cake.

The black man who was wrongly convicted, was exonerated due to the single handed efforts of a temperamental, pushy cop who freely uses racial

epithets when angry, and whose language is often politically incorrect. The innocent guy who was released would probably not care about that, only that he was free. Eric's rough style and exterior disguises a fierce integrity and ruthless commitment to justice.

※ ※ ※ ※

A commitment to truth, whatever the cost, creates enemies. One Sunday night I was bitching about having to drive into Manhattan the next morning to testify in a case. President Clinton was coming to town for something, and massive gridlock in the area of the courts was predicted, so I decided to take the train. Usually flashing my shield and ID worked fine, but just in case, Eric lent me his NYPD train pass. Wouldn't you know, I got a nut job of a conductor, who made a huge deal about my shield/ID number not matching the train pass. The railroad ended up confiscating — my shield, ID, pass, gun, handcuffs, and would only release them to my boss. After my boss got done yelling at the railroad official who took my stuff, he started in on me for wasting his day with this nonsense. I got docked 2 weeks pay. Then forgot about that ridiculous incident.

Not long after that I was ordered to report to Internal Affairs at Police Headquarters. I had no idea what it was about, since I have never abused a prisoner, or accepted any bribes. Well… there was that ugly little coffee mug with pink flamingos all over it, that a parolee gave me after I let him travel to Florida, to visit his sick mother….

The room was full of detectives in expensive suits. I felt very important. They immediately began grilling me: "How much did you pay officer Eric Marshall for the purchase of his train pass? What other NYPD equipment is he selling? Is he just selling his equipment, or renting it out? Does he have many civilian customers? Any convicted felons? Has he rented out his firearm? You better give the right answers if you want to keep your job." I took a few deep breaths. But, it did not help.

I really lost it; "Are you a butch of complete idiots! Marshall is the best cop in the city, none of you are half the cop he is! And probably not half as honest! Why don't you go after the dirty narcotics detectives, or the guys with a dozen assaults on prisoners! You bunch of…." There was a lot of yelling back and forth, until I finally calmed down. When I settled down I realized what was going on. This was a hatchet job — enemies Eric had made found a tiny opening, and were going for the jugular. Being combative would not help him, and they would use the slightest inaccuracy or inconsistency in my statements to try and hang him. So, I just stuck to the simple truth.

They were not happy, and wanted a lot more from their "star" witness. They never got it. Eventually they dropped the case against him, but docked him 3 weeks pay — ouch! He never let me forget that one.

The only thing Eric and I enjoy more than martial arts, is arguing about martial arts. He would say aikido was not aggressive enough, and that if you throw someone, you need to follow up with some devastating blows. I would argue for O'Sensei's battlefield awareness mindset, in which slipping attacks, and instantly turning attention to the next attacker was better than wasting time pounding on the first guy. We must have had this argument a dozen times, over his scotch and my Guinness. Knowing full well that hypotheticals are meaningless, we none the less enjoy arguing about it.

One night, when leaving his Queens detective squad, Eric confronts two knuckleheads sitting on the front of his car, drinking their Colt 45 malt liquor. They refuse to get off the car. His final request was met by a bottle swung at his head. In the next moment, the arm swinging the bottle — and the head of the fellow attached to it, slams into the car door with all the force of Eric's powerful hips.

As the bloody head rebounded from its collision with the car, Eric was already focused on the second guy beginning his move towards him. With eyes piercing like spikes, he commanded "Don't even think about it!" That stopped him in his tracks, and abruptly ended any intention the second fellow had of getting involved.

I thanked Eric for sharing this story, and proving my point for me. He, of course, insisted it proved his point. The arguments continued.

Our various arguments about martial arts tactics in real world combat would usually end with Eric insisting martial arts were mostly for health, not for combat. I would point out all his successful street combat, but he would insist he never used a martial arts technique in real combat, only some of the principles, combined with a lot of luck. I continued to argue the point until one night, he stopped me in my tracks with these two stories:

> "I was a rookie cop working on foot patrol up in Harlem. It was a lot of standing around and waiting for something to happen. I had signed up to fight crime, but was mostly just moving annoying drunks off the sidewalk. Finally, I got my big chance to arrest a guy. I don't even remember why I was arresting him, but since I had my black belt, I did not bother even calling for backup.
>
> His passive resistance quickly turned into active resistance. Then I was fighting for my life. Once his adrenaline got pumping, he went nuts — punching, clawing, biting — not exactly what I practiced for. This maniac ended up on top of me, punching me in the face. As he tried to pull the gun out of my holster, I was fading fast.
>
> Suddenly, a bottle shattered against the big guy's head, knocking him out cold. I pushed the guy off of me, then drenched in sweat, and with my heart still pounding, I looked around. No one else was there. The nearest person was the same bum, as usual on the sidewalk across the street. I was too exhausted to even care what happened. I was just happy to be alive.
>
> Later that night, limping out of the precinct on my way home, I saw the bum from the sidewalk coming down the stairs from the detective squad. What was he doing here? He had a police shield around his neck. As he walked passed me, he grinned and said, 'You owe me a bottle of booze, man.' If not for that cop I would probably be dead."

After that story Eric threw this one at me:

> "After making it to the Olympic trials in tae kwon do, I was leaving the Las Vegas convention center, after impressing spectators with my dazzling sparring techniques. As I turned a corner, I was knocked down, and stomped by two muggers. Before I even realized what hit me, my wallet was gone, and so was part of my rib cage. So much for the invincible tae kwon do master. Like I said, martial arts is fun and great exercise. But, if you believe martial arts alone will protect you from real world violence, then you deserve to get your ass kicked. We need to grow up and stop living in a dream world!"

8. Earth, Fire, and Water

𝕿HE hallway is quiet on the second floor of the Coast Motor Inn. Not exactly a five-star hotel, it is one of the spots where the Department of Social Services places the homeless on Long Island. The sister of the parole violator I am looking for, called in a tip that Ted is staying there. He has relapsed big time, hitting high-class bars, and running up big tabs all over town, before slipping out the back. Several places have filed criminal complaints against him, and there are multiple warrants out for his arrest.

Ted is not a really bad guy, and I want to grab him before he gets himself into more serious trouble. He has no violent felonies — yet. A county cop stands to one side of the door of room #42, where the hotel manager said he

was staying. The young cop can't believe we are doing this alone, but there are no other police or parole units available this morning for "routine" jobs, and I want to jump on this tip before the trail gets cold.

Just listening at the door for a while — a good strategy. There are no clumsy, drunken sounds. No yelling, banging, singing, and I hear no voices inside. Hopefully he is sleeping it off. Very slowly I slip the key the manager gave me, into the door lock — take a nice long breath, before turning the key. I want no sound. If Ted set the security bolt from inside, all bets are off. Then there will be no slipping in there silently, to cuff him in his sleep — my favorite method of arrest.

So far, so good; things are proceeding nicely, and I am actually glad there are no more officers around with all those noisy toys dangling from their duty belts, making all those noisy police sounds. The door responds to a slight push and opens smooth as silk, one inch at a time. Be EARTH — be still, silent, patient. Catch him unaware, and there is no struggle.

This carefully crafted silence is suddenly broken by a blast of static from the young cop's radio. Damn! He sees the glare in my eyes, and instantly flips it off. Frozen in place — we listen for a reaction, for the slightest reaction. There is none. We continue the slow, methodical entry. We get our first visual — the end of the bed. There is no motion, no sound. I see the silhouette of legs under the covers, but no movement. Peering around the corner of the room, a few degrees at a time, ready to pull back in a flash if a weapon comes into view. There is only a sleeping body.

Gears shift — move quickly in FIRE mode. Prepared to use maximum force if he resists. Enter! Overwhelm any resistance, before a fight can begin. My partner is cover officer — hand on weapon, scanning the room for additional threats, covering my back. I am contact officer — focused on Ted. He awakens to a bad dream — he is already handcuffed and under arrest. Bad dream, perhaps, but not a nightmare by any means — We are now polite and low key. It was a work of art. No fight, no struggle. It does not get any better than this!

Now we must carefully search for weapons around him — under the pillow, mattress, the end table, drawer. Next will be a slow, methodical pat down — but first ask, I always ask: "Anything sharp on you, anything that can cut me, stick me?" Then I wait. Any hesitation I take for yes —then everything stops. Little cuts, nicks, or sticks can ruin your day. If he has Hepatitis B or

HIV, it can ruin your life. Search his clothes, then help him get dressed. In five minutes we are on our way.

On our way to jail, I am WATER — soft, easy, and accommodating. Give him his smokes, and a snack. Ask how the relapse happened; then listen well. I am kind to prisoners, because calm prisoners are safer to transport, and because there is no reason to kick a man when he's down. We all screw up sometimes. When I am not judgmental, my prisoners do not have to be defensive or combative. The textbooks say that sociopaths do not feel guilt, but I tell you it is not true. Many guys I arrest express shame and remorse when they have a sympathetic listener, they let go of the macho tough guy nonsense. Many of these guys plead guilty, waiving their right to a probable cause hearing, which they may have beaten on technicalities. They feel guilty that they let me down, so they plead guilty.

Law enforcement is not just about the law, relationships matter. A clean relationship with the individuals I have to deal with, makes my life easier and safer. Nothing touchy-feely, just clean — I am tough but fair, and give second chances whenever reasonable. I try to show empathy in situations where they are usually treated like dirt. The greatest danger for cops is not the knives or bullets, it is the risk of losing your humanity.

9. Navy Seals and Mamba Snakes

HANK was a former Navy SEAL, on parole for armed robbery. He was very good at everything he did. He never did anything halfway. After his service in the Navy, an addiction to crack cocaine came fast and hard. To feed it, he had committed five armed robberies on the same day — like I said, he never did anything halfway.

He was paroled after serving five years of a 5–15 year sentence. My job was to closely supervise his parole — watch him, check him for weapons and drugs, and get him off the street fast at the first sign of relapse. It was none of my business what happened during his tenure as a Navy SEAL, or what caused him to go off the deep end after his discharge. He said he did things he was trying to forget. So, I left that alone.

Hank did his substance abuse recovery program like he did everything — all the way, no holding back. None of the usual whining, bitching, and moaning about being mandated to counseling or having to report to his PO. Dealing with a guy who actually took responsibility for his actions — and held himself accountable was highly unusual, and very refreshing.

His attendance at counseling was 100 percent, and all the drug tests I did on him were clean. He worked hard as a construction contractor, took care of his family, and avoided trouble. During all my inspections of his home and job sites, everything was good. Since I am an animal guy, I enjoyed seeing all his pets, which included dogs, exotic birds, and a big, long mamba snake.

I got the feeling whatever this guy did as a SEAL, he did it in the jungle, because that is pretty much what the inside of his house was. I guess he got the right PO, because I generally feel more comfortable around animals than people. A lot of bosses and POs prohibit parolees from having dogs, or other potentially dangerous animals, but it never bothered me. On the job, it is humans I do not trust. I have told more than one parolee with pit bulls: "I really love animals, so it is important that you know, if you ever had your dog attack me, I would not shoot the dog — I would shoot you." I think they believed me, because I never had a problem with a dog, when arresting their owner.

I had been out of work several months with an injury, when my partner, Richie, called, saying he had to arrest Hank on a parole violation. Few things surprise me in this business, but I was surprised to hear Hank was in trouble. Richie said the chief was glad I was out since I probably would have refused to make the arrest. Now Richie had my attention:

"A neighbor complained about Hank's dogs barking, and threatened to shoot them. (Not a smart thing to say to a Navy SEAL.) Hank was cool, and said he would try to keep them quiet. The next week he found his dog dead, and the vet told him his dog had been poisoned. When the neighbor refused to speak with him about it, Hank ripped the door off the hinges. He must have held the guy in some near-lethal, SEAL choke hold. Putting the fear of God in him, and warning if anything happened to his other animals he was a dead man. The next day, the guy was at the precinct, whining about fearing for his life, and demanding 'the crazy commando guy' be arrested."

I told Richie the boss was right, I would have congratulated Hank on his restraint — he only threatened to kill the guy! Then, I would have gone over and smacked the neighbor myself. But, they handed Richie an arrest warrant, and sent him out to meet NYPD, around the corner from Hank's Canarsie home. When Richie got there, emergency services trucks (NYPD-SWAT) were all over the place, with a command center set up down the block. Guys were running all around with shotguns, automatic weapons, and sniper rifles. Apparently the precinct commander heard "Navy SEAL" and freaked out. They were all hyped up to crash through the front door with a high-risk tactical entry team, using their flash-bang-smoke grenades, dogs, tear gas, helicopters and all those other exciting toys.

Agencies love to set up drama like this, it makes for great press releases and lots of overtime. It also justifies the big money spent on all the high priced exotic hardware. I recall Richie and I stopping at the 81 precinct in Bed-Sty, Brooklyn, one day to get some back up. We wanted two cops to cover the back while we picked up a parole jumper. When the desk sergeant looked at our paperwork and saw guy's rap sheet, he refused to give us two cops. He made a half dozen phone calls, insisting the guy was so dangerous it must be a "special operation". He ordered us to stand down, until the special ESU tactical unit secured the location. This was our typical Brooklyn parole violator, nothing out of the ordinary; a few felony drug arrests, a robbery, and a weapons possession conviction; our usual customer. To the Sgt. this was Al Capone and John Dillinger combined.

They had us wait three hours at the precinct, until the tactical teams were set up at the location. When we got there, we watched the second truck full of SWAT guys finish putting on all their tactical gear, and loading their machine guns. While we waited, I showed a lady sitting on her stoop across the street, our fugitive's photo. "Oh yes, I saw that young man a few minutes ago. He walked out of his apartment past all of those big policemen getting dressed in the black suits. He went down toward Atlantic Avenue." After that fiasco, it took us another six months to track the guy down. Needless to say, we never asked for back up again at that precinct.

As the big special operation craziness was getting organized down the block from Hank's residence, Richie watched the battle preparations unfolding, and wisely got authorization to place a phone call to Hank. With his usual demeanor that could calm an earthquake, he arranged for Hank to surrender peacefully. The conversation went something like this:

> "Hank, this is Collings's partner, Basso. I am down the street from your house with all these SWAT guys, who are really nervous about the whole Navy SEAL thing. Do me a favor; come outside and let me cuff you. If all these ESU-SWAT guys charge into your place, and any of those animals get hurt, Collings will be bitching at me for years." Hank replies; "OK, Basso, but if any of those swat assholes shoot at me some of them are going to get hurt."

With special tactical teams poised for action, Hank walked out his front door letting Richie quietly handcuff him. Then they drove away. All the excitement and drama of another "special operation" ruined, by Richie's calm demeanor and common sense. If he were secretary of the United Nations, I believe world peace would be achieved in about three days.

Hank only served a short time in jail. Rather than testifying against him, I think the terrified neighbor fled to another state. Most important, the mamba snake survived without a scratch.

Morihiro Saito Sensei once said that the best thing about the warrior path was the special people you are privileged to meet, and lifelong friendships you make. He was speaking about people like Ron. Ron endured intense headaches, which no medication could effectively relieve. He had metal plates holding his skull together. A disabled veteran, who often missed training due to his medical issues. When he apologized I would remind him it was my privilege to teach him, and that he need not apologize for any absences. One night, he stayed late after class and shared this story:

"Sensei, I want to explain why I have to miss training sometimes. It is a story about something that never happened. Back when Ronald Reagan was president the US government was afraid of the Sandinistas running Nicaragua because they were friendly with Cuba. A Navy SEAL team was sent there to lay mines in their harbor. That probably was a violation of international law, but warriors follow orders. One of those mines exploded, killing or injuring much of the team. Thirty feet down, one guy's skull was fractured in a bunch of places but he fought to stay conscious. He managed to tow some of the unconscious guys back to the boat. He tried to save their lives. That guy survived, but most of the others did not.

I am sort of the bionic man. I have lots of screws and wires holding my head together. Sometimes it's bad, and I cannot concentrate enough to safely train. But, I can't complain — they told me my injuries were not survivable, and that I should not even be alive. So for me, the headaches are a gift. My being alive is a gift. When I make it to the dojo, I forget all the pain and the nightmares. A dojo is a beautiful place to be. I really love it."

I bowed low. I gave Ron the biggest — longest — strongest hug I can remember. Having him at the dojo was the real gift.

Somewhere in New York, there is a part-time security guard at a federal park site, with medals of valor that only his son will ever get to see. He is the ex-Navy SEAL "bionic man." Few people know that he is a national hero. But, I know. And that seems good enough for him.

10. My Federal Crimes

THE two US Marshals attempting to serve me with a federal subpoena, missed me by only half an hour. So, they served the subpoena on my boss. When I came in, he handed me the papers charging "Officer Collings, Officer Basso, and others" with federal civil rights violations, illegal entry, illegal searches, and a variety of other "official misconduct" (I guess you don't get indicted for "unofficial" misconduct).

I never heard of the first two plaintiffs, Martha and Mary Williams, but I recalled the third name from several years ago, Warren Perkins. I vaguely remembered Warren from a hit day back around 1995. We were moving through Brooklyn housing projects with a handful of arrest warrants, searching for parole jumpers. I remember catching Warren, and arresting him without incident.

Speaking with the other officers we managed to recall some of the facts. He lived with an aunt and a bunch of her relatives in a big tenement apartment. We found him as I usually did, sleeping until noon. That told me he was probably running the streets at night and heading for a fall. I had never had any trouble with anyone at the residence. In fact, his aunt appreciated me checking on him often, rousting him when he was late for his drug program. He had a long history of heroin addiction. However, he had tested positive on the last drug test, and stopped attending his program. After that, as expected, he stopped making his weekly reports to me, and ducked my phone calls.

After the second FTR — "Failure To Report," to scheduled visits to your parole officer, the warrant book comes out of my boss's desk drawer, and in sixty seconds, "presto," I have an official New York State arrest warrant. I remember doing my usual soft knock on the door, showing the warrant to a young girl who opened the door. When she hesitated, after being asked if Warren was there, I knew he was there. Gently nudging her aside I quickly headed down the long hallway, with three other officers following close behind. A quick peek in the doorway and, eureka! Warren was sleeping like a baby next to his girlfriend.

It was a silky smooth arrest. Before he or his girlfriend woke up, he was already handcuffed, and I was already looking for his clothes. No muss, no fuss, and no fighting. We were out of there before any of the other folks even woke up.

At his parole violation hearing, I prepared for the usual one-on-one combat with his defense attorney in front of an administrative law judge at Rikers Island. But against the advice of his lawyer, he plead guilty and admitted he relapsed. He apologized and thanked me for picking him up before he OD'd or got a new felony drug arrest. I heard he did about a year of jail time. End of story, I thought.

To me this was all ancient history. But, as I read the federal complaint, I saw that "profoundly harmed" plaintiffs were demanding two million dollars in compensatory and punitive damages. I was hoping to someday leave this job with a pension, but that might not happen now. The papers looked ominous. The state attorney general's office, which defends state officers in federal cases, had insisted it was just another frivolous lawsuit, and it got buried in a file cabinet. "This will never come to trial. Don't worry about it. Just forget about it, we'll take care of it."

Six years later, a call came from the same office, telling me to get ready for trial. I was called to the attorney general's office, where a young guy, who must have just come out of law school, told me to clear my calendar for the next month for the trial. After reviewing what we did and did not do, this assistant state attorney, (who looked like a kid,) assured me they had no case. It would be a five-minute proceeding in some back room office.

On trial day, at my attorney's request, I wore one of those little, silk ropes around my neck. The kind I see businessmen and government bureaucrats wear. Was this colorful noose a sign of things to come? Aren't these worn by criminals headed for the gallows?

The address on the court papers was: United States Federal Court, Eastern District. I was the first name on the court papers, so I had to be there first. At the federal court, I saw that it was being held in the court room of Chief Judge Sterling Johnson. This would be no back room informal proceeding — Sterling Johnson was famous in New York, not only for being New York's special narcotics prosecutor for many years, but also for being the Executive Director of the NYPD Civilian Complaint Review Board in the 1970s, which investigated police misconduct. They gave our case to the most high-powered guy in the federal court. This was not good.

In the courtroom, I sat all morning, watching juries being selected for the cases beginning that day. They did not exactly look like "a jury of my peers." That would be a forty-eight year old, white law enforcement officer. Most of the jurors were minority people who had no connections or high-powered positions to get them out of jury duty, and they did not look happy about being there. As I sat there, my defense attorney, "the kid," pointed out my adversary. A very heavy, middle-aged, black lady, I had never seen before. Warren never showed up.

Flashing through my mind were the flood of recent police brutality stories filling the news in New York. There was the Haitian immigrant, Abner Louima, tortured in a Brooklyn police station bathroom by a white cop. Then there was Amadou Diallo, the unarmed Guinean immigrant, mistakenly shot over thirty times by white cops. Now I understood why the lawsuit named only "Officer Collings, Basso, and others." The other officers were Black and Hispanic. They wanted only white faces to point fingers at. It was artfully orchestrated, perfectly timed to appeal to the backlash of public opinion against white cops, the ones brutalizing minority citizens. Not good.

Sterling Johnson looked at the jury, looked at me, then looked over at the "injured party," who closely fit the jury profile. He knew exactly what was happening, so he motioned my defense guy up to the bench and quietly said, "I am giving you ten minutes to work out a settlement, because if this goes to trial, it's not likely to go well for your client." That told me I was not just being paranoid, that even the judge knew this looked bad.

The state's attorney returned in fifteen minutes to happily tell me he had negotiated the $2 million claim down to $10,000. I just needed to sign off on the deal. I would be indemnified by the state, not have to pay a cent, and I could go back to work. Just sign it, and I can walk away.

It would have been so easy to sign that paper. But somewhere in there was an admission of wrongdoing. There was no wrongdoing, so, I would not sign. My lawyer and the judge looked irritated. The judge was irritated not because he was too lazy to hold the trial, but because he expected me to get creamed, regardless of the facts. I learned later that he had been an NYPD cop for eleven years. But there was nothing he could do for me now.

The plaintiff's lawyer opened with a barrage of charges, ranging from illegal entry, to terrorizing occupants at gunpoint, and illegally searching through drawers without a search warrant. His client was looking increasingly more frail and worthy of sympathy, while I was being portrayed as a Nazi storm trooper from the privileged class. My lawyer's rebuttal sounded lethargic and hollow. Things could not have been going any worse if Luoima and Diallo were sitting right there in the courtroom. In a sense, they were.

When I was being questioned by the aggressive ambulance chaser, I used Zen breathing to stabilize myself. I had been through hundreds of hearings, and generally do well in trench warfare with seasoned attorneys. Combat usually begins with a series of polite, innocuous questions designed to guide you off balance. Then they get aggressive, and do their best to provoke you, hoping to show your aggressive nature. I know the game well. I am a veteran of this form of combat, and restrained my emotions during the barrage of provocative and argumentative attacks.

For me, verbal courtroom battles are all about breathing. In this arena, Asian disciplines are my secret weapon. I made sure the one element of the trial under my control, my demeanor, would go my way. My big problem was remembering few details or any times related to the arrest. It was more than six years ago, and I did not keep notes from that far back. Answering so many questions with "I cannot recall" sounded bad.

In my effort to stay disciplined and calm, I probably appeared too cool and aloof compared to the plaintiff, who cried on the stand, reliving the "horror" of that terrible day when her apartment was "raided." Horror? She slept through the whole thing! But, she certainly was a more sympathetic figure than I was, recounting how she was "terrorized," repeatedly threatened, and her whole apartment ransacked for more than an hour, as we performed an illegal search for drugs. She was a great dramatic actor, she could have gotten an honest job on Broadway.

The final witness at the trial was my partner, Richie. I knew he would be cool and calm, no matter what the lawyer threw at him, but that would probably not be enough. They had painted a picture of cruel and sustained harassment, brutality, and abuse of authority. It was her word against ours.

She had the dirty details to every little question, answering tearfully but confidently. Although she was lying, her answers sounded a lot better than all my "cannot recall, sir" responses.

During Richie's testimony, a little thing became a very big thing. It was Richie's obsession with electronic toys and gizmos of all kinds. Decades before the advent of the iPhone or Blackberry, he was always pulling some silly little electronic memo pad or computer appointment book thing out of his pocket. I would be making fun of the things telling him they were not even thick enough to stop a bullet, and that a deck of cards would be better protection. He, in turn, would make fun of my toys — my telescoping mirror for peeking around corners, mini binoculars, the pouch sewn into my Kevlar vest for a backup gun, extra ammo, and snacks — lots of snacks. Oh, yes, there was also the telephone book from the trunk of my car, which I occasionally duct taped to my chest on the days I forgot my vest. For some reason, Richie made fun of that too.

Richie got grilled by the lawyer but remained cool, like he always did, but had to admit we did not ask permission to enter the apartment when the door was opened by the young girl, and yes, we opened several dresser drawers without a search warrant. The guy turned to the jury and told them Richie had confirmed that we broke into the place, raided it, and conducted a prolonged and illegal search.

It was the lawyer's last question that changed everything. "Officer Basso, you claim you were only in this apartment for a few minutes, but you have no paperwork to verify that, do you officer. "No, sir." The attorney then happily said "Your Honor, this witness is excused."But, instead of getting up, Richie turned to the judge. "Your honor, I do not have any paperwork from that day, but I do have detailed notes in this electronic memo pad." He pulled out that silly little silver thing I was always making fun of. I almost fell off my chair. Before the lawyer could object, Judge Johnson already had it in his hand, and was studying it. "You use this thing to keep field notes?" "Yes, sir;" Richie replied,"it has a lot of field notes in it." The judge managed to hold back a laugh, but could not stop the smile. "I'll allow it into evidence." He ignored the stunned lawyer's objections and told Richie to turn the thing on, read it, and let the court clerk verify the date and text. After going to the date, then reading through the notes from earlier that morning, he continued:

8:32 a.m.: Stopped at 73rd Pct. Brownvsille, notify desk
Sgt. of next hit address.

8:48 a.m.: Arrive 10 Amboy Street, Bklyn., residence of
Warren Perkins.

8:53 a.m.: Gained access to parolee's 5th floor apartment.

8:59 a.m.: Exited apartment with prisoner in custody

9:10 a.m.: Lodged prisoner Perkins in 73rd Pct. holding cells.

9:25 a.m.: Left 73rd Pct. for next hit at Unity Plaza
Housing Project.

From that point on, the trial focused on the time frame that we entered and left the residence, which Richie's notes had verified was very brief. We were in and out fast, so there was no time for a long illegal search of the place as they alleged. Our defense guy explained about our standard practice of opening drawers just to get clothes for our prisoners, rather than dragging them outside in their underwear.

The jury came back soon, with a not guilty verdict. The plaintiff's lawyer later appealed the illegal entry issue to the New York State Court of Appeals. About a year later, the court clarified New York law, ruling that a law enforcement officer with a lawful arrest warrant may enter a residence regardless of who opens the door, and regardless of whether the adult lease holder granted permission to enter, if the officer has a reason to believe the subject is there. They also said in very fancy, legal language that it was not illegal to open a dresser drawer without a search warrant, to get your prisoner a pair of pants.

Thereafter, I never again referred to Richie's electronic toy as "the silly, little gizmo." I gave it respect, calling it a fine electronic note taking device or the "two million-dollar gismo."

11. Harold T. — "That's Just How It Bends"

HAROLD was recently out of recruit class, so the boss told me to take him on his first hits. "Collings, do not let him get hurt or screw up," ordered the chief. "Yes, sir, no problem," I said. Hits are parole officer talk for grabbing a bunch of fugitive arrest warrants, getting a few POs together, then meeting at 5am to track down some parole violators.

Convicts often jump parole when they are afraid we will do a drug test, or because they assume we know they are out there committing new crimes. Most of the time, we don't know, but they assume we do. So, they stop showing up to their scheduled reports to us, and often move to another town or another state. When they cheat on their girlfriend, rip off a drug customer, or piss off their mama — I often get tipped off where they are hiding out.

The first hit of the day was at a Brownsville Housing Project, the rough Brooklyn neighborhood that produced brawlers like Mike Tyson. As we get to a fourth floor apartment, I could see Harold was nervous, partly because of the danger, but also because this was his chance to show the chief he could handle the job. He was impressed with how I sweet-talked my way right into the apartment, and how quickly we located our fugitive and cuffed him up — before he could hide, start fighting, or grab a weapon. It was all going smoothly as I grabbed some shoes for the guy, when the family suddenly went ballistic.

Now brothers, cousins, aunts, uncles, nephews, were coming at us from all sides. To them, we were not duly sworn officers of the law executing a legal arrest warrant, we were intruders who invaded their home, and were messing with their boy! When things are going smoothly, four officers seems like overkill. But, when the shit hits the fan, you wished you had ten more with you! I pushed Harold and our handcuffed prisoner down the hallway, and out the front door of the apartment. Then I ran back in to help the other guys fight their way out of there. When we got out, I looked around but there was no Harold, and no prisoner?

I ran down the hall to a window, just in time to see the backside of our prisoner running across the courtyard four floors below — no shirt, no shoes, and handcuffed behind his back. Zooming at full speed, with a fifty-yard lead on Harold! How these guys can run like the world's fastest human, while hand-cuffed behind their backs and shoeless is beyond me.

When we got down to the street, Harold was a block away, and our ex-prisoner was just a speck in the distance, two blocks away. "Keep after him Harold!" I yelled, as I ran and got NYPD Central Dispatch on my radio:

"Parole 0714 requesting 10-85, assistance forthwith!."
"What is your condition 0714?"

"In pursuit of male black wearing blue jeans,
    and running east on Linden Blvd.,

73 Precinct" …(I now prepared for the humiliation)…
    "no shirt — no shoes and cuffed behind his back."
    …She tried to muffle it, but I heard somebody
    cracking up in the background.

"0714, you had one under and lost him?" (Great lady, rub
    it in — she was loving it)

"Affirmative Central."…….. "OK, units on route 0714."

As I ran, I yelled to Harold "I'm going to kill you, Harold," but un-fortunately he was too far away to hear me. Closing the distance, I fantasized about doing terrible things to Harold.

Eventually, all the broken glass and pot holes on Brownsville streets took their toll on our fugitive's feet, slowing him down a bit. As we tackled him in a big garbage-filled vacant lot, three squad cars roared up, sirens and lights blazing. I hoped they assumed we had just made the arrest, but the big grins on their faces told me they heard the radio call. "Any more that got away, guys?" This crack was followed by several more jokes, before a merciful sergeant yelled over the laughter; "Forget about it, we all got two or three stories like this." The sergeant's comment didn't help, I glared at Harold with great violence in my eyes. "You are doing all the paperwork on this! I will never let you forget this one, Harold!"

I never did let him forget it, cruel bastard that I am. Not 5 years later when he became my supervisor, and not 10 years later when he became a bureau chief. It became a kind of joke with us, I would bring it up whenever he reminded me of paperwork that was overdue. Unfortunately, the distraction rarely worked, and he always stayed on point. But, it is great fun to have something like that over a boss.

Harold was born and raised in a tough minority neighborhood of New York City, so it is not surprising that bad guys have attempted to rob him. Just like certain styles of dress and music, neighborhoods also have their own manner of speech. In Harold's neighborhood the style of speaking was very slow, like old style jazz talk. Harold does not take drugs, but you would swear he was stoned if you were not used to his distinctive sloooowwww...Brooklyn-ese. But the day a bad guy pulled a gun on him, his slow talking proved very valuable.

There is a martial arts wrist-twisting technique called kotegaeshi. I have been studying it, and trying to perfect it for about four decades. It takes most students a few years before they can execute the technique well. So, Harold is confronted at gunpoint, and the guy is demanding money, screaming "What you got? Give it up! Now! Now!" But, Harold responds sooo slooowwl-lyyyy — wellll....I....doonnn't....reeeaally....haavve....thaaat.... The guy is in a big hurry to get something and run! He cannot handle how slow this thing is going! Out of desperation he makes a major error — he moves closer and sticks the gun right in Harold's face. Harold then just reaches up and twists it out of the guy's hand. Stunned, in shock, and humiliated; the bad guy runs off, possibly considering another line of work.

"Show me what move you did, Harold," I ask.

"That is kotegaeshi, where did you learn that?"

"Which art do you study?"

"That is no art. I don't know any martial artsy stuff,"
  he responds.

"So, where did you learn kotegaeshi?"

"Coat-a-guy what? I just turned his wrist like this.
  That's just how it bends."

A perfectly executed kotegaeshi technique, with no martial arts classes. Harold was obviously ignorant of the fact that it takes years to learn this technique. But, he did not perform a "technique." He just turned the guy's wrist "how it bends." You can't make this stuff up.

VI.

IN THE SHADOW OF THE TWIN TOWERS

1. The Mystery of Life and Death

IT is 8/11 of 2001, and I am on the 107th floor of the World Trade Center, North Tower. I walk into Windows On The World, one of New York's top restaurants. Breakfast at a table by the window, with the awesome view of the New York skyline would be great. But, a $25 breakfast is a little beyond my budget. I would also like to stop and say hi to my neighbor Andy Stern, a bond

trader on the 104th floor. But, I am on the job so better get working, can always visit Andy next month.

This is one of the employment investigations, on my monthly excursion into Manhattan. It is my fun day. No staring down crackheads in the stairwells of scummy Brooklyn housing projects today. Today I flirt with classy Manhattan receptionists, eat at a fancy cafe, and enjoy the spotless air-freshened bathrooms in shiny glass office buildings. I could get used to this!

I am fantasizing about working here. An FBI guy I worked with mentioned that his boss took over as head of security here. I should go talk to that guy — I remember the name, John O'Neill. My friend said he was the smartest guy in the FBI, and knew more about international terrorists than anyone in the Bureau. In fact, he was the expert on some top dog terrorist "Osama" something. The bureaucrats were too caught in politics to listen to him. When O'Neill bitched about it loudly, they forced him out of the Bureau. He sounds like a real trouble maker — my kind of guy! Yes, when I am here next month I will look that guy up.

A jacket and tie is required to get into Windows On The World, but flashing a shiny gold shield, and using my stern "government business" look gets me waived right through. Even wearing my multi-colored, short sleeve aloha Hawaiian shirt. It is so ugly but so nice and cool. No roasting in that disgustingly hot, sweaty kevlar vest today. I look and feel just like a tourist.

The mâitre d' knows me, since I have been here before, checking on Torres. Is he still showing up for work? Still behaving himself? I check the dining room, the bar, the kitchen — but no Torres? I track down the restaurant manager. He tells me the guy was just fired. Oh no — what damage did this guy do? Will I be getting tortured by the chief again for "letting" the guy screw up on my watch? Torres is on parole for manslaughter, so I can hear the boss now: "Why the hell did you allow that guy to work at the World Trade Center! I told you before, you are too damn anxious to get them working!"

The manager says Torres was his best worker. He did the work of two guys. "I was going to ask you for three more just like him, but Human Resources finally got around to his background check. They saw the felony conviction. I told them he was a good worker, but they said its policy — no felons." The guy had worked there eight months — that really sucks. He did his time — fifteen years. He was doing good, and he deserved to keep that job. Life is not easy for guys with a record trying to do the right thing.

On September first I do a late night curfew check. I find Torres at home like always. He is beyond anger, in the depths of despair. "It's no fucking use Collings, I did everything just like you said, not like the other times on parole when I was screwing around. Now I am back to zero. I'm a fucking zero! Lock me up, because I can't do this parole shit anymore." I sit down with him a while. No bullshit pep talk. Just sharing his shit. Sometimes life sucks.

After a few minutes I get up to leave, "We'll figure out something. Just don't do anything stupid. Do not let yourself go backwards! I got some ideas." As I walked out he is still just staring at the floor — not a good sign.

The next week when he failed to make his report I got worried. In two years he never missed a report. I checked his place twice but there was no answer. I went late, past his curfew time, but still no answer — this is not good. A few days later he called, saying he lost his apartment for unpaid rent. He was staying at a city shelter. He gave me the address, and assured me he would see me next week. I still heard deep depression in his voice. I am pretty good at telling when someone is suicidal, and did not think he was. Then again, you never know for sure.

The following day was 9/11. Both towers of the World Trade Center came crashing down. My neighbor Andy Stern was killed. So was the manager of Windows On The World, and all seventy one employees. The only employee who survived was the one they had just fired.

John O'Neill was also killed. But, with him it was different than everyone else. He knew the attack was coming soon. He had told people. Yet, he still chose to be there. The name O'Neill means "champion" in Gaelic. He certainly lived up to his heritage. A true American hero.

It would have been my usual day of the month for employment investigations in Manhattan. I would have been there checking on Torres, visiting Andy Stern, and maybe John O'Neill. If Torres had not been fired, I am pretty sure I would have been there and been killed with them.

When Torres came in the next week his depression was replaced by far more complex emotions. He asked me, "Why did I get fired just before those towers fell? Why did all my friends there have to die? Why…? They were all questions with no answers. I had two questions of my own: Was somebody watching over us ? …..Why us ?

🌾 🌾 🌾 🌾

Shortly after the Towers were attacked came the crash of another commercial airliner in Far Rockaway, New York, which was initially assumed to be another terrorist attack. Then came the anthrax scare in which twenty two people were poisoned, and five died from anthrax laced letters and packages. This extended the fear into our homes, to our own mailboxes and the mail on our kitchen table. These events prolonged and intensified our feelings of threat, vulnerability, and impotence. By 2003, we were still in shock, and most Americans, especially New Yorkers shared a collective Post Traumatic Stress Disorder (PTSD). In such a vulnerable state, irrational decisions are common. You desperately seek easy solutions — simplistic answers — and targets for your rage. A convenient scapegoat can always be found.

Enter George W. Bush, a president of limited intellect and experience, elected in the shadow of his father, president George Bush senior. Humiliated so early in his presidency, George W. needed to prove to a frightened nation, and his father, that he was a strong leader. The gang of right wing extremists who surrounded Bush, the Cheney-Rumsfeld-Wolfowitz cabal, exploited these events to the fullest. The reality that 9/11 was perpetrated by a small band of criminals was quickly rejected, in favor of a much grander approach, fitting the needs of a conquering hero, and better serving the neo-conservatives agenda. Allowing law enforcement agencies to do their job — to investigate, apprehend, and prosecute the perpetrators was much too modest a goal. What was needed was — WAR. A "War on Terror."

Unlike a boring criminal investigation, a war would engage the entire military industrial complex, providing lucrative contracts to a long line of hungry corporations waiting to provide security, and construction for whichever nation we chose to demolish. The problem was, that to have a war there must be an enemy nation — so they invented one. It needed to be easy to defeat, and needed to be an Arab country with a predominantly Muslim population — since Islam was the chosen symbol of 9/11.

After a brief, masterfully orchestrated marketing campaign, the third rate dictator Saddam Hussein was chosen. He was the perfect choice. We knew him well, having supported and armed him in the past. Best of all he was sinister looking, inarticulate, and not very bright. Saddam was easily vilified. A still dazed and terrified America people would not object to our attacking his country. It was a "feel good" war, designed to restore our tarnished image of omnipotence. It was a goldmine for corporate media, a blitzkrieg of "Shock and Awe" which glorified American military might, and restored our pride. TV commentators and politicians jumped on the bandwagon. It was a grand celebration, and great therapy for our post 9/11 feelings of vulnerability, impotence and rage.

Our destruction of Iraq was also a grotesque and shameful act of savagery. We slaughtered and maimed hundreds of thousands of innocent Iraqi men, women, and children who had nothing to do with 9/11. It wasted the lives of several thousand selfless young Americans who had enlisted after the Trade Center attacks, with the intention of providing meaningful service to their country.

To veterans of the Vietnam War resistance, the Bush campaign to sell us this new war — looked, and smelled unmistakably like the fiasco of Vietnam. In addition to writing letters to editors of newspapers and magazines, my old marching shoes came out again. After all these years it was time to hit the streets: maybe America could regain its senses, get centered and grounded again. Soon I found myself at planning meetings for war resistance activities in New York City.

Among those organizing the event were a few of the old guard anarchists, Marxists and militant minority group leaders. They were concerned with agent provocateurs and infiltration of the meetings by government agents, and insisted that any law enforcement officers identify themselves. They were shocked when I stood up and identified myself. I had nothing to hide. I let them know I worked in law enforcement, but that my involvement in the protests was personal. I was not there in any official or undercover capacity. When one of the organizers still questioned my motives, we had this heated exchange:

> "Why are you really here?" he demanded. I felt anger surge up my spine, and took a long breath. "I am here for the same reason as you, to stop death and destruction. Everyone of you has a right to be here, but I have a special obligation to be here — these guys are hijacking the US government, they will unleash terrible violence on innocent people. They will do it in my name, with my tax money. Bush, Cheney and the whole bunch are acting like thugs. They want to attack innocent peo-

ple, and that is illegal. I took an oath to enforce the laws of this state, and this country — to protect people from criminals. Every law enforcement officer should be here marching with us!"

That did not exactly get me a standing ovation, but it ended their concerns about me so we could get down to business. I joined the security team responsible for violence prevention and maintaining an orderly march. Non-violence was crucial since popular opinion toward dissent after 9/11 was very negative, much the same as during the Vietnam War era. Dissent during war time is always considered unpatriotic, it was viewed as disrespectful to the victims of 9/11. Communication is power, and for dissent and civil disobedience to communicate effectively it must not be violent, or it frightens people.

Ironically, non-violent resistance requires all the poise, restraint, and discipline of the warrior. I wore a t-shirt with "Parade Marshal" on the front, and "Security" on the back. I took the job very seriously; it was a great opportunity to practice a warrior's discipline in the service of peace. We helped prevent anything stupid from happening. Almost a half million people marched that day, in a demonstration of American humanity, powerful non-violence. Being part of it, I felt both pride, and deep sadness.

Unfortunately, most Americans sat on the sidelines. Still frozen with collective PTSD, and hypnotized by the relentless drumbeats of "homeland security" and war fever. There were just not enough voices willing to rise up in dissent. More than ten years later we are still paying a high price for the senseless destruction of Iraq, and the squandering of $1.7 trillion (yes $trillion!) of our resources, and the chaos we left behind in the whole region. I am glad the world saw that not all Americans supported such mindless violence.

The day of that march was the same date which I had scheduled examinations at my dojo months before. When I announced the examination would be rescheduled, or held in my absence, both students and assistant instructors were very upset. How could I allow "politics" to get in the way of an important dojo event. To make matters worse, I encouraged others to join me. "Politics have no place in the dojo," they said. I actually lost some students over that. But, it was not politics to me. It was life and death. All the death, destruction, and misery of a war — they viewed as just "politics." I think it was a kind of "emotional armor," protecting them from feeling.

They held the examinations, and had the dojo party without me. I made no apology for my absence. I just shared this story:

> "When I lived in Japan I met a very dignified old gentleman one day, on the train to Iwama. That is where O'Sensei 're-tired' after leaving his military training positions and walking away from the war effort in 1942. The old man had been a colonel in the Imperial Japanese Army. We talked a long time about the war, and his role in it. After a long pause, I asked 'You are an intelligent man, why did you never object to what was happening?' I cannot adequately describe the depth of shame I saw in his eyes. He finally responded, 'because I was afraid, I was afraid I would be killed.' I told my students that I never wanted to experience such shame."

The world has always lived with wars, and there has always been an abundance of warriors. To embrace "warrior" as a model of wisdom and virtue requires great care and discernment; which qualities do we emulate? Which do we reject? German soldiers in World War II were the epitome of discipline, yet their robot-like obedience made them complicit in horrific crimes. While heroic on the battlefield, they were cowards when it came to questioning or resisting the evil they were ordered to commit.

Soldiers of Imperial Japan were incredibly courageous and dedicated soldiers, but their unwavering loyalty to the Emperor (unquestioning patriotism) led to unspeakable brutality towards their prisoners, and savagery toward the Chinese even more horrific than what Germans perpetrated on the Jews.

I have studied the life of Osama bin Laden, trying to understand the evil genius who single-handedly set America on a course of perpetual war — war in Iraq, war in Afghanistan — and a seemingly endless "War on Terror" across the world. He was a well educated, and very religious man. By all accounts he was a courageous freedom fighter and a selfless warrior who joined the Afghan resistance against the Soviet invasion. He gave most of his vast wealth away to the cause. How can such a man turn pure evil?

At some point, he fell victim to the greatest danger for the warrior. He became consumed with hate. His whole world became — Us vs. Them. His spiral downward left him devoid of humanity, an anarchist seeing only death and destruction as the solution to injustice. When your adversaries are no longer seen as human beings, you are headed for pure evil.

I use the term "evil genius" intentionally with Osama bin Laden, because he knew his enemy so well. He unfortunately understood how to provoke Americans into a war against the Muslim world, thereby producing an endless supply of jihadi martyrs. He foresaw how panic from a few terrorist events on American soil could dramatically change the character of our fragile democracy. Did he also foresee how the obsession with security would overwhelm all other American values?

The greatest evil perpetrated by this brilliant madman, was not the destruction of the Twin Towers. His greatest evil act was the creation of a War On Terror, in which torture is no longer an atrocity, perpetrated by Nazis or deranged third world dictators, but sanitized with the obscene name "enhanced interrogation." Now acceptable if the prisoner is a "suspected terrorist." My God, what have we become?

The events of a single day stimulated such panic in us, that we allowed the suspension of fundamental constitutional rights, by implementing the so called "Patriot Act." Motivated by hysteria, we have allowed our government to engage in the broadest imaginable surveillance of our personal activities. If not for NSA whistle blower, Edward Snowden, the idea of government surveilling all our communications would be considered wildly delusional. Sadly, we now know it is true. We have permitted an out of control — ever expanding web of overlapping secretive agencies — CIA, NSA, FBI, DIA, ODNI, and at least twelve others!

Warriors feel fear, but do not allow fear to dominate their actions. By dismantling many safeguards of our democracy, abandoning our highest values, and placing America on a perpetual war time footing, we hand Osama bin Laden success beyond his wildest dreams. He could not destroy the fabric of our democracy, only we can do that. But, in doing so we dishonor the victims of 9/11, and all the brave men and women who fought and died to preserve our values, constitutional freedoms, and democratic ideals.

2. Kevin Shea — Ninja of Rescue One

KEVIN was a nervous young guy in his early twenties when I first met him in the mid 1980's. It was nice to have a friendly, soft spoken guy walk in, after the bums and junkies who often wandered into my ghetto dojo. It was on a bad street in Glen Cove, New York. He stared at my monster bamboo trees, which took advantage of the sixteen-foot ceilings and the leaky roof. I was proud of the carefully arranged plastic sheeting, that caught the rain when it leaked through the roof, and out of the ceiling. The set up funneled the water into hoses along the walls, that watered the trees whenever in rained. Those giant trees drew peoples' attention from the rest of the place, which probably should have been condemned.

The son in law of a friend, Kevin needed my help. He wanted to be a firefighter in the worst way, but every time he went for the physical, his blood pressure went sky high, so he got rejected. Kevin knew we did meditation at my dojo, so he thought the training might help him. He was not that interested in martial arts, and he did not seem at all athletic, but he gave it a try and did pretty well. He liked the falling drills, and put a lot of energy into his meditation training; a lot more than most martial artists do.

I never met anyone who wanted something as bad as he wanted to be a firefighter, and I saw right away that was the problem. His desire was too strong. As the Buddha said, unrestrained desire creates suffering. He wanted something too much, and when we fail to keep "the wanting mind" on a short leash, it gets out of control and causes trouble. As the months passed, I encouraged Kevin to consider other occupations, reminding him of every negative thing about a fireman's job. After a few months, he began to consider other kinds of work.

His falling skills became pretty good, and his Zen practice got strong. He learned to use his breathing effectively to lower his heart rate and blood pressure, a skill which any serious student of meditation can acquire. One day, he came in smiling, to report he had taken the FDNY test one last time and passed! A few weeks later, he was off to the New York City Fire Department

Training Academy. It was a good feeling knowing he got what he needed, and moved on.

I would hear occasionally about how much Kevin loved the job, and how well he was doing. A few years later, I saw Kevin on the evening news. He was in a harness, dangling from a rope, twelve stories above a Manhattan street. He was holding an office worker tightly against his body, both of them dangling from the rope. The guy had climbed out onto a window ledge, to escape a fire in the high-rise office building. The building was too high for ladder trucks to reach him, so they lowered Kevin forty feet down to the guy from the roof.

Kevin was a member of Rescue One, the elite FDNY unit known for doing the impossible. Rescue One is famous for going over, under, around, or through anything that is in the way, when people's lives are at stake. When there is a major fire, explosion, or building collapse in Manhattan, Rescue One is first on the scene. When firemen are trapped and need help, they know Rescue One will somehow get to them. What a thrill it was, to watch Kevin, the guy who kept flunking the physical exams, swinging down from the roof of a huge building like

a modern day ninja to save that guy. A New York Post photographer took an award-winning photo of the incredible rescue.

I thought about Kevin occasionally, and hoped he would stay out of harm's way. Then in 1993 came the first World Trade Center bombing, and there was Kevin again on the evening news. Rescue One was the first to respond to the explosion in the parking garage below the foundation of the Tower, and Kevin was one of the first to go in, searching for survivors. The explosion destroyed several levels of the parking garage, creating a deep crater. He could not see anything for all the blinding smoke and dust, so he had to feel his way through the ruble crawling on hands and knees. As he crawled through the dense smoke, he went right off the edge of the crater, falling several stories down. Strapped with fifty plus pounds of breathing tank and other equipment, he dropped like a rock, landing on sharp broken concrete and hot twisted metal.

They said it was not a survivable fall. He had cuts, burns, and a shattered knee. But, against all odds, he survived. I imagined what it was like alone down there, with fires and falling concrete all around, not able to see or climb out, or even move. He said he had absolute faith his brothers would find him, and not rest until they did.

When I visited Kevin a few months later, he was still hobbling around on crutches, restless as hell, and totally focused on getting back to the job. Against medical advice, he was fighting to get his job back. He wanted to rehab his legs more aggressively, so I suggested he start swimming every day, in addition to the physical therapy to help rebuild his knee. That was a good example of me opening my big mouth too often. "Yes!" he said, and off we went to find a pool. Unfortunately, it was a holiday of some sort, so public pools were all closed. How I lost the argument, and was stupid enough to take him to the ocean, I will never know. The surf was huge that day. I bitched, and moaned, and cursed, as he hobbled across the sand toward the surf. I cannot remember how that day ended, but somehow we did not drown or get swept out to sea. After that, I made no more suggestions to anyone, about anything, for a long time.

Kevin finally did rebuild his legs, and fought his way back onto the job. He served another six years before retiring as a New York City Fire Department legend. Firefighters I met through the years would light up when I asked if they ever worked with Kevin Shea. I would hear, "He spoke at my academy class, he is an icon of the department. I got to shake his hand. Did you really know him?"

When the World Trade Center Towers collapsed on September 11, 2001, Kevin immediately drove to Manhattan, and was one of the first volunteers on the scene searching for survivors. One survivor was a firefighter blown 200 feet by the power of the building collapse, who sustained a broken neck, but miraculously survived. His name — Kevin Shea (a coincidence?). That fellow definitely had good karma.

The fourth day after the collapse, Kevin was still working feverishly to find survivors. He had worked his way down a long slope of rubble, which formed a huge crater, then he panicked. He recognized it, it was the same spot he had fallen into, after the first bombing in 1993. "I felt the fear crawl up my back. I got out the first time, but might not make it out this time. The fear was crippling." Instead of working his way back up the safer slope of the crater, as he had been trained, panic from the flashback sent him frantically scrambled up a dangerous steep mountain of rubble. He had to get away from there!

As he got to the top of the crater, intending to keep running, he encountered a soldier uncovering bodies of two firemen trapped in the rubble. He stopped running. Then he helped the soldier dig. After they finished, the soldier introduced Kevin to another retired fireman, who was searching for his son. His son was a firefighter from Rescue One. The three men spent the rest of the day searching together.

Lt. Kevin Shea was asked to be the keynote speaker at the 9/11 Memorial at Bradenton City Auditorium, and at the Tribute to Heroes Memorial. He did not make any speeches, he just shared the bond that those who face danger know to be the source of their strength and courage.
He told a hushed crowd:

> *"If I said to you I am not a hero, you might call me humble. But you don't understand. It's a fact. What happened to me, no matter how uncomfortable I was or afraid I was, I had the guy next to me. It's always about the guy next to you...firefighters every where are brothers and sisters...and I am not afraid to fail because I know you will not judge me. With support like that, I can do anything."*

3. Magical Thinking and Airline Insecurity

FANTASIES pervade popular culture about the amazing abilities of martial arts heroes, government agents and TV cops. They always seem to beat the bad guys, and to win in the end. That is how we want it to be. Mythology is fun, except when it creeps into public policy. Then it becomes dangerous.

After 9/11, it should have been crystal clear that the FAA is primarily a public relations — trade organization for the airline industry. Its primary mission is not airline safety. It is protecting industry image and profits. When a few guys with two-dollar box cutters and a plane ticket effortlessly slipped into the cockpits of several airliners, turning them into missiles, it became obvious that airline safety was a bad joke. Secure cockpits would have cost a little more money. Policies and procedures prohibiting pilots from opening cockpit doors during flights, might be an inconvenience, or worst of all; it could be bad publicity!

The government and FAA policies that allowed the 9/11 hijackings to so easily happen, were to be corrected after those tragedies. Safety was to be the highest priority. Several months after the World Trade Center attacks, I accepted an assignment transporting a prisoner from a South Carolina jail back to New York's Riker's Island. After leaving New York without his parole officer's permission, this guy traveled down south and quickly committed new crimes. He managed to get himself arrested in a small Southern town, and after serving his sentence down there, South Carolina was anxious to get rid of him. New York officers were to bring him back for a parole violation hearing, then more jail time in New York. My boss gave me the job.

The boss knew I had refused interstate prisoner transports for years, after my first run in with the dirty little secret of the airline industry. While doing interstate prison transports early in my law enforcement career, I was shocked to discover that most prisoners in custody were routinely transported, not on the secure US Marshal flights, but on regular commercial flights without the knowledge of the passengers. Making this practice even more dangerous; the airlines prohibited the use of handcuffs or restraints of any kind.

Passengers are unaware they are sharing their flight with prisoners because they board the flight early, sit in the back of the plane, and wait until all other passengers exit before leaving. It is a successful deception that continues, with passengers unaware they are sharing their flight with fugitives and felons. The airline industry makes millions each year on ticket sales for thousands of prisoners, and their escort officers. They have no public relations problem, since the danger to passengers is well disguised.

The prisoners sit with loaded firearms inches from them, on the hips of escort officers. The officers can only hope they would prevail if a prisoner reaches for their guns. The FAA apparently has decided criminals have the good judgment, high moral character, and law-abiding natures not to grab a gun that does not belong to them.

After losing my first major argument with a flight crew and pilot, for refusing to remove my prisoner's handcuffs, I vowed never to be a part of that dangerous charade again. From then on I declined all transport assignments. The agency could do nothing about it, because of a little rule tucked away deep within most agency policy manuals stating that: "No order need be carried out which is deemed to be reckless or dangerous."

I was not ordered to perform any transport duties for several years. Then, after 9/11, when my boss assured me things had changed, I agreed to do an the extradition from South Carolina back to New York. From the airport, we drove out to the little county jail, showed our paperwork, and took custody of the prisoner. He was not happy to be going back to New York to face more jail time. I reminded him he was going back to the land of corn beef, pastrami, and Coney Island hotdogs — he did not laugh. I would have to watch this guy carefully.

After searching him for the usual hidden lock picks and handcuff keys, he was cuffed and shackled, then off we went to the airport. I asked to see the return paperwork, but there was nothing about a US Marshal service flight! It was a regular commercial flight to New York! How was this possible, after 9/11?

At the gate, a polite flight attendant greeted us, "We have been expecting you officer. Your seats are the back row left. The pilot reminds you to board thirty minutes early, and remove the gentleman's handcuffs." She saw my eyes, and looked frightened. "What year are you living in lady? What the hell is the matter with you? The handcuffs stay on! Let me talk to the pilot. Now!"

When the pilot came out, he repeated the same old airline policy like a brain dead bureaucrat. I confronted him about his responsibility for the safety of his passengers. His logic was astounding, it left me speechless: "We will be at 30,000 feet, going 400 miles per hour; there is no chance of your prisoner escaping. What's the problem?" A bad guy cannot do any harm way up in an airplane, right? Was this a bad dream? I think the airline had given their pilots some strange kool-aid to drink, which suspended normal brain function leaving them in some alternate reality.

Part of this insanity was due to the magical belief that a prisoner could never successfully get the officer's gun since cops are "super heroes." I confronted the pilot loudly at the gate; "You are a fool, and you are endangering your passengers!" He responded with, "Sir, keep your voice down. It is my call, and this is always how it is done." I threw the tickets on the floor, and led the prisoner away from the gate. The passengers listening to our argument looked worried. But, they were probably relieved as I led the prisoner down the hall away from them, still in handcuffs. Even after 9/11, for the airlines it was business as usual!

Our extradition office in Albany was not happy to hear I had just thrown away $1400 in airline tickets, and rented a Hertz Crown Victoria sedan to New York. A bureaucrat in the Albany — Interstate Travel Office, demanded an explanation. Unfortunately our phone connection was bad, and we were somehow disconnected. "What... what... I can't hear you....

I have never told a supervisor who gave me a reckless order to go fuck off, instead I politely ignore the order. If I had to respond, I used a brilliantly conceived linguistic device. Perfected over many years by my colleague PO Sly Burns, who deserves full credit for the greatest "non-response response" ever conceived: "No Problem." Close to perfection, it is my absolute favorite silky smooth — non-contentious method of ignoring foolish requests.

Have you noticed that cops on TV never have to go to the bathroom? The trouble with transporting prisoners long distances by car, is that unlike a plane, there is no lavatory a few feet away. My intended scheme to address this little issue was to speed down the interstate in our unmarked vehicle at eighty five mph, get pulled over by a state trooper, then get a police escort to the nearest state police barracks to relieve ourselves. Maybe even get a snack, and relax in a secure location. An excellent plan.

After traveling through North Carolina and Virginia at eighty five mph without being stopped, then Delaware and Maryland at ninety mph, we all really needed to go badly. If I was off duty going sixty-six mph, I probably would have been pulled over. But doing ninety for 300 miles, we seemed to be invisible. I did not want to march a prisoner in cuffs and shackles, jingling and jangling, into a coffee shop or service area. I did not care about embarrassing our prisoner or freaking people out; it is just not safe. You just never know when you will bump into one or more of his old friends, or old cell mates from the various facilities he has been in.

As we entered New Jersey, I was pushing ninety-five mph on the Jersey Turnpike — passing cars and trucks like they were standing still. No way we would not be stopped here! My mother got a speeding ticket there doing 68 mph. But, we had apparently entered a strange zone beyond time and space, some strange dimension which was invisible to all state troopers. I wish I could have bottled and sold it. But my euphoria at being invisible was constantly interrupted by a painful need to relieve myself.

I was afraid to push the Crown Vic over a hundred, so we said the hell with it and pulled into a service area. Two armed parole officers, walking into a McDonald's with a guy in leg irons and waist restraint, jingling and jangling like St. Nick's sleigh. The manager was not happy, and a few customers looked freaked. We did not care — we all had to go really bad. The feeling when relieving ourselves was worth it. To console the manager, I bought five deluxe burgers on the way out. One for my partner, one for our prisoner, and three for me.

We made it all the way to Rikers Island in just a few hours. Amazingly, not much longer than the flight would have taken. On that day, a world land speed record was set between South Carolina and New York. I should probably contact the Guinness Book of World Records. It could only have been accomplished by someone trying his best — but failing, to get pulled over for speeding.

That crazy ninety-mile-an-hour trip should never have happened. All interstate prisoners should be flying on the US Marshal — secure flights. A few weeks before this trip, my NYPD pal, Eric, had also been ordered to remove handcuffs from his prisoner — a murder suspect he was transporting back to New York from Florida. He was angry as hell about it, and co-signed my letter to a dozen senators, congressmen, and the director of the FAA. The letter was not subtle or diplomatic; it expressed outrage at the disregard for passenger safety.

The letters apparently hit a nerve. Eric was soon taking a lot of heat from NYPD brass, who apparently got nasty calls from airline executives. The bosses did not care about the danger to the public, only Eric's breach of protocol. He had gone outside the chain of command, and in a bureaucracy, the chain of command is sacred. Eric did not fail to remind me this was just one of several occasions, in which his association with me landed him in hot water. I had little sympathy, since he is a born trouble maker, just like me. Besides, disciplinary action against him quickly evaporated after receiving a thank you letter from Washington:

It is nice to know we played a small part in improving airline safety. It is very nice no longer having to check the back seats of planes for unrestrained criminals, when the family flies somewhere on vacation. Sometimes, it takes a couple of loud mouthed hot heads who ignore sacred protocols, and break the chains of command, to accomplish something useful.

U.S. Department
of Transportation
**Federal Aviation
Administration**

800 Independence Ave., S.W.
Washington, DC 20591

Mr. Thomas Collings

New York

MAY 3 1 2002

Dear Mr. Collings,

Thank you for your letter offering comments and concerns regarding mandatory removal of handcuffs from prisoners being transported by law enforcement officers on commercial airlines. Please accept our apologies for the delayed response.

On February 17, the newly created Transportation Security Administration (TSA) assumed responsibility for civil aviation security in the United States. TSA's responsibilities include..... As part of the transition, the regulations governing air carrier security were recodified .... effective February 17, 2002.

The policy on hand restraints is covered in 49 CFR 1544.221(g), enclosed. It now requires each armed law enforcement officer escorting a prison and each aircraft operator to ensure that the prisoner is restrained from full use of his or her hands by an appropriate device .... If you observe that these rules are not being carried out, please notify the Federal Security Director or one of their Federal Security Agents at the applicable location immediately.

Please accept our appreciation for taking the time to share your thoughts with us. Your help and support is an important contribution to ensuring safety and security of the nation's aviation system.

Sincerely,

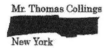

Kenneth W. Peppard
Director
Tell FAA Task Force

Enclosure

VII.

MODERN WARRIORS AND PEACEMAKERS

1. The Sword That Gives Life

𝕿HE blade has been a part of the man for fifty years. He is not of Japanese descent, but the sword is a part of his soul. As a boy growing up in Brooklyn, he found a retired Marine instructor to teach him the way of the knife. That is a basic coming of age skill on the hard streets of East New York. Later it became fencing, and then Japanese kendo. Then, it was on to find a vocation for a modern day samurai. His path of service would be medicine.

In medical school, surgery training taught him the intimate relationship between the body and the blade, with a depth few swordsmen ever learn.

He routinely cut tissues, organs, muscle, and studied the precise location of arteries. The intent was to heal, yet the practice was learning to cut. The intricate tapestry of nerves throughout the human body became his greatest fascination and expertise.

Hundreds of hours in the operating room tends to desensitize surgeons to the act of penetrating flesh, the flow of blood, and the cutting of tissue and organs. The usual human inhibition against slicing through the human body disappears, as it does with battle hardened warriors.

Returning to his Brooklyn apartment building one evening, Dr. Dave is unloading some expensive medical equipment from his car. His appearance is every bit the physician; a slim, bespectacled man in conservative dress with a brief case. His building is where he grew up, on a street in one of New York's roughest neighborhoods. He is aware that his actions will catch the attention of any street predators in the area, but leaving this equipment in the car overnight is not an option.

As he carries the equipment, a casual demeanor does not reveal his battlefield awareness which has highlighted two young men down the block, as they cross to his side on the street. The few glances as he walks into the building provide all necessary data — age, sizes, relationship — who is leader and follower, and a myriad of subtle cues all relevant to preparation for combat. The mind of the warrior has extraordinary radar.

As the predators enter the building, they are focused on their chosen victim. They are unaware that their every move is closely monitored by their intended victim. They are also unaware how close they are to death.

The doctor joins several people getting on the elevator, with his adversaries now part of the group. He knows when they will make their move. It will be when he or the others get off the elevator. Predators of all species follow the same pattern — separate, isolate, then attack. Their predictability is a weakness. Up close he sees they fit the description of two men who have committed several robberies in the building recently. These are not just thieves, they cut one victim after getting his money — they are violent predators. The doctor's decision is resolute; at the right moment he will attack.

He knows there is safety in numbers, and that he may avoid confrontation if he gets off the elevator with the others. They will then choose another time and place, and another victim. The samurai in him decides to stay as the others get off.

With the closing of the elevator doors, battle lines begin to form. They prepare to make their move. It will be just before the doors open at the next floor, so they can make a fast escape. But, they are already several moves behind. They are preoccupied with their plan of attack — they fail to notice the long folding knife, opened and ready. Laying flat against their target's right thigh. It is held lightly, expertly. But, it is held so subtly it is virtually invisible. His sword has been drawn, but it cannot be seen.

They feel some kind of problem, but it is hard to discern. As seconds pass, their unease intensifies. It is the focus, and stillness in their intended victim's eyes. There is neither the denial, nor desperation of normal prey. They know something is terribly wrong.

They are, however, too close to their goal to abandon their plan. As the elevator stops, they pull their knives, and block the door. Their moves were predicted, and they are now in perfect alignment for the samurai's attack — one deep thrust to sever the closer target's aorta, he will be dead before hitting the ground. The movement of his second target will lead directly into his knife. Two short movements, two kills.

The predators waste precious time glancing at one another, losing focus and initiative. Their hesitation and indecision is clear. Their weakness and desperation changes the equation for the samurai. There may be an alternative to killing.

Fully prepared to kill, he chooses to let his polished blade become visible, and assumes a full combat stance. Revealing intent and readiness, his attack is now psychological. They receive the full impact of a warrior's demeanor. It is unmistakable. In his eyes they see "satsujin no ken" — the sword that takes life. They can feel death.

There are dimensions of time in combat which are unlike ordinary time. A milli-second before he attacks, he further weakens both their resolve and focus. His free hand takes the wad of small bills from his front pocket, and tosses it passed them into the hallway. Their eyes follow the money, a successful decoy leaving them more vulnerable to attack. They glance at one another again. One quickly turns and runs. The other follows. They rush to grab a few bills as they flee the building. Accepting the consolation prize that saved their lives.

These young fools stumbled into confrontation with a modern samurai and miraculously survived. They did not deserve the reprieve. They owe their lives to a samurai with "katsujin no ken" — the sword that gives life.

O'Sensei spoke of a place beyond winning or losing, beyond contest and beating an opponent. The warrior resides in this special world. It is a world of conflict and resolution, where many choices are available. This is the freedom of the warrior.

2. In Harmony with Bums, Psychos, and Rowdy Drunks

TERRY Dobson, that big bear of a man who spent ten years with O'Sensei in Japan, loved to share stories of woman warriors. One of his favorites was of a petite female flight attendant having to deal with a big, belligerent, drunken Texan. Everyone on the plane was terrified of the guy, who got drunker and meaner as the flight continued. When the meals were served, instead of quieting down he got worse, yelling about the bad food. As the flight attendant passed, he stabbed his baked potato with a fork, holding it up in front of her in a threatening manner. "This damn potato is no good; it's bad! What are you going to do about it?"

That whole section of the plane went silent, as fear took hold of everyone. She looked at the big guy, then at the potato. Then she snatched the potato from his hand, and smacked it several times. "Bad potato! Bad potato! This potato will give you no more trouble, sir." She handed it back to him, and walked away. With his whole mindset rattled, he chuckled a bit, then began laughing hysterically. As his laughter gradually faded, so did his energy. He nibbled at a little food, then fell asleep for the rest of the flight.

I asked Terry how she did that. He said he did not know, that her actions were just like O'Sensei — "I don't understand it but I am in awe of it. It is the highest form of combat; it is aiki". I asked if that was what he did that day he was teaching a big seminar in conflict resolution at a school gymnasium, when a drunken bum wandered in off the street. He was hassling people and heckling Terry. It was very impressive when Terry walked right up to the guy, and putting his arm around him like a brother, just walked him out. It was amazing. "Was that aiki too?," I asked. With a big grin he responded, "Oh, sure. It was very impressive wasn't it. But, would you like to know what really happened?":

> "When I went up to the jerk, and walked him to the door I
> held a $10 bill in my hand. It was probably more cash than
> he had seen all year. He was not really moving with me, he

was moving with the $10. When we got to the door I told him he could have it if he got the hell out of here. That's why he was so cooperative. But, to everyone watching it looked like magic."

Another of Terry's favorite aiki stories is about the skin heads in the park. I was never clear if he saw this or heard about it. A guy is walking in a city park when he comes upon three skin heads beating the hell out of a black guy. One guy is clubbing the fellow with a 2x4. The skin heads are big and will probably kill him too if he tries to stop them. So, he goes up to the one with the 2x4 and says; "You are just fooling around man, let me show you how to really beat the shit out of a nigger." The idiot with the 2x4 smiles says "hey brother take a swing," and hands it to him. The guy then knocks the skin head to the ground with the 2x4, and the other two run away.

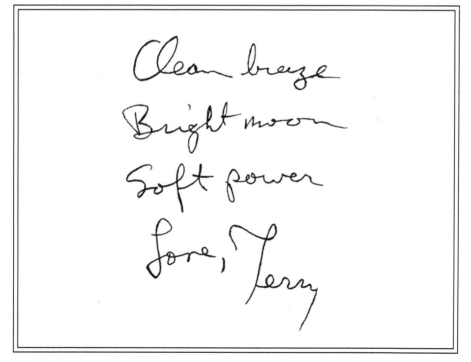

Note from Terry Dobson I kept in my locker at work

This "aiki" often has an absurdly amusing quality to it. A doctor I know was doing his rotation in psychiatry at Brooklyn's Brookdale Hospital, the closest treatment center for the shooting/stabbing victims and drug overdoses of Brownsville and Canarsie. A patient admitted to the psych ward was a Vietnam veteran who, due to drugs, alcohol and PTSD was completely psychotic. Screaming and threatening staff, he was far too irrational to understand anything being said to him by the nurses or doctors. With his mind manufacturing devils everywhere and his world spinning out of control, attendants and security staff gathered for a physical altercation.

My friend detected a faint essence of soldier still within this guy. He recalls walking right up to this guy, who was deeply lost in a psychotic rage. With a commanding tone he blasts out — "Attention!" The response was automatic — the patient snapped to attention. "Private Arnold, you will go to your quarters and lie down on your bunk until further orders! Is that clear private? Instantly emerging from the depths of insanity, came a response without hesitation, "Yes sir." My doctor friend finished with "dismissed!" The patient immediately returned to his bed as ordered.

Was it intuition, or my friend's stern warrior presence? Whether warrior wisdom or aiki it even penetrated madness!

3. Mike V. and The Dalai Lama — All they meet are Old Friends

WARRIORS often sense things that other people cannot. It is a kind of intuition. With this power you can sometimes redirect and lead the mind of others. O'Sensei perfected this power. Healers often have it, and holy men like the Dalai Lama. The Dalai Lama once said he treats everyone he meets "like they are my old friend." My friend Mike V., can do this, too.

Mike and I supervised group homes for juvenile offenders in residential care. Mike is not a big guy, and is blind in one eye. So, when he was parked in the street working on a car engine, he should have been an easy target for the predator sneaking up on him with a knife. Mike was sprawled out over the engine, focused on his work.

Creeping up from behind to rob a mild mannered, visually impaired man who is immersed in his work — should have been easy. Mike is not a cop, or a martial artist. But he knows the streets, and tends to stay alert. He also has advantages that disabilities offer. The body and mind have great powers of compensation. Due to his visual impairment, his hearing is much more acute than average hearing.

He abruptly turned to his rear, interrupting his attacker's approach and disrupting his mind set. "Yo, how you doin'? It's me, Mike! I haven't seen you for a long time, how you been, man? You know my brother, right? I got to tell him I saw you, bro. What you been doin'?"

His reality rattled, intention derailed, our mugger's will and purpose is clouded. He falls into confusion. He is crippled with uncertainty. His focus is obscured by the possibility that he may know this guy, or maybe his brother. Intention turns to awkwardness. The knife slips back into his pocket: "Oh...yeah...uh...good...I'm good...how you doin'?...uh...peace, bro." His retreat is accompanied by a trail of awkward small talk. He feels relieved that he narrowly avoided making a big mistake. He does not remember this guy, but he must know his brother? He wanders off, in a kind of fog.

I asked Mike, "You never saw the guy before in your life?" He answers, no. "Then, where did that come from? Did you plan to use that trick if you ever needed it?" His reply was, "No, I have no idea why I said it. It's all I could think of at the time."

Mike is not a Buddhist. He is a Hispanic guy from New York. He is not a student of the Dalai Lama, but he is like the Dalai Lama. When ever the need arises — he can instantly turn strangers into old friends!

4. Files, Folders, and Peace Officers

THE office across the hall is quickly filling with armed officers, engaged in an intense standoff with a screaming convict. They are trying to arrest him on parole violations. The POs order, then coax, then plead with him to turn around, and place his hands behind his back. The parolee ignores all commands, continuing to respond with " why! why should I... why?"

This had been going on for several minutes, and it was becoming annoying. My partner, Richie and I are stuck in the office all day to catch up on a big, nasty pile of the paperwork this office generates. We would rather be in the street "protecting the community," as the agency mission states, but we promised the boss. For

the tenth time we promised the boss we would absolutely, positively, stay here until all reports were written, forms were filled out, memos answered, expense vouchers submitted etc., etc.

Unlike most days, when our best of intentions to do paperwork get pushed aside by hot tips about criminal activity, or where a fugitive is hiding, today we get this done! We hope this will be a day with no frantic girlfriends calling to report they were just assaulted. Today we will let nothing come between us and those files — folders — and paperwork!

We do our best to block out the craziness across the hall, but it is just keeps getting louder. "Why, what did I do? Why? What did I do? " As his resistance escalates, he is approaching pure irrationality — when nothing is heard, and nothing computes. At this stage of confrontation, words are just gasoline poured on the fire, and verbal commands just escalate the situation. But out of frustration, or fear, the officers keep repeating their ineffectual commands.

I do not have Richie's ultra-cool DNA. This was my damn paperwork day, which I want to get over with. But it is not going to happen until the craziness across the hall ends! When I look over at Richie, he knows I am about to drag him into another mess. We get up and head toward all the noise and commotion. We are neither heroes nor fools, but on this day we are untouched by the unfolding drama, and easily avoid the battle of wills. Some situations are like being caught in a thick fog, you just cannot see. Yet, to an outsider things can appear so simple and obvious.

Every situation is framed by the context and environment where it takes place. This place is the stereotypical parole office, with folders and files piled everywhere. A "palace of paperwork." So with paperwork in hand, and muttering something about a lost folder, we walk unnoticed not only through the crowd of yelling officers, but right past the screaming convict. We are the perfect caricatures of the bureaucrat, seemingly oblivious to the confrontation taking place in our midst. Concerned only with finding a folder we are invisible. I cannot believe he let us walk right past, and behind him. "Excuse me, guy," as we brushed past, not even looking at him. It defies logic, but it worked.

After picking up and fumbling with a few folders on the file cabinet behind him, we simply turned around and handcuffed the fellow. He was so busy with his confrontation he hardly noticed he was handcuffed! We did a quick search and removed a box cutter from his front pocket. Then, walked out as casually as we had entered. I never noticed if we left those officers relieved, embarrassed or confused. Perhaps it was disrespectful to ignore the gravity of their confrontation, to walk right through it as if it had no significance. But that is precisely what allowed us to do what we did.

Back across the hall, we managed to knock off almost half the overdue paper work before an emergency call came in, sending us into the streets. Passing my boss's office on the way out, he spotted us and yelled, "You said absolutely, positively all paperwork today!" As we disappeared down the stairs he could hear that familiar old refrain "No problem..."

5. Responding to Aggression — Takemusu Aiki I

For most of my adult life I have worked in law enforcement, psych wards, or youth detention facilities. All these jobs have the common thread of working with people who feel desperate, and sometimes lose control. There are excellent violence management systems available that provide practical training in de-escalating violent situations, and providing physical intervention if needed.

Three good systems are CPI (Crisis Prevention Institute), NAPPI (Non-Abusive Physical and Psychological Intervention), and TCI (Therapeutic Crisis Intervention). I have found all of these to be consistent with the philosophy of O'Sensei. There is concern for the welfare of the individual posing a threat, as well as our own safety and that of our coworkers.

These training programs are open to anyone working in law enforcement, health care, child care or education. Our skills for responding to aggressive behavior cannot be confined to a mugging situation, since conflict and

Monk Gensai, 1750-1837

anger are common in the workplace place, as well as social situations. We need to learn strong skills for assessing and defusing aggression, rather than just reacting to an attack.

In the Cornell University Therapeutic Crisis Intervention System (TCI), aggressive behavior is differentiated into two distinct types. Each has different dynamics and requires different responses. The first type of aggressive behavior is REACTIVE AGGRESSION, which is characterized by high emotional charge, loss of control, and little motive other than the release of anger.

Reactive aggression is exhibited by an agitated psychiatric patient, a driver filled with road rage, an angry drunk, or anyone (including friends/family) whose emotions are overwhelming their ability to cope. The target of this rage is usually whoever is in front of them. It erupts like a volcano, there is no planning or motive other than releasing anger.

The second type of aggression is termed PROACTIVE AGGRESSION, characterized by little or no emotion, a clear motive, and more mental and physical control. This is the bully using violence or the threat of violence for intimidation, or the predator skilled in violent assault. The target of proactive aggression is carefully chosen. So is the time and place. If the victim shows signs of being a "hard target" — early recognition of danger and some response to that awareness — the violence is often aborted or directed elsewhere.

While both Reactive and Proactive types of aggression have the potential for violence, the likelihood of physical aggression is strongly influenced by our response. A volatile situation can go either way. Violence is an INTERACTIONAL PROCESS. It does not occur in isolation. The manner in which we respond affects their behavior, for better or worse.

 ## BEING EARTH

The best response to the reactive emotionally charged individual is to be calm and stable. O'Sensei symbolized this attitude using the square, representing the qualities of EARTH. The rage of the emotionally charged individual can usually be de-escalated when we allow them an outlet, an opportunity to vent those emotions. The most powerful method I have found to help an emotional person keep control is — listening. Just LISTENING.

Listening does not sound like much, but it takes great strength and discipline. To stay open and listen to someone screaming at you requires great stability. It is easy to be reactive, defensive, or argumentative when someone is loud and threatening. It is common knowledge among mental health professionals that helping someone express strong emotions verbally, lowers their need to act out physically. I have been in countless volatile situations which were resolved through the powerful discipline of listening.

It is easy to tell an angry person to: "Calm down." But, this phrase rarely helps, and often makes things worse. "Calm down" indicates you are more concerned with their (loud) behavior than with their feelings; it trivializes their feelings. FOCUSING ON THE FEELINGS that are driving the behavior immediately opens communication; the relationship instantly changes. Its hard to view someone as your enemy when they really listen and show interest in your feelings.

Rather than attempting to quiet down highly emotional individuals, I do the opposite. I encourage them to vent, to release their rage verbally — even if it is loud and harsh. If safety is the priority, then screaming, yelling, and even threats can be viewed as an alternative to violence. It allows the same rapid discharge of emotional energy as physical violence, but without the damage. In extreme cases even destruction of property can be seen as a sign of self control — the alternative chosen rather than harming a person. Viewing release of anger in this way helps us to avoid over-reacting.

As someone vents, it is easy to tune them out, especially if their words are unreasonable or irrational. But ignoring someone's pain intensifies their anger. Pretending to listen is not much better. Our non-verbal communication does not lie — tone of voice, facial expression, eyes, and demeanor tell all. Better to listen — not to the words, but to their feelings. It is possible to listen well, without agreeing — disagreeing — or responding. This is an important skill to develop.

O'Sensei's student Terry Dobson, described how he would "become earth" in volatile situations as a bouncer at rowdy bars. "Doing nothing," remaining calm and attentive, was often his most effective response when dealing with wild and crazy drunks. Even with these guys he found that an attitude of empathy was his most effective tool. Disciplined listeners are like mountains. Standing still in the face of all the sound and fury. Remaining open and silent.

GIVING TIME

Listening takes TIME. There will usually be someone around who wants the commotion ended quickly. They are often bosses, supervisors, or administrators whose job is the "business" of life. They feel pressure to get back to "business as usual" as soon as possible. These concerns must be ignored. They neither understand nor care about the dynamics of emotions and violence. In situations of potential violence, safety takes precedence over everything else — BUSINESS as usual must be PUT ASIDE. People, not business, takes priority. Time is a small price to pay to avoid violence.

The lead negotiator of the NYPD Hostage Negotiating Unit used to follow this rule:

"I deal with desperate people as if we have all the time in the world."
Under his watch all incidents ended peacefully.

GIVING THEM SPACE

Emotionally charged individuals usually telegraph their physical intensions. This is fortunate for those around them because reaction time is critical to safety. Giving an emotionally aroused person more space gives us more time to react. In Japanese martial arts there is one term for both space and time, "ma-ai"(lit. space-time.) This term emphasizes that in violent engagements space and time are one (space=time.)

Giving the explosive person more PERSONAL SPACE serves two other important functions. First, it significantly LOWERS their STRESS level. In cases of psychotic or paranoid individuals moving away can instantly de-escalate the situation. The second impact of backing away from a volatile person is it provides them immediate feedback about their behavior. With high emotion comes a loss of self awareness. Backing away is a simple, clear communication their behavior is inappropriate and threatening. It is powerful non-verbal communication. The message often helps them begin to calm themselves.

BEING WATER

Listening — Time — Space are a highly effective "Riai," or "integrated strategy" for helping an angry person maintain physical control. But, if rage overwhelms self control we must provide physical control, until their self control returns. It is a kind act — because the consequences of violent behavior are serious.

The rage-filled attacker has lost their mental balance, resulting in tenuous physical balance. Out of control physical force requires resistance of some kind to maintain balance. We do not want to provide that resistance, therefore, a soft, non-resistant physical response usually works best. It does not provide the stabilizing resistance they require to continue their aggressive behavior. When O'Sensei said attackers were destined to fall, this is what he meant. We do not fight them with resistance that would help them keep their balance.

The element of WATER represents this approach, symbolized by the circle. Water (unless frozen) does not offer much support, as a drowning person sadly discovers. The yielding exercises of tai chi, and blending exercises of aikido are effective training for this skill. They offer practice in receiving and guiding aggressive energy with poise and balance.

This soft approach is very effective with highly emotional individuals. Proactive predatory aggression, however, requires a different skill set and a different spirit. We must project a very different kind of energy.

BEING FIRE

Proactive aggression of the bully, or predator has an entirely different dynamic. Softness is interpreted as weakness, and can intensify aggression. An EARLY and FORCEFUL response is essential. O'Sensei spoke of fire being an essential element of the universe, and an essential quality of his aiki. He symbolized fire with the triangle (spearhead.) Fire is — energy — focus — intensity. These are the essential qualities for skillful action in some situations.

The FIRE element has been largely rejected by modern aikido, which has adopted a one dimensional view. But expressions of FIRE are evident throughout O'Sensei's martial arts and daily life: His thunderous kiai shouts, powerful atemi, intense sword and staff work, ruthless self discipline, intensity, and fiery yet purposeful temper — all express the qualities of FIRE.

Fire is not necessarily destructive. In human interaction it is initiative, assertiveness, and resolve. Working in plain clothes on ghetto streets, I was often approached by crack addicts and gang bangers. Before they got close I would blast out "BACK OFF," with a tone and demeanor that sent a crystal clear message: "You are warned!" It stopped 90% of them in their tracks. They figured it just wasn't worth it. O'Sensei described this action as creating a protective space or "moat" around us. When the intense energy of the fire element within us is released without inhibition — it is rarely ignored.

> Projecting the quality of FIRE to a bully or predator communicates:
> > This target is AWARE of potential danger
> > (regardless of my attempts to deceive or distract)
> > > This target already KNOWS my intentions
> > > (before I can get close)
> > > > This is a HARD target.
> > > > (Better to choose someone easier.)

A forceful warning expressed with a voice and demeanor of pure FIRE, will forestall much aggressive behavior, and can often prevent violence. This is not mere theory. Early in my law enforcement career my gun was frequently drawn in response to a threat. With experience, I discovered that — my hand on a holstered weapon, with a fierce demeanor and deadly serious tone — had far more impact.

TAKING THE INITIATIVE

While predatory violence requires us tapping into the "harder" part of our nature, TIMING is often the deciding factor. We must respond EARLY.

Predatory behavior involves choosing the place and time of assault, and relying on the prey reacting too late. Distraction and deception are used to close distance. Asking for a quarter — for directions — for some other assistance — are all common ploys to get close. This is where magical thinking permeates most martial arts and police training: "If I learn a defensive movement well, reacting in time will be no problem." This is a pervasive myth, reinforced by the subtle choreography of formalized, telegraphed attacks, and the illusions created in demonstrations.

The reality is, if you wait until the (final) attack takes shape, it happens too fast to react in time. My own research, as well as that of the respected Calibre Press police training and research organization, have demonstrated this countless times with both veteran cops and skilled black belts. In close proximity ACTION IS ALWAYS FASTER THAN REACTION.

We must trust and act on our intuition. Our gut feelings are highly developed — primal, early warning systems. If we respond to, rather than ignore or deny our feelings of fear or uneasiness, we have time to issue a forceful warning "Stay Back." If our warning is ignored — we have confirmation the threat is real. We now have options, because we have created space and time. We can call for help, run, deploy a weapon, or strike first. We may use deception and distraction (atemi) as a prelude to a defensive technique or escape.

CONTROLLING TIME

Students of O'Sensei reported that he looked passive only because his initiating actions were so subtle and deceptive. My teacher, Kazuo Chiba remembered Ueshiba admonishing him, "It is NOT budo if you begin your movement AFTER the strike (attack) is in motion." In doing so he essentially moved beyond technique, taking control of the time and space elements of the engagement.

In mastering the time element of his engagements O'Sensei was borrowing from ancient military classics such as the 4000-year-old Art of War by Sun Tzu, who believed it was necessary to "dictate the nature" of the battle. His strategy was — lead the adversary to unfamiliar ground, and compel them to fight on YOUR TERMS.

The American combat strategist, John Boyd, was a modern master of this strategy. By controlling the "tempo" of the encounter — staying one step ahead — he forced his adversaries in air to air combat to continuously react to him. He became a legend at the Top Gun Air Combat School where he instructed. He was never defeated.

Boyd coached generals and government officials at the highest levels in planning the Desert Storm invasion of Iraq. His strategy kept Iraqi generals off balance and guessing — controlling the "decision making cycle" of battle from beginning to end. This strategy is credited with ending the war quickly, and minimizing loss of life on both sides.

Exploring the time dimension of encounters reveals how moving EARLY is an effective alternative to moving QUICKLY. But it seems fast. When I attacked the Shingu Dojo headmaster, Michio Hikitsuchi with a fast, explosive thrust, he moved very slowly. Yet, his fist was at my eyes before my strike reached him. It seemed to defy logic.

Martial arts can be useful for self defense, but we must also develop skill of identifying the nature of the aggressive behavior we face, and choosing the best response. Training should strengthen our capacity for maintaining a quiet stable presence when appropriate, and explosive, dynamic action when called for. All the qualities necessary to respond effectively are within each one of us.

6. Responding to Aggression — Takemusu Aiki II

TAKEMUSU Aiki is the principle which forms the foundation for O'Sensei's unique Budo. It is generally regarded as an abstract esoteric philosophy, or oversimplified as merely generating unlimited martial techniques. My experience suggests it is much more than this — it is a practical guide for identifying and releasing the vast energy resources within us. With unrestricted and uninhibited access to these powerful resources we can respond effectively in situations of conflict or danger.

Martial arts training usually involves practicing self defense techniques, then hoping our techniques are good enough to meet the threat. Very few dojos, regardless of style train students in threat assessment and tactical decision making. But, accurately assessing the nature of the threat is critical for wise, decisive action. Avoiding confusion, over reaction or under reaction is key to decisive action. This is more important than our technical skills.

What follows is a short-hand guide for rapid threat assessment. It has helped me survive physically, emotionally, and legally during 30 years of law enforcement work on the streets of New York and mental health work in psychiatric settings. It is based on both O'Sensei's Takemusu Aiki principles, and studying the criminal histories of hundreds of convicted felons:

What is the Nature of this Threat?

What is my Best Response?

FOUR DIFFERENT AGGRESSIVE THREATS
1) FACING ANGER AND HOSTILITY

Conflict is a fact of life, and cannot always be avoided. Facing the anger or open hostility of someone is unfortunately not uncommon. It is an inherent part of many jobs such as law enforcement, education and mental health work. But, almost any work, whether it be in education, health care, business or any form of public service sometimes involves interpersonal conflict where emotions run high. We need to be skilled in managing these situations, both for reasons of safety, and minimizing stress in our life.

Whether it is the wrath of a customer — client — student — patient — coworker — relative — or stranger on the street — the dynamics of anger are the same. The motivation for directing anger at us is RELEASE OF EMOTION, and VENTING of the anger. It is actually quite rare for a loud, angry person to become a threat to our safety, because the verbal expression of emotion helps them keep (physical) control. This understanding is important to avoid over reacting.

Many emotions such as sadness — grief — loss — disappointment — embarrassment — or fear are painful. It is helpful to recognize that when you are facing an angry individual you are facing someone in pain. Help them release their pain. The best way to do this is to LISTEN. Just listen. It is the most powerful method I have found for de-escalating potentially violent situations.

How do you feel when you are very upset, and the person you are with listens to you? Really listens. Without talking, interrupting or arguing. It is a rare and wonderful experience. It is rare because it takes strong self discipline. The kind of strength martial arts is intended to develop. It is the purpose of all the "shugyo" training in traditional martial arts.

Motivation	→	Releasing emotion / Expression of emotional pain
Safest Response	→	Disciplined Listening / Use of centering / breathing skills
Takemusu Aiki Quality	→	EARTH (quiet and stable) /
Challenge	→	Over Reacting / Arguing / Defensive anger

2) FACING RAGE

Anger can escalate suddenly or gradually beyond an individual's capacity to cope. Then they can become IRRATIONAL. At this level of emotion they neither hear nor respond to verbal communication. Words only serve to further agitate them. Whoever is nearby becomes the target of their rage. Whether a motorist with road rage, a homeless or hospitalized mental patient, or mean drunk, the dynamic is the same — they are UNPREDICTABLE.

In this situation our NON-VERBAL COMMUNICATION becomes very important. A stable posture with a defensive — but non-aggressive arm/ hand gesture works best. I always combine this with backing away. CREAT-ING SPACE — a safety buffer, usually lowers the anxiety level of a person struggling to maintain control. Space also provides critical reaction time in case of violence.

Aggressor Motivation	→	Explosive release of anger / Agitation / Delusions
Safest Response	→	Non-Verbal: Back Away / Stable Non-aggressive Posture Prepared to run /or fight if pursued
Takemusu Aiki Quality	→	EARTH (stability) retreat without argument
		FIRE if pursued — run or fight
Challenge	→	Under-reaction — Drawn into verbal exchange — Failing to immediately create buffer of safety

3) THEFT (Robbery)

Theft of our property is infuriating, and the threats and intimidation which may accompany a robbery are frightening. Keeping presence of mind for accurate threat assessment is critical:

Is there URGENCY to get PROPERTY — your money, wallet, watch, iPhone etc ?

Are they focused on getting the property and FLEEING?

These are indicators of LOW to MODERATE level of danger. This is the drug addict or thief who wants to get away asap. Harming you is not the priority. The thief wants to "take the money and run." If we DO NOT RESIST — we help them keep control of themselves, and leave quickly.

You do have the legal right to resist. If you choose this option the likelihood of violence is high, and the chance of injury or death to someone is high. It could be you, or them — violence is always unpredictable. In robbery situations the CHOICE to resist or comply is usually YOURS. If you feel deeply that your wallet is worth fighting for — do it. You must take responsibility for the consequences of your decision.

Keeping some presence of mind, complying, and giving police a good description of the perpetrator is usually the safest course of action in cases of theft.

Aggressive Motivation	→	Material gain / get Property and quickly flee
Safest Response	→	Tactical Compliance: If Confronted — Toss property toward thief and flee in opposite direction (highly effective distraction) If Held — Stay calm/and compliant which helps them stay calm
Takemusu Aiki Quality	→	EARTH (stable, calm)
	→	WATER (compliance/ nonresistance)
Challenge	→	Over-Reaction — Anger / Panic / Impulsive (non-tactical) resistance — Emotional attachment to property

Some martial artists students question the recommendation to comply when confronted with theft. They feel it is their "right" or "duty" to fight. This is usually the fault of macho instructors with little experience dealing with real world violence. Research shows compliance is clearly the safest response to aggressive behavior motivated by desire for property.

Martial artists who believe it is their "duty" to fight over property or reputation, have been poorly trained. To them I say — material objects or reputation have nothing to do with honor or budo. There are better ways to prove your manhood than engaging in unnecessary violence. Do not be a prisoner of your ego. Real warriors choose their battles carefully.

4) VIOLENT PREDATORS

This is the worst case scenario, and can usually be quickly identified. A truly violent individual uses robbery, kidnapping or home invasion as an excuse for violence. The purpose is to hurt, terrorize, or kill. Fortunately, they make up only a tiny percentage of the criminal population. They are the violent muggers, rapists and serial killers. They may be a predatory bar fighter masquerading as just an obnoxious drunk, or a wolf pack of gang bangers.

The dynamics of this aggression are unique. This behavior is premeditated, and usually well planned. This situation LACKS the "TAKE AND FLEE" URGENCY of the common thief. Predators are well practiced in violence. When property is offered — without immediate response, you are likely dealing with a violent predator.

There will often be "Herding Behavior," similar to that of predators in the wild. They move prey to a more advantageous location. They will order (pull/push/drag) you to a less public/more private spot. Taking the time to

MOVE YOU is a precursor to the HIGHEST LEVEL OF VIOLENCE. This is no longer mere theft, this is life or death.

We have a significant tactical advantage when dealing with predators. Unlike the thief who takes advantage of the element of surprise to strike and run. Herding behavior takes time. The element of surprise has been lost. You now own it — use it wisely:

* Recognize the severity of the threat

* Choose your moment tactically/ to move EXPLOSIVELY
>   — attacking or escaping
>   —Use distraction/
>   misdirection / kiai/
>   atemi/screaming

* Use whatever weapon is available — keys/pen/finger
>   nails/teeth

* Release primal survival instincts — "jaws + claws"

* Primary Targets of attack are eyes/throat (hands/fingers if you are held)

Aggressor Motivation	→	Violence/ Domination/ Inflicting Pain
Safest Response	→	Explosive Action — Timing is critical
		Use of distraction/misdirection as prelude for attack/escape
Takemusu Aiki Quality	→	FIRE (explosive action)
Challenge	→	Under-reaction / Mistaking predator for common thief /Denial (denying gravity of situation) /Failure to release (violent primal) survival instincts

STRENGTHENING DECISIVE ACTION

Most of us have a deep rooted inhibition against harming another human being. A high stress moment when confronting violence is a bad time to decide how far you are willing to go to survive, or save the life of someone else. NOW is the time for soul searching, personal exploration and clarifying your most deeply held values about using violence to protect self or others. This will free you to act decisively. Whatever actions we then take will be powerful, and free from hesitation or guilt.

First, let us dispel two illusions about violence:

Myth: Aikido / tai chi are non violent arts therefore they can be applied without injuring anyone.

Reality: If you choose to apply aikido, tai chi or any "nonviolent" physical intervention practiced in a gentle manner during training, you must be prepared for the person being seriously injured or killed when they fall. Real combat is always unpredictable. The consequences of your actions will be judged less by your intention — than by the "reasonableness" of your decision to fight.

Myth: I am not big enough, strong enough or skilled enough to protect myself against a violent criminal, so it is always better to comply.

Reality: Anyone can inflict distracting pain/or devastating injury on another person regardless of size. It has more to do with willingness to release primal survival instincts than size or skills:

* Case History — Westbury, NY — Small women escapes, after biting off the finger of a predator holding her at knifepoint in her car.

* Case History — Bushwick, Brooklyn, NY — Small man escapes, after blinding large knife wielding predator with a handful of dirt.

CLARIFY YOUR VALUES

Am I willing to fight — and accept the consequences of combat if:

> Insulted?.........Challenged?........Embarrassed?.........Humiliated?.

Am I willing to fight to protect my:

> Wallet?........Watch?........iPhone?........Car?

Am I willing to use maximum force — which may result in injury or death if confronted with:

> Robbery?......Home Invasion?.......Rape?......Car jacking?.

Am I willing to use force — even Lethal Force — to survive a violent assault:

> against Me?.....…......my Family?.........Friend?...........a Stranger?

If the situation is beyond my martial arts skills — am I willing to use my most violent animal instincts to survive:

> Claws?.................Jaws?............Most lethal martial techniques ?

This exercise has no right or wrong answers. The "right" answer is what is honest and true for you. As a wise fellow once said "Know Thy Self" — This is especially true when facing danger.

REFERENCE GUIDE FOR MANAGING AGGRESSIVE BEHAVIOR:

(POST — At your work place and share with co-workers)

FACING ANGER & HOSTILITY: ⌑

Motivation	→	To Be Heard/Release of Anger
Takemusu Aiki Quality	→	EARTH Quiet-Stable-Balanced/Empathy
Safest Response	→	Disciplined Listening/Use Breath and Centering skills
Challenge	→	Over reacting/Arguing/Defensive anger

FACING RAGE: ⌑

Motivation	→	Emotional pain/Emotional release
Takemusu Aiki Quality	→	EARTH Stability/Non verbal communication/Give space
Safest Response	→	Back away without argument/Stable posture — prepared to run or fight if pursued
Challenge	→	Under reacting/verbal altercation/failing to create space (safety buffer)

THEFT (Robbery): ⬤

Motivation	→	Steal property and quickly flee
Takemusu Aiki Quality	→	WATER Non-resistance
Safest Response	→	Tactical compliance, Quietly comply/ or throw property down and run
Challenge	→	Over reaction/Emotional attachment to property

VIOLENT PREDATORS: ▶

Motivation	→	Violence/Domination/Inflicting pain
Takemusu Aiki Quality	→	FIRE Explosive energy — to escape or attack
Safest Response	→	Pre-emptive action/Use distraction-misdirection-kiai-atemi-jaws-claws
Challenge	→	Under reaction/Denial — mistaking predator for common thief

7. The Will to Survive

I have a habit of picking up ghetto dogs, and trying to get them adopted. The nastiest, mangiest critters never get adopted, so I am stuck with them. My wife has the patience of a saint about this. After giving them a bath, and buying them a pretty collar, I take them to the shelter for adoption, but leave my phone number. On the tenth day, I usually get the call, " Tomorrow is the last day before we destroy him, if you want to pick him up…" Then I go back, disgusted that they failed to get it adopted. We then have our usual argument over me paying an "adoption fee" for a dog I do not want!

But they usually turn out to be great dogs, and every one of these creatures has taught me something. It does not take long for wild critters to become lazy homebodies, even the pit dogs get used to the easy life, and mellow out.

If I asked you whether a swan could handle two pit bulls, what would you say? How about an alley cat against 3 dogs? No contest, right? A swan hit the telephone wires above my house, then tumbled down my roof, landing right on Blacky, as he ate his dog food outside. He went after the swan, and soon my other pit mix, Rambo, heard the commotion and joined in. The swan needed a moment to get oriented from the fall, then fired that long neck forward at any target within range, slamming it's big beak into their faces each time they moved in. It also gave some real good shots with its elbows, at the base of its wings. Having lost a little chunk of my left wrist from attempting to break up a dog fight between two Alaskan malamutes, I sat this one out. The swan lost some feathers, but successfully fought them off. With no teeth, and no claws it fought them to a stalemate. What it had was superior combat state of mind, and more focused intent. The dogs were messing with it, but the swan was fighting for its life.

That swan was so riled up that when I approached to get it out of my yard, it almost took my arm off, so I called animal control. They said they did not handle hyped up swans because they are so aggressive, and gave me the number of a wild bird rescue service, who would send someone. While waiting, I tried again to move the bird, but neither I nor the dogs could get near it. In a few minutes a little Volkswagen pulled up. An old lady got out. She had no animal control equipment. I warned her, but she just grabbed a bath towel from her car, and ignored my warnings. As she approached, the swan made the same aggressive gestures, and intense hissing sounds that kept me and the dogs away. But, she just walked right up to it, scooped up the big bird in the bath towel, and carried it herself to her car.

Was she deaf, and not able to hear those intense hissing sounds? Was her eye sight so poor she did not see the threatening aggressive gestures? How could this little old lady so effortlessly do what I could not, and two aroused pit dogs could not do? She was more decisive. She had superior intent. She had the mind of the warrior.

> In the beginning of all things, wisdom and knowledge were with the animals, for Tirawa, the One Above did not speak directly to man. He sent certain animals to tell men that he showed himself through the beasts, and that from them, and from the stars and the sun and the moon should man learn...all things tell of Tirawa.
>
> *Eagle Chief (Letakos-Lesa) (late 19th century) Pawnee*

A few years later, a stray cat wandered into the yard, and got cornered by my three ghetto dogs. I heard the high pitched screech of a cat fighting, and ran outside. There was a hell of a commotion as I raced around back to find all three dogs in retreat. Two were bleeding from around the eyes. The cat was now on the top of the fence, slowly walking away. Leaving me with $600 in vet bills. Against all odds, the cat released a ferocity that caught the dogs off guard, overwhelmed them, and dominated the encounter. For a few moments it was not an alley cat, it was a mountain lion.

I observed it again yesterday while working. A cat was sitting in the middle of the road as I walked by, when a big dog keyed in on it, and moved quickly toward it. The decisive action of the cat was not to run, which would triggered the dog's predatory chase instinct. Instead, with exquisite timing, when the dog was about six paces away, the cat arched its back, seeming to double its size. Along with this action came a piercing gaze which burned right through the dogs limited intent. The dog was stopped in its tracks. It turned and retreated, its body language indicating "it ain't worth it."

This will to survive can manifest unimaginable power. A small creature gave me the most dramatic demonstration of this, again, in my own back yard. It was during a cold wet November in New York. I barely noticed the strange sound at first, which continued relentlessly for three days, until it began to drive me crazy. It emanated non-stop from the garden located behind my garage, about 50 yards from the house. At first I thought it was a cricket, but the sound had a long, whiny, ghostly quality to it that continued past daybreak.

On the third day I hunted for the source. There was nothing behind the garage, and nothing in the garden? As I got close the sound momentarily stopped, but then started again. It was coming from my compost patch, the big pile of dirt and kitchen scrapes which eventually becomes my fertilizer. It took a bit of digging, but deep in the middle of all that mud and garbage was a tiny black furry creature of some kind, perhaps a mouse? The sound stopped when I picked it up. There was no movement, but two small bright green eyes were open and glaring at me.

I brought it in the house and washed all the mud off, still unsure what it was. My wife took out her hair dryer and blew warm air on it for a while, and it finally started to move. With the wet mud washed off and the fur dried we could see it was a three day old jet black kitten. A cat must have given birth to a litter of kittens in the compost patch, which generated a little heat even in cold wet weather. This was the lone survivor. It just would not give in to its fate, it refused to give up. It would drive any humans within earshot crazy until they responded. It simply refused to die.

Ikkyo grew into the biggest, strongest cat I ever saw. My friend Bill adopted him, and they remained best buddies for sixteen years. Through those years Bill told stories of all the things that strange and wonderful creature taught him. He was my teacher too. From him I learned that the will to survive can be infinitely more powerful than I ever imagined.

❦ ❦ ❦ ❦

The power of intent, purpose, and focus is clearly seen in the animal world, but it makes all the difference with us so-called "civilized" creatures too. Nick was a middle-aged Italian gentleman, who was my supervisor at a hospital counseling clinic. He did not look like it, but a few decades before, in his bad old days, he had been a streetwise dope dealer. One night he took his wife out to a nice bar and grill. When he returned to their table with drinks, a pair of obnoxious drunks (off-duty cops) were all over her. He explained that she was his wife, and asked them to leave, but they ignored him with a casual "go fuck off". Two tough street cops, with size, police training, and probably armed. Nick had done a little boxing in his youth, never practiced martial arts, and had no gun. So, what are the odds?

Nick walks away without an argument. They chuckle at their victory.

Combat begins with the chair from the next table slamming into the first guy's head; he was unconscious before his lifeless body hit the floor. The second adversary jumps up out of his seat, just in time to see what was left of the chair shatter his jaw. Game over. Duration of the battle: about fifteen seconds.

He could have chosen other options; there are always options. Nick said that being sued, and having to pay the $5000 medical bills of those jerks, was worth the price of defending his wife. We must all get better at finding non-violent solutions to conflict, but I cannot help feeling the universe smiled just a bit, as that chair accomplished its mission. Demand someone's wallet or watch, and they may give it to you without a fight. But, threaten their family or humiliate them, and you may pay a very high price.

Nick's story illustrates the vast difference between martial arts or sport fighting vs. real world combat. Outside of a dojo or an MMA cage, a real warrior creates his or her own rules, as the situation demands. The warrior is free of rules, or free to change the rules any time. Whether the response is violent, or creative non-violence, it is what O'Sensei described as takemusu aiki — "unrestricted response."

It is Saturday night, and I take my daughter to her favorite place, (my least favorite place) the Shopping Mall. As we leave the mall is closing. We enter a darkening parking lot, passing a place of special significance to me. It is a heroic battleground. Just a few years ago, a woman was returning to her car at just about this same time, when she was accosted at knife point. The predator dragged her inside her car, holding the knife to her face. She suddenly bit off one of his fingers holding the knife. Stunned, he could not react in time to prevent her escape. Police followed the blood trail, finding him cowering behind the building, clutching his bleeding hand. Against all odds, a warrior again prevails.

This essence of the warrior, this power of intent and purpose was never more evident than during the Vietnam war. The reason America lost was because the Vietnamese people had an unrelenting sense of purpose, and superior intent. As a country, our sense of purpose quickly wore thin, and our commitment grew weak, while our adversary's focus and commitment was unwavering. The reason is — our purpose was abstract; "Communism is bad," while their's was concrete; defending their homeland. To the Vietnamese people Americans were just the latest in a long line of invaders for over a thousand years; the Chinese, the Japanese, the French, among others. How arrogant we were to believe we could break their will when so many invading armies had tried and failed. We were blind to the fact that they wore down every invading army eventually.

My friend John had the better equipment, better food, better medical care, and was physically stronger than any rice paddy Charley in sandals and pajamas. But after two hours, when he had piss he climbed out of his fox hole, and got blown apart pretty badly while pissing behind a tree. His Vietnamese counterpart lived in his hole for days, perhaps weeks at a time, pissing and shitting on himself, and living for weeks on a little ball of rice. Until just the right moment, then he would jump out behind enemy lines, sometimes right in the middle of an American encampment, and let loose all kinds of hell with his low tech AK-47 rifle.

We could not match that level of self disciple, and internal strength. Even with all our B-52 bombers, helicopter gunships, and tons of defoliating chemical weapons, we could not match the warrior spirit of that adversary. We had all the advanced hardware (external strength) and our soldiers had Army discipline, but the Vietnamese had a stronger sense of purpose, and stronger self-discipline (internal strength.) To the few who knew anything about the Vietnamese people and their history, the outcome of that war was a forgone conclusion. But we had very little knowledge about them, and little interest in knowing. Modern culture is focused on appearances, and outward strength. Asians, and perhaps all cultures with a connection to ancient roots, seem more attuned to substance, and less distracted by superficial attributes. The computer age is focused on technology, while ancient wisdom focuses on the mind.

We have so much yet to learn about real strength, and what it means to be a warrior. But, when we look with eyes open, we see it all around us. In the behavior and actions of wild creatures to survive, in the spirit of ancient cultures, in little old ladies with bath towels and steel nerves, or young women who refuse to be victims — so much warrior wisdom available for us to learn.

8. Warriors Die Well

I have had two near-fatal injuries, one life-threatening illness, and have come within a few inches of being hit by a speeding train. Each incident served as a reminder that death is always near. Brushes with death are sobering reminders of the temporary nature of all things. I watch the beautiful fall colors; the blazing gold and orange leaves sailing down from the big maple outside my window. This is death, but it is not ugly, not frightening; it is beautiful and natural. We are no different from those bright blazing leaves at their end.

To be part of nature is to be temporary. The thought of my end is hard to comprehend, but easier than the thought of infinity. Never ending life with no limits, no boundaries? That is terrifying. Endings are everywhere in nature — things coming — going — passing away: clouds, seasons, storms. Endings feel natural, whereas "forever' is incomprehensible.

We all have private moments when we are frightened by the thought of our own passing. The warrior ethic embraces this fear, and uses it as fuel for living well — living fully now, because there is no time to waste! Carlos Castaneda described it masterfully in his books about the Yakui Indian warrior, Don Juan Matus, who kept death close at hand "just over his right shoulder." Death was his advisor, his ally — available at times of confusion. And able to banish all that is petty and superficial.

How does a real warrior die? Not in novels or folklore, but in real life, in our time? Fortunately, there are many wonderful examples of modern day warriors living well and dying well:

Ann Rivers was an eighty-eight-year-old lady from the Green Mountains of Vermont. I only met her in death, but her son recounted how strongly she lived. She rebuffed all his attempts to have her leave the cabin, and move in with him, or into a retirement community. In 1997, a state trooper checked on her, and found her dead. He heard there was a physician training up in the hills who could sign a death certificate. He found me and my training partner Dave. We accompanied him back up to her cabin.

Her cabin was still warm, from a hot wood-burning stove, with a large pile of freshly split wood next to it. She had just split more wood the previous night, before going to bed.

Mrs. Rivers appeared to have passed away in her sleep during the night. Her face was old and wrinkled, but her body was muscular. Especially her hands and arms. She had obviously been splitting and carrying wood, as well as performing lots of other heavy physical work for many years. She was strong, independent, and not afraid of living alone. An easy, comfortable life had no appeal to her. She died as she lived, simply and naturally. Unlike so many old folks these days, she died with her dignity intact.

When I lived in Japan, I used to marvel at the old men who attended **Ueshiba Sensei's 6:30 a.m. class** each day, at the Hombu Dojo in Tokyo. Why so many old men? It was because they trained through their youth, through middle age, and just never stopped training. Martial arts was not a hobby for them, it was a life style, training was their life. It was not uncommon for an old man to die while training in that class. It was not tragic, it was by choice. They died doing what they loved. They lived fully to the last moment. Wonderful lives, wonderful deaths.

Joy Johnson ran the twenty-six miles of the New York Marathon last week at age eighty-six, as she did every year. At mile twenty, she fell and banged her face and head. After medics bandaged her up, they insisted she stop running, and let them take her to a hospital. She thanked them, then ran off to join the other runners. She had only six miles to go.

There must have been a special joy in that accomplishment. That night, she died in her sleep. Mrs. Johnson could have lived the comfortable, safe life of a "normal" old person. She could have quit running at age forty or fifty as society expects. She could have played it safe, and gone to the hospital. But eighty-six-year-old marathon runners do not play it safe, and do not do what is expected, they live! Warriors are free to take risks, they are not prisoners to "playing it safe."

The last few years of his life, **Tom J. Collings,** my father, became increasingly fearful of losing his memory, and becoming senile. Common memory lapses, such as misplacing his keys, reinforced his fears. It became his preoccupation. For a ruthlessly independent workaholic, aging and retirement can be a painful time. A worker with no work is lost. Society praises a "good family man" who lives only to work and attend to his families needs. But, the retired family man with grown children has lost his identity, his purpose. A preoccupation with physical or mental changes fills this void, as well as financial concerns. Those last years were difficult for him, but in the last year of his life there was a dramatic change.

My mother was hospitalized for several months with serious heart problems, which blew away all dad's other preoccupations and concerns. Although no longer able to drive very well, he managed the ten-mile roundtrip drive to the hospital twice every day, seven days a week. Attending to mother's medical needs overshadowed everything else, and gave meaning and focus to his life again. Now he had to make meals himself, take care of the house himself, and monitor the quality of care she received at the hospital. He did it without complaint, and at eighty-four, seemed stronger and healthier than he had been for a long time.

After several months my mother finally came home, and Dad continued to focus on her needs and her recovery. But I noticed that his appetite was becoming poor, and his usual hyperactive energy was gone. He resisted going to see a doctor but finally went, receiving a long drawn out series of tests. Before the first doctor visit, he casually mentioned that he would die soon, and that all the tests were a silly waste of time. This seemed like more neurotic anxiety of a preoccupied old man; after all, he was not doctor, and had no serious symptoms other than poor appetite and a little fatigue.

As months of tests passed, he became more focused and calm than I had seen him in years. He insisted I pay attention without comment as he reviewed his finances, his will, and his detailed instructions for helping my

mother manage bills, finances etc. Contrary to any definitive medical information, he insisted he would be gone in a few months, and needed to get all his business in order. I finally stopped protesting; he knew something no one else did, even the doctors. In fact, during all the months he had focused on my mother's needs, he knew exactly what was happening to him, but kept it to himself.

Finally, a doctor gave him a diagnosis of terminal stomach cancer, with a prognosis of two months to live. His reaction was simply, "I told you, I knew that. Enough already with the doctors, now let's go home." From that day on, he had no more concerns about losing his memory or becoming senile. He was relieved. Even his preoccupation with my mother's financial security faded, as he placed his trust in my sister and me to look out for her interests.

The month before he died, I took a leave from work to be with him every day, and help my mother care for him. His abdominal wall became hard as a rock, and he could not eat anything, but he did not have much pain.

Since he always enjoyed his Pepsi with lemon, he got a big Cola-morphine cocktail each day. Judging from the smile on his face, and his frequent question "When is it going to start hurting?" I guess they worked pretty well.

I returned from the store one day to find that he had slipped into a coma. His breathing was very loud, with a strange sound I had never heard before. The visiting nurse explained that as the body approaches death, it often make a last, valiant attempt to revive itself through powerful breathing, before slipping away. In a few minutes, the sounds of his breath gradually faded, and he was gone. His death was harder for the family, than for him. I feel privileged to have closely witnessed a man face his death, as a welcome end to a good life.

🌿 🌿 🌿 🌿

My mother, **Catherine Collings** carried on an active life for about ten years after my father's passing, reaching the age of ninety-five before becoming too unsteady to walk. In the hospital, surgeons told her they could not restore circulation to her legs, and would need to amputate them to save her life. When I learned of her diagnosis, the doctors had already scheduled a variety of preoperative procedures, and scheduled her surgery for later in the week. We were instructed to review a bunch of forms with her and have her sign them. For several days, my sister and I discussed her condition with her, but when it came to signing the forms, she would just say, "Let God decide." After a few days, everyone was getting impatient, since without the signed forms no procedures could begin.

During our last attempt to have her sign the papers, and her continuing to say "Let God decide," I finally woke up and understood. She had expressed her decision clearly several days before, but our own fears and emotional issues clouded our understanding. I probably had known all along what her decision would be, but had trouble facing it. Realizing the strength of her faith and power of her spiritual life, it became so obvious. There would be no "heroic" attempts to prolong a wonderful and fulfilled life of ninety five years. Spending her final days in a nursing home as a double-amputee, was not prolonging any kind of meaningful life. For her, it was a no brainer. She was ready to go.

We got her out of the hospital fast, to the great irritation and dismay of all the doctors involved in her care. "Stop worrying, honey; I will be with God soon. I hope you will be OK." She spent her final weeks praying a lot, but not out of fear. For her, it was going home. We made sure she got meds to keep her reasonably comfortable. She died a few weeks later.

It was the depth of her faith, and lack of fear, that was so hard for all of us to handle, especially the medical staff. We have so few models of such spiritual power and warrior courage. She lived in a different dimension, which most of us can only imagine. But, she showed us what is possible. Courage is not really an accurate term for her attitude toward dying. When you have no fear, you do not need courage. Her only concern was our welfare. This level of consciousness is beyond warrior, it is more accurately described as enlightenment.

The original body
Must return to
Its original place:
Do not search
For what cannot be found.

No one really knows
The nature of birth
Nor the true dwelling place:
We return to the source,
And turn to dust.

Many paths lead from
The foot of the mountain
But at the peak
We all gaze at the
Single bright moon.

If at the end of our journey
There is no final
Resting place
Then we need not fear
Losing our way.

"Skeletons" by Zen monk Ikkyu 1394–1481

VIII.

TRAINING AND TEACHING
WITH INTEGRITY

1. O'Sensei's Battlefield Awareness

"Swallowing the field of vision I am blind.
Through me Life sees."

I never met my grandfather, Lt. John Barclay Clibborn. He fought with the 3rd Canadian Mounted Rifles in World War I. He was killed in France, by a sniper. My partner, Leon, had a gun put to his head, as he intervened during a robbery at a Brooklyn restaurant. As he confronted the perp, another member of the robbery team came from behind. He just barely survived. The majority of street muggers whose parole I supervised, preferred to accost victims from the rear; yoking — choking — clubbing — or placing weapons to their head from behind, as they did with Leon.

Whether engaging sword wielding adversaries in the chaos of the battlefield, or a sniper hundreds of yards away, the attack of choice is always your adversary's blind side or rear. Hunters and predators of all species — whether lions, wolves, or human street predators, instinctively know to approach from the blind sides or rear.

Soldiers and cops quickly learn (if they are lucky) they must resist becoming consumed by what is in front of them. The science of battlefield survival taught in traditional Japanese schools of swordsmanship recognized this problem. A critical skill was identified, known as " happo zanshin." It is a visual/mental skill which counteracts the danger of tunnel vision when under stress. Early bujutsu techniques were not developed for dueling, but to survive the multiple threats of the battlefield, since a dueling "one on one" mentality on the field of battle had lethal consequences. It is as true today, as it was then.

Happo zanshin is a fluid, rather than fixed awareness. A soft gaze with a broad visual field. Within this skill set, "strong" focus is not as useful as the ability to easily release focus, refocusing on the next threat. The vast array of katas and practice exercises seen in most martial traditions, consisting of continuous turning and reorienting, is training in happo zanshin. These practices have survived through centuries because warriors with multi-directional awareness and the widest field of vision were the survivors.

In the 1950s, a brilliant military strategist and top fighter pilot, John Boyd, was confounded by the ten to one kill ratio that he and his fellow fighter pilots achieved against Russian MiGs during the Korean War. The MiGs were superior aircraft in almost every respect. Except visibility. The American aircraft cockpits offered a spacious 360-degree view, whereas the MiG cockpits were small and restrictive, limiting the pilots' vision. The Americans based their air combat strategy around this one advantage. Taking maximum advantage of their superior field of vision, they stayed one step ahead of the MiG pilots in tactical decision making. Broader vision, and initiating action (being first) proved to be the deciding factors in Korean War air to air combat.

Col. Boyd, who became an aeronautical engineer and test pilot, relentlessly championed this successful "see more and stay one step ahead" tactical decision making theory. He incorporated this strategy into all military aircraft he designed. Resisting the prevailing trend toward greater size, power and loading aircraft with ever more complex technology, he championed small, simple agile aircraft which gave pilots an open expansive view. Because aircraft he designed were far cheaper than those proposed by aircraft manufacturers and the generals in their pockets, he ferociously fought battles within the pentagon — earning the title "Genghis John."

Boyd eventually influenced the US military's overall approach to battle strategy. His "broad view — act and keep them reacting" strategy radically altered the tactics of the US Marine Corps.

O'Sensei also viewed the qualities of awareness as deciding factors in human interaction, basing his aiki budo martial art on this understanding. He saw sparring and competition as too closely resembling dueling and confrontation in its dynamics and mindset. This is not consistent with battlefield survival, therefore not budo. From his perspective, dueling arts such as kendo, boxing, judo (or MMA), while excellent for exercise, encourage absorption in one direction, reinforcing the battlefield weakness of tunnel vision and narrowing awareness.

As awareness training, the soft kata based discipline of tai chi, with its circular orientation and continuous turning is stronger budo training than any sparring arts. Competition has referees to enforce a prohibition against attacks from the flanks or rear. By prohibiting the possibility of attack from the areas of greatest threat, fighting sports of all kinds should be viewed as games, rather than budo, because "one on one" contests, reinforce the narrowing of awareness. Likewise, a cop easily drawn into "confrontation" (notice the root word "front") does not fare well on the street.

A similar dynamic exists with artistic/demonstration oriented martial arts as it does for competitive arts. Focus is narrowly centered on one's own grace, artistry or acrobatics. This performance orientation has strongly influenced the mind set, practice and techniques of modern martial arts. By removing the acute sense of danger — threats from the flanks and rear, the essence of budo is lost.

A strategy which simultaneously protects us from the front, rear and flanks, was a clear priority of Morihei Ueshiba. It is a significant departure from Daito Ryu Aiki Jujitsu, which is far more linear than Ueshiba Aiki Budo. A common training method from the Ueshiba Iwama Dojo, was three person rotation training or "san-nin mawaru." This training method has a second partner attacking from rear, as the first attacks from the front. If a technique fails to protect the defender from both front and rear, it is not the aiki discipline of Ueshiba. Few, if any, other martial arts (including many styles of modern aikido) can meet this criteria, which is why san-nin mawaru training is so rare today.

O'Sensei's weapons curriculum included staff katas, bokken "happo giro" (8 direction cutting) exercises, and the unusual Yagyu based stance of "hanmi." Along with his three person practice, these methods are all designed to instill multi-directional awareness and a "healthy fear" of the rear.

A related practice is the aikido randori exercise, in which multiple training partners lunge or strike at the defender simultaneously, requiring not only a stable, relaxed posture, but a free flowing attention. Engaging any one individual for more than an instant results in entanglement, becoming bogged down, and overwhelmed by the multiple threats.

O'Sensei insisted on the training posture of hanmi, from the Yagyu

Sword School because it places the body on an oblique angle to the person in front, fostering a softer peripheral view of the front, rather than direct — confrontation view. This stance (mental as well physical) seems intended to soften "eye to eye" contact with the adversary, reducing tunnel vision. Hanmi, if practiced correctly enhances broader awareness and a more inclusive visual field. The disciplined use of hanmi helps protect against the all consuming engagement of attention to the front, which paired practice tends to reinforce.

Battlefield awareness, which protects against the tunnel vision of confrontation, transcends victory on the battlefield; it is part of spiritual practice. During situations of danger or conflict, the narrowing of awareness results in ego being easily drawn into confrontation and power struggles. Conflicts arise, and altercations erupt from the front — the realm of emotion, passions, and delusion. Hence the term "con-front-ation." If an eye to eye mentality stimulates passions of the ego, it follows that a softer, broader awareness allows human interaction to be less personalized, less emotional, and less ego driven.

O'Sensei's focus on "battlefield awareness" in the service of purification reflects a lineage dating back to ancient times. In the cultural lore of Japanese swordsmanship, the "Tengu" hold a prominent place. These legendary mountain demon-spirits attack the heart and mind of warriors at vulnerable moments. They are particularly attracted to warriors who become mountain ascetics, attempting purification. Tengu attack from all directions using distraction, misdirection and all manner of deceptions.

Tengu were similar to the elusive "Mara," the demon of attachment and delusion who attacked the mind of the Buddha during his quest for liberation. Mara employed a multitude of ploys, trickery, and disguised attacks. Both the Tengu, and Mara come from all sides, preferring subtle and indirect attacks to catch their victim unaware. The iconic statue of the Buddha in meditation shows his left hand open, in front of his center — willing to receive any hardship and endure all temptation. At the moment of greatest struggle, he reaches down with his right hand touching the earth, infusing his mind with all the strength from the earth. With a stable mind all Mara's attacks fail.

Buddha touching Earth

When he achieved victory over the forces of Mara, the Buddha was asked how his enlightenment made him different from ordinary people. He replied "I am ordinary. The only difference is that now I have a 360-degree view of all things."

mist rolls down

the sleek flanks

of Silver mountain

parts cleanly

round the clearing

where the Tengu cabal

dust shuffle

feather ruffle

2. Deep Roots of Budo

to the high meadow where
a giant snarled oak
that lightning wounds each year
pushes out green buds again
the sleek flanks
of Silver mountain
parts cleanly

SHORTLY after returning from my last trip to Japan, Hurricane Sandy blasted up the East Coast of the United States to New York. It ravaged

the shore of Long Island near my home. That night I listened as powerful winds howled outside, and worried about the old sixty foot oak tree that towers over my house. I waited to hear a crash on the roof.

That old oak is not a pretty tree. Its long limbs have so few leaves it hardly seems alive. In contrast, I had no worries about a newer tree; the beautiful pear tree in the front yard. It was thick with leaves and flowers emanating from every branch. I went to sleep and hoped for the best.

In the morning, there was no power. I looked out my window to find the pretty pear tree had blown over, taking with it phone wires and power lines for the whole neighborhood. It was on its side, with the base ripped out of the ground. Exposed were all its shallow roots. I was amazed to see the ugly old oak tree had handled the storm well. The roots must have been very deep. The unadorned limbs must have been less affected by the high winds.

Long ago my teacher Chiba Sensei scolded us when we criticized soft, "flowery" styles of martial arts, mocking them as "eye candy." He defended them, insisting it was a wonderful thing that people were attracted to artistic and beautiful styles. He called them the "flowers and branches" of the art. He insisted "this life needs beauty and creativity." He then added, "But there must be a small group that focuses on the roots, to keep those roots healthy and strong. Without healthy roots the tree will die. Without strong roots the tree will fall."

What are these roots, this foundation that forms the essential core of budo? Part is the intensity and chaos of the battlefield. Part lies in the silent halls and corridors of the monastery. Both components are necessary. A dojo at its best, simulates danger of the battlefield but without death, and minimizing injury. The fierce heightening of all senses, presence of mind, and hyperalertness are all present. This energy is used both in the service of combat effectiveness, and "shugyo," self purification. Without the internal struggle of shugyo martial art is not budo, it is just fighting. Without a battlefield sense of danger, it is also not budo. It is only recreation.

> *When you know who you are;*
>
> *when your mission is clear and you burn with the inner fire of unbreakable will;*
>
> *no cold can touch your heart;*
>
> *no deluge can dampen your purpose.*
>
> *You know you are alive.*
>
> — native American warrior, 1899

Precision and awareness support safety within this zone of "controlled danger" which is the dojo. Deep stillness, calm, and sensitivity, developed through sustained shugyo practice provides balance to the rigorous, and sometimes explosive nature of budo training. This deep realm of practice strives to achieve balance within the elements of O'Sensei's Takemusu Aiki — Earth (stillness) Fire (explosiveness) Water (resilience).

The roots of true budo are indifferent to all embellishments added for dramatic or acrobatic effect such as "flying kicks" in karate, and high falls in aikido or jujitsu. Performance and exhibition have little relation to serious core practice. You are safely near the roots when it is all about training and substance, rather than appearances.

The foundation of a discipline consists of research, struggle, risk-taking, trial and error, and thousands of mistakes. A joyful struggle. It is not performance. The beauty of martial arts lies not in artistry, but in the extraordinary self discipline exercised during practice.

shu

gyo

3. Unbreakable: Conversations with The Undertaker

ITTING alone in my dojo late one night, I received a call from a fellow named Mark. He said he was a professional wrestler looking for a new trainer. As a kid I used to watch pro wrestling all the time on TV, and even got my dad to take me to some arenas. Those guys seemed like big mindless hulks, but they sure put on a good show. When I got older, and learned it was "fake" I lost interest and stopped watching it. The guy on the phone could not be one of those guys; he was bright, articulate, humble, and a real gentleman.

We talked for a long time about martial arts training. He was particularly interested in the skills of falling, avoiding injuries, and how to keep an aging body together. He asked a lot of questions about O'Sensei and martial arts masters I had trained with in Japan. Mark was fascinated by how good aikido black belts executed powerful joint techniques and dangerous throws without injuring their training partner. He clearly had great respect for that.

I still lived a little like a monk back then, and did not watch much TV. When he mentioned his stage name was "The Undertaker," it meant nothing

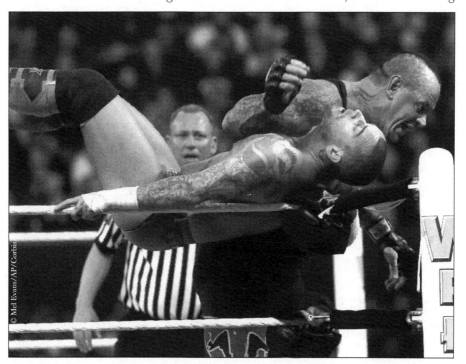

to me. I laughed and said, "that's good, I like that." I figured he was a martial artist contemplating a wrestling career, since his humility gave no clue who he was. I was completely ignorant of the fact he was already a legend, at the top of his game, and that he had turned "The Undertaker" into a multi-million dollar enterprise. Perhaps it was refreshing for him to speak with someone not star struck. Someone who did not want anything from him.

The next day I asked the first student who walked in, "Have you ever heard of a wrestler called Undertaker?" I quickly learned just who this guy was. What was most fascinating to me was his martial arts knowledge, and his depth of understanding. He had a unique point of view on so many things. When he watched the old films of O'Sensei, Mark Calaway did not see an old man with magical power tossing around helpless attackers, as most aikido students do. Nor did he see a phony, choreographed performance with make believe attacks and guys just falling down — as some do.

What he saw was an amazing interaction between people. He saw the tremendous concentration and energy, and how precisely attuned one was to the other's every movement and nuance. Where others saw magic or collusion, Mark saw high level teamwork, and masterful coordination. He was thrilled to see such excitement, energy, and drama — without injuries. He saw O'Sensei through the eyes of a professional athlete and master performer.

Our dialogues explored the level of interaction between two people where communication and coordination reaches spontaneous — unrehearsed action. This was natural for O'Sensei, but rare for the rest of us. In Asian disciplines this is first practiced as "ki musubi," or tying together of energy. When mastered it becomes "takemusu aiki," spontaneous — creative — response.

I related how a paired sword form at a fundraiser demonstration had evolved from prearranged kata to something approaching takemusu aiki. I had practiced the kata hundreds of times with a friend who is a skilled Yagyu swordsman. During the demo, while cutting at full speed, I inexplicably began cutting in totally different ways from the practiced form. It could have been a disaster, ending in serious injury. Yet, my partner spontaneously improvised — flawlessly matching my every movement. As if we had practiced that way a thousand times. How did he do that?

I doubt anyone watching believed all those cuts and parries were spontaneous and unrehearsed. I found it hard to believe myself. How did he so perfectly and unexpectedly adapt? These were strange esoteric Asian concepts to me, but not to Mark. You cannot send your three hundred pound body flying fifteen feet across a wrestling ring, from the top of five foot high ropes, onto your opponent's throat — without a unity of interaction approaching ki musubi and takemusu aiki.

Mark knew I had taken falls for O'Sensei's son, grandson, and other masters during my years in Japan, so he figured I must know something about avoiding injury. "When you get some success, it's easy to get lazy and complacent," he said. This guy must have been reading my mind, because I had been telling myself, and my black belt students that for years. He asked if I was available for private lessons, saying "I can pay whatever you want." That I had not heard before. Assuming he was just another martial arts bum like me (unaware he was a multi-millionaire) I said "don't worry about money. I have a day job, so come by anytime and we'll train." I also gave him the names of one or two guys who were better than me.

These days, I watch him snarl, growl, and radiate his dazzling insanity before the cameras, and appreciate what an *amazing* actor he is. I also know how much incredibly hard work and intense training goes into his wrestling matches. Those guys are not only great showmen, but amazing athletes and very good martial artists.

That The Undertaker has remained at the top of his game for decades, outlasting almost everyone else, is no accident. One reason he has been able to take such brutal punishment well into middle age is because he is a master of ukemi. This term usually denotes the ability to fall, but at the highest level it is a form of masterful cooperation, or "becoming" whatever is being applied to you. At this level both participants create the outcome. And this skill is not just for show — it allows the hardest, and most dangerous training to safely happen. Very few martial artists understand this.

Kobudo, Japan's oldest and most battlefield oriented martial arts emphasize non-competitive paired forms rather than sparring, why? Total commitment of attack is required to honestly simulate the extreme aggressive energy of the battlefield, whereas competition involves caution and holding back out of concern for being "over committed."

The more confidence you develop in your falling skills, the more honestly and accurately you can simulate unrestrained aggression. You move through — rather than up to the partner. You know your balance will be taken if the receiver avoids collision (non-resistance) with your power, but you commit anyway — TO MAKE IT REAL. When balance is lost you instantly change from heavy to light, and from hard to soft, for a safe fall. This transformation is another manifestation of O'Sensei's Takemusu Aiki.

Kaishi waza, or "reversal techniques" in martial arts are really not techniques at all. It is an attitude of nonresistance, where joining can become escaping, leading, or reversing. It is becoming an "active participant" in whatever the partner or opponent is attempting. When you give up the concept of winning/losing, nothing is done "to you," only with you. The difference is huge. It is a kind of cooperation that makes you nearly indestructible. As close to injury-proof as it gets. This allows a sixty-three year old guy like me to train hard with young guys. I can be very heavy or very light, whatever the moment requires.

I once assisted an extraordinary Chinese martial artist to prepare for a national tournament. In my mid fifties, I had no interest in sparring, but none of his students had enough falling skill to train with him at his level. None of them could handle his incredibly powerful throws and sweeps. It was great to discover I had no difficulty handling such power; I felt like a leaf riding the winds of a storm. Leaves don't break — they just get blown around. I stayed light, and let his power send me airborne. It was great fun. He was doing all the work — and I got to fly! (High fall in Japanese is "tobu," the verb "to fly.")

Giving a training partner the opportunity to blast out uninhibited power is about the best gift one martial artist can give to another. Our training was fantastic. Until I decided to become a better "competitor." I decided I should offer more resistance. Big mistake.

As his lightning fast leg sweep exploded under me, I dug in and held my position. I stayed strong and grounded. That decision cost me a $5,000 knee surgery, and six months of rehab. He won the tournament, and thanked me for my help. But, I got more out of that training than he did. The lesson was learned deep in my bones that day — you must give up your position to be indestructible. I never made that mistake again, and have had no serious injuries since.

Those who attacked O'Sensei said he just seemed to "disappear." The great tai chi master Professor Cheng Man-Ch'ing taught: for real strength you must "invest in loss." They were both teaching us that there is great strength in resilience. Falling **skills** are useful, but an **attitude** of non-resistance is essential. Then, go beyond nonresistance to "active participation" in whatever throw, sweep, pin, or attack is directed at you — so that NOTHING is done TO you — ONLY WITH you.

It is ironic that most martial artists seek to win by resisting being thrown — yet, "The Undertaker" does the opposite. He uses non-resistance and cooperation as the secret to his success and longevity. He reminds me that as we age, not only balance but falling (well) becomes an essential physical skill. It becomes our most useful martial arts skill. My mother never recovered from a fall. Hospitals and nursing homes are filled with bodies broken from falls. This is so unnecessary.

We should learn from small children. They fall a thousand times while learning to stand and walk, yet rarely get injured. The more they fall — the better they fall. Yet, an old person falls — and it is often catastrophic. Why? Because somewhere between childhood and old age, we stop falling. Then, we forgot how to do it.

So, please excuse me now — I am not young anymore, so I must get to the dojo. Like my friend "The Undertaker," I have to get in my hundred falls before supper!

4. Martial Arts Fact and Fiction

A martial arts teacher recently described a failed attempt to use a self defense technique outside his dojo. Things did not go well. His comment was, "It's easy to create myth in the dojo." The statement expresses both honesty and clarity. He reminds us that shared fantasies and mythology often overrides truth and common sense. That can get people hurt.

A combination of respect, loyalty, and fear of authority conspire to perpetuate some very unhelpful fantasies. In disciplines with long tradition, questioning accepted forms and training routines may arouse hostility, or create conflict with our teacher and fellow students. Who are we to question the tradition? The curriculum? The master? As a result, erroneous training exercises, useless affectations, and ineffective techniques creep into even the best martial arts. They contaminate the system, and degrade it's integrity.

In an effort to separate myth from reality, I offer a few hard won lessons from the school of hard knocks. For those who worship tradition, or are just "thin skinned," I apologize in advance for my irreverence. I have chosen a few "sacred cows" from three martial arts I have studied. This allows me to offend true believers in all three styles equally:

Myth #1: Karate

In Okinawan karate, a central practice is the Sanchin kata. This wonderful kata was originally an internal Chinese qigong standing meditation practice, from the art Pangai-noon. It was adopted and "hardened" by Okinawan karate teachers, who renamed it "strong man" kata. It seems to have been further hardened as it entered Japanese styles.

The mythology of our dojo was that the unusual pigeon toed stance, and dynamic tension made one virtually immoveable. During demos, boards are broken over the practitioners' arms and legs to "prove" this. To further demonstrate "invincibility," we would plant kicks to the abdominal area of the one performing the kata, with seemingly no affect. We were true believers.

Many years later, a friend, who was not a true believer, asked to test the "immovable" stance of a strong, confident black belt with twenty years of

Sanchin training. Just one well-executed, upward tai chi push sent the powerful looking black belt slamming into the wall behind him.

I love the practice of Sanchin more than ever, and practice it as a serious qigong breath and movement meditation, for health, release of tension, and deep muscle relaxation. I let go of the foolish "immovable" strong man nonsense. It is far too valuable a practice to be turned into some kind of childish performance of strength.

Myth #2: Tai Chi

This example is from a tai chi man who has never quite fit the correct tai chi image. Although he can move with unbelievable grace and beauty, his thousands of hours of Chen soft-hard practice shows through. He won national form and push hands competitions, but was disqualified several times for being "too forceful." He did not fit a New Age image of passive, ever soft, and yielding tai chi.

While a relaxed upper body is central to the gathering of power in tai chi, real world application is not always gentle or graceful. As with most authentic Asian disciplines, the essential core skill sets are usually quite severe. Far from the candy-coated, recreational version. My friend could have softened his appearance and demeanor to better fit the image, expectation, and mythology of the judges. He could have easily won more tournaments. Instead, he chose to drop out of tournaments and exhibitions. Now he just trains.

About ten years ago, a long-brewing dispute between he and a coworker erupted in his office. The large man charged across the room at him. A half step before he reached my friend he ran into the "steel wrapped in cotton" or "fajin," of true tai chi. That one strike knocked the big fellow down, breaking several bones in his face.

There is a time to be soft and receptive, and there is a time to be hard. There is a time to be subtle, and a time to bring the ground up through you slamming into an attacker. My friend was not bound to the tai chi myth of "all soft all the time."

Myth #3: Aikido

Aikido may not be burdened with more myth and fantasy than other martial arts, but it often seems that way. Much of standard aikido practice is far more ritual, ceremony, and performance art than budo. This can be very dangerous for students. In 1974, I was an attendant on a psych ward. A psychotic patient saw me as the devil and began firing kicks at me. I managed to get him down on the ground, then proceeded to pin him with the standard technique taught at most aikido schools. Face down with his arm up against my chest. Then I proceeded to twist from the waist, bending his arm just as I was taught. I would stop when he calmed down and tapped out, just as I was taught.

He never did tap out. Instead, he screamed in pain as the muscles and tendons of his elbow and shoulder ripped. His body involuntarily twisted with the pain. As his body contorted I lost all control. He successfully escaped the torture (his logical perception) and with a partially damaged arm jumped up to continue the fight. As he got up he was screaming at me for trying to break his arm. He was now even more filled with rage, and harder to control. The ensuing fight was not pretty.

But he was supposed to tap! Then he was supposed to relax, and give up, like my training partners. Unfortunately, he had never read the aikido rule book. From his point of view, I had successfully pinned him down, then tried to bust his arm. It took a student of O'Sensei who was not a teacher — but a Tokyo cab driver, to show me the practical old aiki budo pins that do not cause pain, just immobilize. That is what a pin is supposed to do!

Forty years later the same flawed arm bending/twisting "pin" is still the standard finish taught in most aikido schools. Shame on all those teachers for sending students out into the world with such a poorly conceived, and obviously untested tool for self protection. It took a crazy, psych patient, and a cab driver who actually had to use his budo to teach me the reality of pinning.

In the film Harakiri, the samurai Hanshiro Tsugumo confronts the corrupt Lyi Clan regarding their brutal actions towards his son in law Motome. In retribution, he disgraces their three top sword masters in combat by cutting off the top knots of their hair, rather than killing them. Describing their samurai status as only a "facade," he comments:

"A swordsman untested in battle is like the art of swimming mastered on dry land."

Many martial arts teachers, especially "professionals," have never had to test their techniques outside of the dojo. They live sheltered lives. They do not have jobs where they must "get their hands dirty" confronting real world threats. Therefore, they have no idea what is practical and what is just "art." It is their students who pay the price.

Dojos are social institutions. They offer students support and valuable relationships, but like any institution they have shared mythologies, with some practices which become corrupt over time. To learn we need an open mind and some faith in our teacher, but we also need to keep a critical mind. Anything purported to be a means of self protection should be viewed with skepticism until proven effective in the real world. A teacher or school unwilling to periodically review its curriculum with a critical eye is not worthy of teaching serious students.

It is also a good idea to pick the brain of any graduates you may find of that most esteemed institution of higher learning known as "The School of Hard Knocks."

5. Reality Check: Your Martial Art on Adrenaline

MURPHY'S Law states that anything that can go wrong — will go wrong. This is particularly true when attempting something requiring precision, when under stress. Martial Arts were originally created from battlefield experience and the study of human behavior under the stress of combat. A clear understanding of this foundation is essential to keep our practice methods and curriculum valid for use as protection outside the dojo.

Not long ago I wrote an article about responding to aggression using Morihei Ueshiba's concept of Takemusu Aiki. The urgency I felt about this issue was puzzling, since the danger level of my law enforcement job had not changed, nor had any other conditions in my life. So, where was all this tension coming from? Right after completing the article, the murder of twenty six students and teachers at the Sandy Hook School in Newton, Connecticut, occurred about an hour drive from my home. Was it a coincidence? Did I somehow feel something of that young man's insane rage, as it boiled toward explosion? I don't know. What I do know is the PERCEPTION OF DANGER is a mysterious and amazing power. It triggers a series of internal events with the potential to save us or paralyze us.

Sensitivity to danger is most highly developed in creatures who need it most — animals in the wild who rely on it for daily survival. Most humans, with the exception of battlefield warriors and street cops ignore all but the most obvious signals of danger. But anyone can become more attentive to these signals, if awareness is a higher priority than comfort, since the signals of danger are physically and emotionally uncomfortable. This multi-sensory awareness comes to us through an extraordinary, and largely unconscious process. It is an early warning system — a kind of HUMAN RADAR which includes: sound — sight — feel — smell — and other senses researchers are only beginning to discover.

Anxiety is imagined danger, which has no survival value. But FEAR is a response to real and immediate danger, that triggers a unique set of body/mind dynamics. It intensifies many of our capabilities to an extraordinary degree, while crippling others. This phenomena is referred to in military and police training as the ADRENALINE STRESS RESPONSE (ASR.) Without taking into account the powerful effects the fight/flight response has on our body and mind, any preparation or training for this event will be at best flawed, and at worst completely worthless. Training not designed specifically for, and consistent with ASR will provide only the illusion of enhanced safety.

THE ADRENALINE STRESS RESPONSE

When we perceive the slightest cues of imminent danger, everyone — including cops, military special forces, and trained martial artists — experience a RADICAL TRANSFORMATION IN BRAIN AND BODY CHEMISTRY. The change is involuntary and sudden. A powerful mix of stimulant hormones and enzymes flood the system. In many ways we become a very different organism than we were moments before. A slight increase in stress generally improves mental and physical performance, but the intense biological changes in reaction to a threat to our physical safety infuse our system with "nitro fuel," giving us both "super" capabilities and significant disabilities.

During ASR, our most PRIMITIVE BRAIN AND PHYSICAL FUNCTIONS are ACTIVATED. There is hyper-vigilance, with all sensory perceptions heightened to a remarkable degree, enhancing — hearing, smell, visual focus, night vision, muscular strength and stamina. There is a surge in the power and speed of GROSS MOTOR FUNCTION — simple large movements like pushing, pulling, turning, and running speed. The fight/flight response enhances our physical ability to "struggle" or flee.

On the negative side our higher brain functions such as coordination and precision movement are impaired. Both our MOTOR COORDINATION (performing a series of movements) and FINE MOTOR COORDINATION (tasks requiring precise finger movement) are seriously degraded. This deterioration in coordination is due in part to the DRAMATIC INCREASE IN HEART RATE which leaves our body literally "vibrating." BREATH becomes faster and shallow, which further increases heart rate to more than double our resting state.

Extensive training under conditions of stress can mitigate some of these effects, especially when breath training is a central component of practice. Skilled breathing can moderate the rise in heart rate — a core skill of any true budo. Whether it be the "dragon breath" practice of Shaolin monks, or the "combat breathing" of US Special Forces and elite sniper schools, specific breathing skills are a critical component of any effective training for high stress situations.

ASR intensifies VISUAL FOCUS, creating tunnel vision and a corresponding LOSS OF PERIPHERAL VISION — an essential element of battlefield and street survival. For this reason both police and military training emphasize protecting one's FLANKS AND REAR. The effort to compensate for this loss in peripheral vision is seen in the circularity of Chinese disciplines, the multi-directional nature of most martial arts katas, classical Japanese sword schools, and the sword based martial art of aiki budo (aikido.) All these disciplines attempt through training to compensate for the tendency toward TUNNEL VISION which survival stress stimulates.

THE DISCOMFORT OF SURVIVAL MODE

When training emergency responders PREPARING THEM FOR DISCOMFORT is vital. To function well in EMERGENCY MODE you must EXPECT AND ACCEPT the unpleasant biological effects of the aroused state: Dry throat — pounding heart — disruption in breathing — tight chest — nervous tension — must not be misinterpreted as weakness, or it becomes a self-fulfilling prophecy leading to a loss of confidence, self doubt or panic. The

UNPLEASANT FEELINGS must be accepted as the body's NATURAL and UNAVOIDABLE response to danger.

Unlike a street attack where immediate action is required which discharges much of the survival stress, managing aggressive behavior in a work setting may be a long, drawn out affair, with a continuous build up of adrenaline stress during our efforts to deescalate the situation. There is no stopping this intensive build up of adrenaline stress in such tense situations, we can ONLY MANAGE IT using breath and grounding skills.

Another ASR effect is the EXTREME CHANGE IN METABOLISM which immediately shuts down digestion and enters protective mode. To prepare for possible injury both the bladder and intestines may spontaneously empty, a critical survival mechanism to prevents rupture if of the organs are struck. The common phrase "I was so scared I pissed/shit in my pants" has a firm basis in reality. REAL WARRIORS do piss and shit in their pants — it has nothing to do with a lack of courage or competence, and everything to do with survival during combat.

"THE FREEZE" RESPONSE

Another common reaction to sudden danger is freezing. This is an instinctual reaction to being startled. It may be for a moment, or leave us "frozen" in place. The extreme form is fainting. Freezing probably evolved for its survival value in avoiding predators, since becoming frozen in place (motionless) in the forest makes us harder to see. Falling down and appearing dead (fainting) makes us less threatening, and can reduce fear based aggression in some animals. In human encounters, however, freezing seriously interferes with our ability to respond effectively.

To counteract the freeze, warrior training has traditionally incorporated various forms of "war cry" to "JUMP START" the body — mind — and breath. In budo training KIAI both frees us to act, and becomes an effective DISTRACTION WHICH CAN CREATE A FREEZE RESPONSE IN THE ADVERSARY. Kiai is an essential core skill in budo, strengthening our actions on many levels, and counteracting negative effects of ASR.

The intensity of O'SENSEI'S PIERCING SHOUTS during aiki budo training is legendary. Yet, as his art was modernized this critical component of Ueshiba's aiki system has largely been removed. Explosive breath and sound does not fit the casual recreational atmosphere found in modern styles of aikido. The removal of KIAI from martial arts training seriously weakens our capacity for effective action when confronting real violence.

LOSS OF COORDINATION

The marked difference between training performance and real world application is dramatically seen in the use of firearms, and highlights how SKILLS NOT SPECIFICALLY DESIGNED FOR HIGH STRESS SITUATIONS QUICKLY DETERIORATE under conditions of combat. Although the profound difference between a shooting range and combat may seem obvious, firearms training has historically been oriented toward sport and target shooting. The results are striking: Police officers with extensive training on the firearms range experience nearly a 300% drop in accuracy in real gun battles. About 1 in 6 shots hit their mark — in mostly close contact encounters!

Statistics from World War I show an even greater deterioration in skill during combat, in which seven thousand shots were fired (yes 7000) for every enemy casualty. In Vietnam there were 50,000 rounds fired for every enemy casualty. This highlights how many skill sets which are practiced and mastered in training — do not hold up under adrenaline stress. ONLY ASR SPECIFIC SKILLS — that is, skills specifically designed for high stress situations, SURVIVE the transition from training to real world application.

THE TRUTH ABOUT KNIFE DEFENSE

Few instructors let students know they are LIKELY TO BE CUT when defending against a knife. Is this fact concealed in a misguided attempt to build the student's (false) confidence, or is the instructor ignorant of this fact? TELLING STUDENTS THE TRUTH is important for many reasons. The most important being — knowledge is power. When a student knows he/she is likely to be cut in the course of surviving a knife attack, they are less likely to panic if it happens. Being cut is rarely fatal, and often has little effect on one's fighting ability because ASR dramatically INCREASES THE CLOTTING FACTOR OF BLOOD. This limits blood loss in all but the most catastrophic arterial bleeding. I have personally experienced this.

Knife defense training in both martial arts and police defensive tactics too often involves the weapon being presented and clearly visible during the attack. But when interviewing those attacked by edged weapons you commonly hear "I never saw the knife." Weapons defense must emphasize reading the body language of "palming" and other forms of subtle weapon preparation. Making the weapon clearly visible prior to attack instills the dangerous mindset "out of sight, out of mind." We must instill the BUDO MINDSET that: ALL ATTACKS ARE WEAPONS ATTACKS.

Practicing specific "weapons techniques" is a weak defensive strategy. ANY TECHNIQUE NOT TACTICALLY SOUND AGAINST A WEAPON should be DISCARDED. A last minute selection of a "weapon technique" or last moment re-adjustment for a weapon is unrealistic. An effective skill set involves a SMALL REPERTOIRE OF BROADLY APPLICABLE TECHNIQUES. Unfortunately, it is the nature of martial arts organizations to add ever more elaborate curriculums, with large numbers of variations required for advancement through the ranks. Yet, in the realm of life and death it is QUALITY RATHER THAN QUANTITY that keeps us alive.

Teachers must free themselves from the mythology of legend, and influence of "action heroes." Evasion and escape (survival) is challenging enough, without added complexity. Many impressive looking disarming — throwing — pinning techniques involve complex motor coordination suitable only for demonstration and the controlled environment of the dojo. Surviving edged weapons requires the simple, effective movements found at the CORE of most traditional martial styles — FREE FROM THE ARTISTIC EMBELLISHMENTS AND ACROBATICS which often surround and cover it. Do we want to impress students, or save their life?

PAIN COMPLIANCE AND PRESSURE POINTS

It is important to understand that ASR SIGNIFICANTLY REDUCES the PERCEPTION OF PAIN. On one occasion when I sustained a deep gash across my forearm exposing four inches of bone, I felt no pain for almost a half hour while in survival mode. After a major car accident I spent several minutes assisting occupants out of the other car before becoming aware of the big gash in my leg. In other high stress situations I have had teeth knocked out, and dislocated bones which I only noticed later on. This state of "feeling no pain" is well known to anyone who has ever been drunk, or injured in some highly charged situation.

While this altered perception of pain has survival value, it also helps the bad guy. I have applied powerful wrist locks to criminals resisting arrest — that HAD NO EFFECT. Half that much torque in the dojo has had most black belt training partners howling in pain. Understanding these ASR dynamics gives us a realistic expectation for pain compliance and pressure point techniques. Pain based techniques outside the controlled environment of the training class are unpredictable at best.

The wonderful teacher and veteran police instructor Sensei Robert Koga used to say: "DIRECTIVE PAIN which leads motion by offering an escape route has worked well for me, while applying pain for compliance or to immobilize, has not worked well." Although prominent in many martial arts curriculums, pain compliance and pressure point techniques should have a very limited role in any self defense curriculum.

WAITING FOR THE ATTACK: THE "REACTIONARY GAP"

Police street survival research has shown that even well trained officers need at least 21 feet of space/time to react to a sudden assault. Military research confirms this natural gap in reaction time. Perception > mental preparation to act > selection of specific action — can take several seconds. This is a lifetime in the world of combat or street survival. Anything that can shorten this gap is effective training, likewise, anything that extends it has no place in a budo curriculum.

While the large, clearly defined attacks found in most traditional martial disciplines can be effective body movement training, they artificially remove the reactionary gap of real world encounters. When this is the primary mode of practice — dangerously misleading expectations are created. In real aggression the attack is rarely clear (grab, strike, push, tackle, etc.) until the final moment of engagement. By then, it is often too late to successfully react.

All forms of practice which involve "reacting and responding" are essential passive, subjecting us to the reactionary gap. Our practice is then reinforcing a PASSIVE REACTIONARY response regardless of one's technical skill. One alternative is attacking at the first perception of danger. Another effective ALTERNATIVE is seen in Ueshiba's aiki budo system — ACTIVE ENGAGEMENT of aggression by INITIATING ACTIONS WHICH PREEMPT and DISRUPT THE ATTACK. This effectively transfers the reactionary gap to the aggressor. Although extremely challenging to practice, it is a very effective protective strategy outside of the dojo.

IMPLICATIONS FOR MARTIAL ARTS TRAINING

Practice can mitigate some of the effects of survival stress, but only when practice occurs under conditions of similar stress. For skills TO TRANSFER EFFECTIVELY to a real defensive situation the training ATMOSPHERE NEEDS TO SIMULATE DANGER, arousing a minimum level of "learning stress." Dojos with a casual, purely recreational atmosphere ignore this reality. True budo challenges students to practice skills of mental/physical relaxation within a tense atmosphere of danger.

Yet, even with quality training ASR will always occur, and adversely affect our coordination to some extent. Therefore, the nature of the action being attempted becomes a critical factor. The SIMPLER the ACTION, the more likely it will be successfully executed under conditions of high stress. Martial arts teachers and black belt students take great pride in their ability to perform difficult techniques, which took years to master. How many traditional martial arts schools focus on what is simple and easy, where is the "art" in that?

Who would that impress?

This is exemplified by aikido black belts boasting that iriminage, a technique central to the curriculum, is "the twenty year technique." This attitude is a great disservice to students who need useable protective skills within a reasonable time frame. It also reflects poor understanding of their own curriculum, since any valid martial style grew from a SMALL CORE of RELATIVELY SIMPLE — "USER FRIENDLY" battle tested SKILLS. As time passes elaborate artistic embellishments and acrobatic permutations encroach upon the budo system with a performance orientation.

While artistry and the drama of impressive acrobatics may have a place, it should be distinguished from, and separated from the self protection part of the curriculum which must be simple, effective core skills. Dojos would do well to follow the old military training axiom:

"PRACTICE must closely resemble WHAT YOU NEED TO PERFORM outside of training." Sending students out the door with any lesser preparation is fraudulent and cruel.

CONCLUSION

With a clear understanding of what happens to our mind and body under adrenaline stress it becomes apparent that ASR favors size and brute force. The precision movement, poise, and mental/physical stability — all required for martial arts are adversely effected. This knowledge is essential when reviewing curriculum with a critical eye — to ensure both WHAT we teach and HOW we teach it is consistent with realities of survival stress.

6. SAVING TRADITIONAL MARTIAL ARTS

WHY have traditional Asian martial arts lost their popularity? Where are the young men and women? Why have so few traditional dojos survived? The few that survive must cater to children, who leave in there teens. Without children to support an anemic, and withering adult program the dojo would not survive. Will there be any traditional dojos left in twenty years?

I do not have the answers, but traditional martial arts teachers and organizations must be held accountable for some of the decline. The modern emphasis on demonstration oriented training — emphasizing artistic

Yukiyoshi Takamura

beauty and acrobatics has left most traditional disciplines far removed from the realities of real world violence. Traditional martial arts instructors tend to rigidly adhere to the inherited curriculum they are invested in, even though many techniques have only the most indirect and specious relation to modern threats their students will face.

So students leave, and we say "they did not have what it takes" or "they did not have the patience." In truth, they often leave to find training more relevant to their needs. They leave because modifying and updating our traditional curriculum would be blasphemy! It would be disrespectful to our teachers and lineage — we would be corrupting the art! This attitude leaves traditional curriculum nothing more than a hollow, lifeless set of dead forms.

My fifty years in traditional martial arts, and twenty six years of street work attempting to apply it, gives me some of the courage (or arrogance) needed to propose changes to traditional curriculum. But someone far smarter and more accomplished than me urged this many years ago, and his concern for the fate of traditional martial arts in America has been born out. The brilliant jujutsu master YUKIYOSHI TAKAMURA, several decades ago challenged teachers to have the courage and creativity for what he termed "INNOVATIVE TRADITIONALISM." That is — keeping a traditional Asian system vital and relevant by FOCUSING ON core PRINCIPLES that define the art, RATHER THAN (archaic) TECHNIQUES.

Takamura changed many techniques of his family's centuries old budo system, adapting it to the time, place, and needs of his students. All traditional martial arts teachers should follow his lead:

"Any martial art is really a set of concepts and principles. Physical techniques are important but not the defining elements of a style...it's how they perform the locks (techniques) that differentiate the styles. When I came to America, I discovered that many traditional techniques were simply not applicable to the realities facing my students. Jujutsu techniques in their original form were not intended to address modern situations. At first, I was not sure that I had the answers..."

"I was focusing on Jujutsu techniques when it was Jujutsu concepts that were the solution...new techniques could be devised to address new realities while embracing time honored concepts that form the art's core."

"This would not be abandoning the art. This would allow the art to maintain its effectiveness and relevance to a new generation and era...I am not concerned what other teachers think... I am most concerned with the welfare of my students and living up to the responsibilities that have been entrusted to me. I am comfortable that my students can actually use the art they are learning. The same cannot be said about the students of teachers who embrace a strictly classical approach."

PRACTICE EXERCISES FOR
INNOVATIVE TRADITIONALISM

*T*HE following training exercises are a transition from basic technique and fundamental skills to applied skills for practical use. These exercises are appropriate for intermediate and advanced students, and require a SLOWER training speed for safety than basic practice. A mouth guard, eye protection, and other safety equipment is recommended:

1) Alternate paired practice with what O'Sensei termed "SAN-NIN MAWARU" (3 partner rotation) in which a secondary training partner strikes from rear/or side as the primary partner comes from the front. Begin the practice with the simple blending/turning (tai no henko) exercise and gradually expand to other techniques.

2) RANDORI (free practice) at a very slow speed — with realistic (non classical) attacks and without any waiting or hesitating if nage appears occupied by another attacker. Getting hit or knocked off balance — and continuing to move — is an important skill. The focus of this practice is evasion — blending — leading rather than completing throws or pins.

3) Periodically substitute PADDED CLUBS / BATS for martial arts strikes, and substitute (controlled speed) "HAYMAKER" — lunging type punches for open hand side strikes.

4) Practice "CREATING" SHOMENUCHI (rather than waiting/reacting) by INITIATING upward sword movement toward aggressor's face — who must then raise arm to protect himself (shomen as defensive movement by attacker.) For safety - begin this practice as a slow sword-matching exercise.

5) Uke ADDS realistic STRIKES with free hand to the WRIST GRAB exercises, begin this with basic turning exercise Tai No Henko.

6) Uke ADDS realistic STRIKES with free hand to the shoulder/lapel grab exercises

7) Practice FIRST HALF of techniques ONLY — which is the EVASION/ ESCAPE stage. This significantly reduces complexity of techniques, making them more "user friendly" under high stress conditions. It also makes them more applicable to work situations where injury (from fall) to student-patient-customer must be avoided.

8) Practice REALISTIC KNIFE ATTACKS. Begin with knife out of view, thrust/stabs are withdrawn after each movement, thrusts/stabs happen in short/repeated movements

9) Practice TACTICAL RETREAT — walking away from a fight which ends confrontation or — draws out attack into a more "user friendly" form, as attacker reaches or lunges to stop you. Retreat should be lateral — to left or right, rather than moving backward.

10) Practice CREATING grabs/contact rather than passively waiting to be grabbed. Actively engage uke — entering into uke's space with sword raising movement toward face, which forces/elicits a response. This is the Aiki skill of engagement ON YOUR TERMS.

11) Practice "happo zanshin" expanding visual field using shiho/happo giri — 4/8 direction cutting exercises with bokken, and multi-directional staff katas. Most Karate katas and Tai Chi forms are also excellent practice for happo zanshin.

12) Interrupt predictable patterns of movement: right side-left side-right side-left side and omote-ura-omote-ura that encourage partner to resist and "set up." Making direction of movement less predictable makes practice more realistic and improves ukemi.

IX.

GLOSSARY OF BUDO TERMS

ASR: Adrenaline Stress Response — Research based psycho-physiological changes in the mind and body of humans and other mammals to the perception of danger.

AIKI BUDO: The martial art developed by Morihei Ueshiba which preceded modern aikido. (see BUDO)

AIKIDO: A modern, less martial form of the Ueshiba aiki budo martial art, developed largely by Kisshomaru Ueshiba and Koichi Tohei during the post-WWII years, to preserve and popularize some of Morihei Ueshiba's legacy. Development of the art was strongly influenced by restrictions set by the American postwar occupation, and the passive, war-weary attitude of postwar Japanese society.

AIKIKAI: The umbrella organization of modern aikido developed by Kisshomaru Ueshiba and Koichi Tohei after WWII, emphasizing the physical fitness, artistic, and performance aspects of O'Sensei's aiki budo.

ATEMI: Strikes used in martial arts to distract and unbalance the attacker.

BATTO (also referred to as batto jutsu): The older term/form of the Japanese art of iaido, that involves drawing the sword from a traditional seiza kneeling position. (see IAIDO)

BOKKEN: Wooden practice sword used in Japanese martial arts.

BUDO: The Way of the Warrior. A Japanese term for battlefield arts comprised of rigorous physical training and intensive mental disciplines, with an associated lifestyle and mindset.

BPM: "Beats Per Minute" A measure used in police and military combat research, indicating the level of stress produced by the perception of danger.

BUSHIDO: Samurai code of conduct, ethics of the warrior in Japan

DOJO: A training hall for the study of budo, with elements of both a temple and battlefield.

CHI KUNG (Chi Gong/QiQong): An ancient form of Chinese standing yoga, containing the mental and physical building blocks for most Asian martial arts. It is the primary form of traditional health care in China.

DHARMA: A term dating back to the ancient Vedic religion of India. It is a concept central to most religions of India, including Buddhism, meaning "cosmic law" or "truth." In Buddhism it refers to the path of righteousness, and skillful (virtuous) action.

DESHI: Student of a traditional Japanese martial art (also see uchi deshi)

EMBU: A Japanese term for demonstration, specifically martial arts demonstration. The term has a negative connotation for some traditional martial arts masters, such as Morihiro Saito, who believed modern aikido training had become too artistic and performance oriented, referring to it as "embu style."

GAIJIN: Term used by Japanese people meaning "a foreigner."

GI: Traditional Japanese martial arts training uniform.

GASSHO: Japanese term for the attitude and physical expression of gratitude/appreciation, with palms placed together in front of the chest, often accompanied by a bow.

HOMBU: Large aikido school in Tokyo led by K. Ueshiba, the son of O'Sensei, and until 1974, Koichi Tohei. Also known as Aikido World Headquarters.

IAIDO: The drawing of the Japanese sword from a formal ground-sitting posture, dangerous to practice with a live blade (sharp sword) without total attention and precise movement.

IWAMA: A small village in Japan, about two hours from Tokyo. The location where Morihei Ueshiba built a farm and dojo after resigning his military teaching positions in 1942. Iwama is where O'Sensei lived, trained, and taught for most of the last twenty-five years of his life.

KAISHI WAZA: The term generally used to describe techniques for reversing a martial arts throw or pin applied to you.

KIAI: A loud powerful exhalation used in martial arts to focus energy, unbalance an attacker, and raise energy level during training.

KIRYOKU: Moral energy, will power, spiritual energy.

KOKORO: Character, inner strength.

MMA: A commercially successful form of sport fighting, reflecting the culture's obsession with winning, power and dominance over others.

O'SENSEI: A term of reverence for Japanese swordsman, military trainer, and martial arts master, Morihei Ueshiba. After resigned his high-profile teaching positions during WWII, he spent the next twenty-five years of his life studying budo as self-transformation, and exploring its possibilities for conflict resolution.

QIGONG: See Chi Kung..

RIAI: "Unified strategy" in combat, using space-timing-focus-sound.

SANCHIN: An ancient Chinese internal moving meditation form brought to Okinawa and later Japan, integrated into several styles of karate as a power-oriented kata with dynamic tension.

SEISHI TANREN: (see tanren)

SEIZA: Formal Japanese ground-sitting posture, which involves sitting on feet. It is the best posture for deep abdominal breathing and strengthening core body muscles.

SEMPAI: A senior student, one who began on the path before us. A combination of mentor, and drill sergeant.

SENSEI: The Japanese term for teacher in the study of martial arts or Zen. More than instructor, the title conveys a sacred trust, and responsibility as a role model.

SHIHAN: A title given to Japanese black belt holders of sixth degree or higher. The title is sometimes awarded to non Japanese by martial arts organizations, for significant service to the organization.

SHINGU: The village near O'Sensei's birth place of Tanabe, where O'Sensei often taught.

SHUGYO: Intensive mental and physical training that includes meditation, chanting, prayer, breath work, and other inner disciplines.

SOJI: Applying the focus and precision of martial arts or Zen to cleaning or other chores in the dojo or Zendo.

SHINKEN: Samurai (real) sword with live blade.

SHINKEN SHOBU: lit. "Deadly combat," a budo training attitude of "dead earnest."

TANREN (seishi tanren): Spirit forging, intensive physical training beyond what is expected or required, which pushes and extends one's capabilities.

TAKEMUSU AIKI: A favorite phrase used by O'Sensei in the latter part of his life to describe his art and his vision of complete freedom. An English translation could be "unrestricted, creative response"

TOKONOMA: An alcove or special area centrally located in a Japanese home or dojo, where an altar or objects of special significance are placed

UCHI DESHI: A live-in disciple at a martial arts school

UKE: A term used in aiki jujitsu or aikido, referring to the training partner who attacks and then receives the aiki technique. The one who is thrown or pinned.

UKEMI: The martial arts skill of attacking and falling safely.

X.

REFERENCES

REFERENCES:

Quotes and photo of Yukiyoshi Takamura are from the Takamura ha Shindo Yoshu Kai website of Toby Threadgilll

Photo of firefighter Kevin Shea is from the New York Post

Research on Col. John Boyd from: Boyd, by Robert Korn
Genghis John, Proceedings of the U.S. Navy Institute, by Chuck Spinney

Poems in chapters O'Sensei's Battlefield Awareness and Deep Roots of Budo by sword master John Mackie Evans

Selection from the poem "Skeletons" by monk Ikkyu, translated by John Stevens

Aikido history referenced from:
Budo, by Morihei Ueshiba
A Life in Aikido, by Kisshomaru Ueshiba
Traditional Aikido, vol. I – V, by Morihiro Saito
Interviews with Morihiro Saito, Masao Umezawa, Kazuo Chiba, and Terry Dobson

ADDITIONAL REFERENCES:

Aikido journal.com, editor and historian Stanley Pranin

How We Won The War, by General Vo Nguyen Giap

Japanese Swordsmanship, by Donn Draeger and Gordon Warner

Sharpening The Warrior's Edge, by Bruce K. Siddle

Street Survival, by Calibre Press

The Gift Of Fear, by Gavin De Becker

The Open Way, by Hogen Yamahata

The Sword of Wisdom, by Sheng Yen

The Tactical Edge, by Calibre Press

Therapeutic Crisis Intervention, TCI Instructor Manual
Cornell University

Trog, by sword master John Mackie Evans

ABOUT THE AUTHOR

Tom Collings was born in the Forest Hills section of New York City in 1951. He began martial arts training in the 1960's, studying Isshin-Ryu karate, Tae Kwon Do, and later Aikido under E. Hagihara and Yoshimitsu Yamada. After earning a black belt in 1976, he moved to Japan, immersing himself in martial arts, Zen practice, and Japanese sword. For several years he studied with the son and grandson of aikido founder Morihei Ueshiba, at Hombu Dojo, Tokyo. He later lived and trained at the Ueshiba Iwama dojo with O'Sensei's closest disciple Morihiro Saito.

His training included six months of private study with Kazuo Chiba and his Zen master Hogen at Chogen-Ji Zen Temple, in Kannami Village near Mt. Fuji. He received a Shidoin teacher's license from Y. Yamada in 1989, and 6th degree black belt from Doshu Moriteru Ueshiba in 2007.

Mr. Collings occupations have included martial arts teacher, body guard, police defensive tactics instructor, psychiatric social worker, supervisor of a youth detention facility, and twenty six years as a New York State law enforcement officer. He is a graduate of SUNY Buffalo, Adelphi University Graduate School, and Cornell University TCI (Therapeutic Crisis Intervention) Instructor Training Program.

He continues daily training in Aiki Budo, Aikido, QiGong-Tai Chi, live blade Seigo-Ryu Iaido, and Zen practice. After 49 years of training he insists his only area of "mastery" is kitchen pot washer, at his favorite monastery.

Tom Collings may be contacted at:
tbcoll@verizon.net
web site: liasc.org

Made in the USA
San Bernardino, CA
12 December 2016